American Drama/Critics:
Writings and Readings

By

Bert Cardullo

Cambridge Scholars Publishing

American Drama/Critics: Writings and Readings, by Bert Cardullo

This book first published 2007. The present binding first published 2008.

Cambridge Scholars Publishing

12 Back Chapman Street, Newcastle upon Tyne, NE6 2XX, UK

British Library Cataloguing in Publication Data
A catalogue record for this book is available from the British Library

ISBN (10): 1-4438-0035-X, ISBN (13): 978-1-4438-0035-8

TABLE OF CONTENTS

REALISM, NATURALISM, MODERN AMERICAN DRAMA—AND MODERN AMERICAN DRAMATIC CRITICISM

American drama, for all practical purposes, is twentieth-century American drama, as I trust this collection of essays illustrates. To be sure, there were plays written and performed on the American continent well before there was a United States; and during the nineteenth century the American theater was widespread and active, with theater buildings and resident companies in virtually every city of more than village-size. But, as was also true in much of Europe, this theater was, with rare exceptions, not the home of a particularly rich or ambitious literature.

Serious American drama at this time, at its most ambitious, reached the level of blank-verse, pseudo-Shakespearean tragedy along the lines of George Henry Boker's *Francesca da Rimini* (1855) or large-scale costume melodrama filled with spectacle, like Steele MacKaye's *Paul Kauver* (1887); at its less ambitious, it produced broader melodrama of the cheer-the-hero-hiss-the-villain kind, like George Aiken's enormously popular dramatization of *Uncle Tom's Cabin* (1852). Much of American comic drama, for its part, was built on variants of the situation established in Royall Tyler's *The Contrast* (1787): the triumph of a supposedly uncivilized American (or Westerner, or Yankee farmer) over sophisticated Englishmen (or Easterners, or city slickers). Among the many of this type were Samuel Woodworth's *The Forest Rose* (1825) and J. K. Paulding's *The Lion of the West* (1830).

The theater was a broadly popular light-entertainment form, then, much like television today. It is possible to do artistically ambitious work on American commercial television, but television is not likely to be the first medium to come to the mind of a serious writer—just as the theater was not for the serious writer of the nineteenth century. This is not to say that the playwrights of the nineteenth century were without talent, but that, like television writers, they were more likely to be artisans skilled at producing the entertaining effects that audiences wanted, rather than artists looking to illuminate the human condition or challenge received values. The reasons for this general absence of literary depth or quality were many and not restricted to America: in Britain and on the European continent the eighteenth and nineteenth centuries were also generally fallow periods for dramatic literature.

Yet in America, as in Europe, a change in the kind of literature being written for the theater began to become apparent in the last years of the nineteenth century. (Ibsen in Norway, Chekhov in Russia, and later Shaw in England rediscovered the theater as a vehicle amenable to ambitious dramatic literature, serious or comic.) As with many historical and artistic developments in American culture, this was much less a matter of an organized "movement" than of trial and error and accidents of time, place, and personality. That is, an individual writer might not consciously be innovating, but something in his work might attract audiences or inspire other writers, so that, as a result, the art form lurched forward a step.

There is, for example, little evidence that James A. Herne considered *Margaret Fleming* (1890) revolutionary in any way, but with hindsight we can see that his version of the mildly sensational melodrama typical of the period raises moral questions that its contemporaries do not, and that those questions— about marital infidelity, sexual and economic exploitation, the relationship between class and moral obligation, and the nature of the maternal instinct— give the play a distinctly twentieth-century feel. The process was slow and unsteady, with false starts and relapses, but by the second decade of the twentieth century artistically ambitious writers were venturing into drama and finding it able to carry a weight of psychological insight and philosophical import that it had not been asked to carry before.

This was very much the rebirth—or the very birth—of an art form; with little in the recent history of the genre to build on, the first generations of twentieth-century dramatists had to discover for themselves what shape twentieth-century American drama would take. It is not surprising, then, that the years from, say, 1900 to 1930 saw a great variety of dramatic styles and vocabularies, as playwrights experimented with epic drama, symbolism, expressionism, verse tragedy, and the like, finding out as they went along what a play could and could not do. Foremost among the experimenters was Eugene O'Neill, of whom it is only a slight exaggeration to say that during the 1920s he never wrote two plays in the same style.

O'Neill, whose father had been a star actor in the nineteenth-century theater, and who thus had a sharp awareness of its literary limitations, was consciously experimenting, trying to shape and stretch the medium so that it could do what he wanted it to do—express his profoundly thoughtful insights and philosophies. But even the less determinedly innovative writers of the period found themselves making up the rules as they went along. Following the lead of European experimenters and staking out new stylistic and technical ground of their own, they and O'Neill redefined the boundaries of the medium, finding new artistic vocabularies with which to address new subjects, discovering what various styles of drama were capable of achieving and what was better left to the novel, the short story, and poetry.

Inevitably, some experiments failed. One reason O'Neill himself kept changing styles was that many of them disappointed him, while some of the "-isms" that were briefly successful in Europe proved unamenable to American topics and tastes, or they were simply uncommercial. Through trial and error, however, one particular dramatic mode came to the fore. Theatrically effective, easy for audiences to relate and respond to, remarkably flexible in its adaptability to the demands of different authors, the natural voice of American drama was revealed by the 1930s to be in realistic or naturalistic, contemporary, lower-to-middle-class domestic drama (and, to a much lesser extent, comedy, of whose anarchic or critical potential there has been strikingly little exploration in any period of American drama—owing in part to the competition from both silent and sound film, and in part to the mistaken belief, understandable in a young dramatic literature that wanted to be taken seriously, that comedy is not a serious art form).

Realistic or naturalistic, contemporary, lower-to-middle-class domestic drama—each of those adjectives is worth examining and defining. "Realism," for one, does not mean the uncensored photographic and phonographic record of external reality. Dramatic realism is an artifice as much as any other artistic mode, violating reality in order to give the illusion of reality. To take one simple example, characters in realistic plays generally speak "unrealistically": one at a time, and in complete, grammatical sentences. The important point about realism, though, is that the illusion of reality is maintained; realism avoids gross violations of the laws of nature (people don't fly, for instance) or the introduction of purely symbolic characters or events (say, the Little Formless Fears of O'Neill's *The Emperor Jones* [1920]), while presenting characterizations and behavior that are at least possible. And thus a realistic play asserts the claim that it speaks the truth, that what happens on stage is a reflection of the world its audience inhabits on an everyday basis.

(For the sake of style and convenience, I shall use the term "realism" here to represent both realism and naturalism, but the word should be the otherwise awkward "representationalism." This is because naturalism is distinguished from realism by its depiction of proletarian, as opposed to bourgeois, characters; its greater emphasis on heredity, environment, and the sub- or unconscious in the determination of human character and action; by its tendency to substitute the episodic "slice of life" for the "well-madeness" of climactic realistic drama; its attempt to imitate the way most people, but particularly those of the lower classes, speak: in fragmented or disjointed, often ungrammatical sentences, sometimes spoken simultaneously by two—or more—different characters who are not listening to each other; and by its inclination to be pessimistic, instead of realistically optimistic, about the improvement of the human condition and thereby the state of the world.)

Historical plays themselves were a mainstay of nineteenth-century American drama, and continued to be written in the twentieth; most Broadway seasons in the 1920s saw at least one play about eighteenth-century France or nineteenth-century Mexico, and the 1930s had a thin but constant stream of plays about Washington, Lincoln, or other American heroes. But the overwhelming majority of twentieth-century plays are set in the present, again implying a close parallel to the real world. Moreover, a play set in the here-and-now is more likely to reflect the external reality of the here-and-now, be it the Depression of the 1930s, the middle-class anxieties of the 1950s, or the profound social changes of the 1960s. And one of the first important discoveries about domestic realism was precisely this: that it could address large and contemporary sociopolitical issues, even historical ones, on its own theatrical terms.

Shakespeare, of course, wrote about kings, and even O'Neill wrote about Lazarus and Marco Polo, as did Maxwell Anderson about Elizabeth I and Mary Queen of Scotland. But the overwhelming majority of modern American plays are about people from the same socioeconomic world as the playgoers— the urban middle and working classes. This is not a narrow range, and it can stretch from the barely-getting-by and underemployed to the comfortably well-off. But the extremes of the economic ladder, along with other fringes of society—blacks and rustics, for instance—are rarely represented before the 1960s, except as stereotypes, and infrequently thereafter except in plays specifically addressing minority subjects. Audiences for American plays were, and are, likely to see themselves or people like them, or people they might believably, with good or bad luck, be like.

Of all these adjectives being defined, "domestic" may be the most significant. For not only are American plays about recognizable people in a recognizable world, but they are also about the personal lives of these people. Whether a play is actually set in a living room, with a cast made up solely of family members, as an extraordinary number are, or whether the "domestic" setting extends to an office and a circle or friends or colleagues (as it does in Ben Hecht and Charles MacArthur's *The Front Page* [1928]), the issues and events are presented in small and localized terms. Whatever the deeper meanings of an American play, then, on one solid level it is about love and marriage, sickness and death, earning a living, or dealing with a family crisis.

Of course, Americans did not invent domestic drama. Ibsen and Chekhov (to name just two, and to limit our discussion only to the nineteenth century) had written of realistic characters in domestic situations, and had even hinted at larger social and moral issues through this mode. The gradual discovery of American dramatists themselves, starting in the 1930s, was that domestic realism was their most effective vehicle for talking about larger issues—that small events in the lives of small people could be presented in such a way that they reflected the world outside the living room, and that playwrights therefore no longer had to wrestle with epic theater or other non-realistic modes in order to achieve wider relevance, let alone undying universality.

Put another way, this insight becomes more than merely technical. Dramatists discovered that the real story of, say, the Great Depression was not in financial statistics, mass movements, or large social changes, but in the ways it affected a family in its own living room. From there it was a small step to the discoveries of the 1940s and 1950s that purely personal experiences, even those seemingly without larger social implications (as in *Long Day's Journey into Night* [1941], which in the end is as much about immigration, religion, commerce, and art as it is about Eugene O'Neill, his mother, his father, and his older brother), were valuable and dramatic in themselves; that a group of people acting out their private lives not only could have its own inherent power and importance, but could also draw a picture of the world outside—the larger, public context—which was affecting and even determining those lives.

It is worth noting, at this point, that few American dramatists aspire to high tragedy; indeed, the other characteristics of American drama already enumerated, particularly realism and the domestic setting, militate against any such ambition. A deeply democratic impulse is at work here, in the assumption that the important events of life, the things worth writing plays about, are the things that happen to essentially ordinary people in their everyday existences—not to heroic individuals in their extraordinary exploits. But there is something else which militates against the writing of high tragedy in the United States, and that is the fact that modern liberalism—particularly of the American kind—entertains *non*-tragic premises insofar as it puts its trust in science, reason, and technology. The modern viewpoint, that is to say, is too optimistic for tragedy, which speaks not of secular dilemmas that may be resolved through rational innovation, but of the unfaltering bias toward inhumanity and destruction embedded in the very drift of the world.

Modern liberalism, by contrast, has been inveterately melioristic in its outlook. Denying that evil and suffering, hardship and wrongdoing, are absolute and inalterable, the liberal viewpoint has proposed to remove or moderate the very conditions that make tragedy possible. In the American drama, it does so in the form of domestic realism's most dominant sub-genre: the problem play, which originates in the desire of late-nineteenth-century European dramatists to find a solution for the increasingly overwhelming problem of human social and economic misery; and which finds its natural home in a pragmatic, problem-solving American state dedicated to promoting the life, liberty, equality, and (material) welfare of all its citizens. And promoting them in the drama, I might add, in the "modern" sense: by examining representative sociological and psychological problems as just that, representative sociological and psychological problems that beg for secular solutions, not as purely personal deviations from the norm—sins or even crimes—that call for religious repentance, on the one hand, or divine intervention, on the other.

As with the rebirth of serious American drama at the beginning of the twentieth century, the discovery of domestic realism's power and potential, especially in the form of the problem play, was not the result of conscious artistic manifestos or collusion among writers. The form worked, so individual artists were attracted to it; indeed, in a number of cases dramatists who began as non-realistic writers or who went through a period of stylistic experiment found themselves drawn back to domestic realism in later works: Eugene O'Neill most strikingly, but also Edward Albee, Sam Shepard, and others. (The obvious exception in this instance is not Thornton Wilder, but Gertrude Stein, as I trust my essays on these two will make clear.) The remarkable accomplishment of domestic realism thus lies in its richness and adaptability, as writers as different in their verbal styles, thematic choices, and artistic ambitions as O'Neill, Tennessee Williams, and Arthur Miller were all able to say what they wanted to say by using this mode.

Just as there have been few stylistic schools or movements in American drama, so too have there been few conscious agreements among writers about specific subject matter. Individual dramatists wrote about what interested or moved them, and cases of direct influence (e.g., Williams on William Inge) are far less common than situations in which playwrights responding to a similar reality independently found their way to similar subjects and approaches. Still, similar realities by themselves are likely to produce some similarities in style and theme among artistic contemporaries. It is both coincidental and (with hindsight) inevitable, for example, that the Great Depression of the 1930s would lead dramatists to explore the particular socioeconomic forces that were affecting the lives of millions of people—and to criticize those responsible for them. This drama of social, political, economic, and cultural criticism remains today the most significant part of the serious American repertoire.

For various historical and artistic reasons, then, the stylistic outline of twentieth-century American drama has a clearly discernible arc. An art form that was essentially born afresh at the beginning of the twentieth century went through a period of exploration and experiment culminating in the discovery that one style was more amenable to American tastes and more adaptable to the demands that different writers made on it. That style—realistic, contemporary, lower-to-middle-class domestic drama—was to become the dominant and artistically most fertile and flexible mode, the one in which the greatest American dramatists were able to create the greatest American plays, and in which writers with varying agendas could offer compelling psychological insights, political criticism, or social counsel. So absolute was the superiority for American dramatic purposes of domestic realism that when, soon after the middle of the century, some significant historical events led to another period of experiment and exploration, the artistic center held.

I refer to Absurdism—the idea that man is entrapped in an irrational, hostile, impersonal, and indifferent universe where the search for ultimate truth is an exercise in futility—which seeps into American drama, with Jack Gelber's *The Connection* (1959) and Albee's *The American Dream* (1961), when our post-World War II euphoria wears off, the Korean war erupts in the midst of the Cold War, and the Vietnam debacle looms on the horizon, not to speak of presidential assassination followed by the political disillusionment of the Watergate era. Artistic discoveries were made at this time—some of them greatly enriching the dramatic vocabulary—but domestic realism retained its place as the native and natural American dramatic style as new generations of dramatists continued to discover its flexibility and power. Whatever the subject, however dominant the social or political agenda, however particular or unconventional the life experience being investigated, the overwhelming majority of American plays continued to find that their concerns could best be dramatized through the everyday, personal experiences of ordinary characters—even as playwrights continue to discover the same today, well into the twenty-first century.

That said, one could argue that American drama these days is in serious trouble, not because it lacks talented artists in every area of activity (actually, the number of such talented people has rarely been higher), but because it lacks an informed and committed criticism—theater criticism, that is, not dramatic criticism of the kind practiced by me in the majority of this book. I shall concentrate, for the remainder of this essay, on the theater critic, just as my interviews and essays do the same in part two of this collection (even the one on dramaturgy, as dramaturgy is nothing if it is not a kind of in-house criticism), because the theater critic's work is more difficult than the drama critic's and is at least equally important—in some ways more important.

Theater criticism is more difficult, in judgmental essence, because it must be done under some sort of time pressure, whether of an hour or a day or a week or a month or a quarter-year, and because there is not often a useful body of precedent criticism on a production to help or helpfully irritate the theater critic. His criticism is at least as important as the (scholarly) dramatic criticism that may follow long after because, to a considerable degree, it determines what that subsequent criticism will be—by which I mean, which plays it will treat. The theater critic, even if he writes for a quarterly (as the great John Simon once did), is what I would call a frontline critic: anyone who comments on a play or production within, say, a year of its appearance is in my view a frontline critic. He has the primary, crucial task of winnowing wheat from chaff—in effect, of selecting the materials that will eventually become the subjects for drama critics.

To be sure, the best of theater critics make mistakes, but it's in the front lines that most of the crucial decisions are made. Still, the mere possibility that one such decision can be mistaken, can sentence an otherwise fine play to an early and undeserved death, sends a shiver up the spine. That shiver confirms the theater's critic's importance, responsibility, and need to be competent. That shiver also confirms his prime motive for being: to find and foster the good. It is he, the best theater critic—as type, not as individual—who largely determines which plays will be studied, will be written about by professors, will be revived in the theater. To the handful of great theater critics the American stage has had—George Jean Nathan, Stark Young, and Eric Bentley; Stanley Kauffmann, Robert Brustein, and Richard Gilman—we owe most of our knowledge of the permanent American (as well as world) drama of our time, and in most cases even the opportunity to see or read it.

These men practiced what I call above an informed and committed criticism. And by committed I do not mean only being committed to expressing one's opinions about a play or a performance. As the German poet Heinrich Heine once wrote, "The reason we can no longer build Gothic cathedrals is that they were built from convictions and all we have is opinions." What a potent distinction: between an age characterized by passionate beliefs and one characterized by purely personal views. The American theater critics I've named had plenty of views or opinions, as we know; and some of their dramatic opinions were wrong or misguided (see Brustein on Marsha Norman's 'night, Mother [1982]). But they had convictions in addition to personal views, and that is why we still read them today. They had a vision of the theater, that is, which was larger than their estimate of individual plays—larger than themselves, as it were.

There are few, if any, such critics of the American theater today, and it is my view that the quality of our drama is suffering as a result. (I am not prepared to answer the question of whether too much bad theater drove the critics away, or whether too much academic [read: graduate] education has produced too few good theater critics.) How else do you explain the elevation of such molehills as Tony Kushner and Paula Vogel (to name just two) into mountains? Or the sanctified self-segregation of the overrated and repetitive black dramatist August Wilson, to the point where he didn't want whites to direct his plays (or pay to attend them, either?), let alone criticize them in print? Good theater critics, unaligned and unafraid, would have made sure that false messiahs and peddlers and charlatans like these were shown as such. And only by doing so could such critics have made way for the real messiah to arrive. As I write, we still await his (re)appearance.

PART I:

PLAYS AND PLAYWRIGHTS,
OR TEXTS AND CONTEXTS

CHAPTER ONE

GLOBAL FUTURISM, DIVINE COMEDY, GREEK TRAGEDY, AND . . . *THE HAIRY APE*

"[*The Hairy Ape*] remains one of my favorites. I have an enduring affection for it—always will have—and an enduring respect for it as drama, the more so because so few people have ever seen what it is all about."
—Eugene O'Neill, in a 1944 letter to Theresa Helburn.

There are four aspects of Eugene O'Neill's *The Hairy Ape* (1921) that, because of the play's strong naturalist-expressionistic stylistic component, have hitherto been neglected or completely ignored: first its "comedy," as O'Neill describes it in the subtitle, "A Comedy of Ancient and Modern Life in Eight Scenes"; second, its connection, or opposition, to Italian futurism; third, its choice of so lowly a protagonist as Robert "Yank" Smith to symbolize humanity itself; and last, the relationship of *The Hairy Ape* to ancient Greek tragedy.

Starting with *The Hairy Ape*'s "Italian connection," or connections, O'Neill not only ironically invokes Dante's *Divine Comedy* (1321) but also implicitly responds to the futurist movement in the arts (including drama) founded by his contemporary Filippo Tommaso Marinetti. Originally called simply *Commedia*, like *The Hairy Ape*'s own subtitle, "A Comedy," Dante's masterpiece was reissued in Venice in 1555 with the adjective *divina* applied to the work's title for the first time, thus resulting in the title still used today. The characters whom Dante meets on his journey in the *Commedia*, moreover, are drawn largely from ancient Roman as well as recent Italian history and even from contemporary Italian life. Hence this narrative poem could itself be called "A Comedy of Ancient and Modern Life," just as O'Neill describes his play.

Additionally, even as O'Neill succeeded in *The Hairy Ape* in forging an urban American argot that assimilates the spoken English of immigrant Germans, Jews, Scandinavians, Frenchmen, Dutchmen, Italians, Cockneys, and Irishmen, so too, from a reverse angle, did Dante enrich courtly Italian with his native Tuscan dialect to create a serious literary language that would take the place of Latin and become the ancestor of modern Italian. In fact, Dante's use of language was one of the reasons for the "low" title of *Commedia*, for in this work he treated a serious subject, the redemption of man—one normally reserved for "high" tragedy—in the low and vulgar language of Italian, not Latin as one might expect.

Finally, although in structure a journey to, or through, the Beyond of hell, purgatory, and paradise, the *Commedia* is actually a realistic picture and intense analysis of earthly human life. But Dante's literal journey, of course, is also a spiritual one: an allegory of the progress of the individual soul toward God and of the progress of sociopolitical mankind toward peace on earth—hence the "comedy," or happy-cum-heavenly ending, of the poem. Similarly, Yank takes a literal as well as figurative journey in *The Hairy Ape*. Like Dante, he also begins in hell—the inferno-like bowels of the stokehole of a transatlantic liner, as O'Neill describes it in Scene 3:

> The stokehole. . . . murky air laden with coal dust . . . masses of shadows everywhere . . . [The men] use . . . shovels to throw open the furnace doors. Then from these fiery round holes in the black, a flood of terrific light and heat pours full upon the men . . . [as they] hurl [coal] into the flaming mouths before them. (187)

It is in hell, furthermore (a hell, appropriately, where men seem condemned or cursed to an eternity of hard labor, in the sweat from which they will slowly roast), that Yank meets Mildred—or, it could be said, that this Adam ("naked and shameless" [191]) meets his Eve ("dressed all in white" [180]), who turns out to be something other than Dante's idealized Beatrice. For Mildred not only violates the atavistic, animalistic Yank's territorial space, she also gives Yank knowledge or consciousness of himself—or of himself as others view him—for the first time, and with it the power to think. But "Thinkin' is hard" (230) for Yank, so hard that at least five times in the play, subsequent to his single encounter with Mildred, O'Neill has his protagonist sit "in the exact attitude of Rodin's 'The Thinker'" (193). This 1881 sculpture is often considered to be optimistic, even uplifting—the epitome of contemplative, intelligent man—but one must not forget that Rodin designed it as the central piece of his monumental work *The Gates of Hell* (1880-1917), which would portray brutish man attempting to puzzle out the truth and meaning of human existence. So construed, thought or self-reflection is a kind of hell that separates or alienates humanity from nature, in contrast to the union with nature enjoyed by all other animals.

Yank, however, is identified with the machine or the machine age; he "belongs" (one of his favorite words) to the age of steam, power, and speed. In the stokehole of this particular ship, moreover, he is the supreme being and unquestioned ruler—"fiercer, more truculent, more powerful, more sure of himself than the rest" (166). Or at least he was until Mildred's simple look of revulsion and her words "Oh, the filthy beast!" (192) topple Yank's confidence and self-respect, completely changing his perspective on his life and work. Just as Mildred descends the evolutionary ladder, so to speak, to see "how the other half lives" (184) in the nether regions of the ocean liner, so too does Yank ascend from the bowels of the ship, shortly after his encounter with her, to discover a world on high he never knew really existed and in which he does not fit. To be sure, he begins his actual as well as metaphoric journey in a quest, at first, for revenge against Mildred's upper class, only to have that journey become, more and more, a search for self.

His journey takes Yank from hell progressively back through the evolutionary scale to four places on "earth," in New York City—Fifth Avenue, the prison on what was then known as Blackwell's Island (Roosevelt Island today, in the East River between Manhattan and Queens), the meeting hall of the International Workers of the World on the Brooklyn waterfront, and the zoo (possibly the Bronx Zoo, but probably the closer one in Central Park, because he spent the previous night on a bench in Battery Park at the southernmost tip of Manhattan)—purgatories, all, that lead to physical punishment (as opposed to spiritual penance) for Yank's "sins" and ultimately to his death. ("I ain't on oith and I ain't in heaven', get me?" Yank tells a gorilla at the zoo—his closest "relative" in terms of appearance, strength, and outlook, and what the "evolved" but overbred Mildred saw in the stokehole when she looked into Yank's "gorilla face" [191]—"I'm in the middle tryin' to separate 'em, takin' all de woist punches from bot' of 'em. Maybe dat's what dey call hell, huh?" [230-231]. Maybe, but it could just as well be what they call purgatory.)

"Christ," Yank asks as he is dying at the hands of the uncaged gorilla, "Where do I get off at? Where do I fit in?" (232). The answer lies, not in the uniting of his immortal soul (if he has one) with God, but in the freeing of Yank from the prison-house of self and the reunion of his mortal body with the elements of nature. After what he has been through, one could say, this is heaven enough. As O'Neill himself once explained, Yank *while alive* had "lost his old harmony with nature, the harmony which he used to have as an animal"—and that the stoker Paddy thinks was the ancient order of things on sailing ships, when "a ship was part of the sea, and a man was part of a ship, and the sea joined all together and made it one" (175). O'Neill went on to say that

> Yank can't go forward and so he tries to go back. This is what his shaking hands with the gorilla meant. But he can't go back to 'belonging' either. The gorilla kills him. The subject here is the ancient one that . . . is man and his struggle with his own fate. The struggle used to be with the gods, but is now with himself, his own past, his attempt to 'belong.' (*New York Herald Tribune*, 26 March 1924)

Yank can't go forward, O'Neill says, by which he means that this stoker can no longer identify himself with the modern world of machines, materialism, and technology (a world, it must be said, that eventually would replace him, or the job he does, with a machine). Mildred has seen to that: as Yank himself puts it, "Sure—her old man . . . makes half de steel in de world—steel—where I tought I belonged . . . Steel! *It* don't belong, dat's what! Cages, cells, locks, bolts, bars . . . holdin' me down wit him at de top!" (217-218). But neither can Yank go forward by identifying himself with the labor radical Long's Christian socialism, which enlists the Bible in the proletarian struggle against the Capitalist class. Yank's loss of self and stature is strictly loss—it's not replaced by anything. Once his illusion of supremacy in the world gets shattered, nothing can take its place—certainly not the worship of a new, or another, Superior Being.

Yank can't go forward, then, and he can't go back: he "ain't got no past to tink in, nor nothin' dat's comin', on'y what's now—and dat don't belong" (230). Indeed, he's caught, as O'Neill's subtitle tells us, between "Ancient and Modern Life." But his comedy is obviously not divine—"Hell! God!" (196) is Yank's contemptuous response to Long's religious belief—as was Dante's. Dante's faith resolved the tensions in his *Commedia* between ancient Roman paganism and contemporary Catholic harlotry—and a harlot is what he called the Church of his time, in addition to supporting a secular ruler for Italy in place of the pope. (A heretic is what the Church called Dante, whose *Commedia* audaciously consigns seven popes to the Inferno, and who himself was consigned to exile for such audacity.) Yank, by contrast, has no faith in anything anymore—neither in God, Nature, Man, Woman, or Machine.

Furthermore, it is Yank's peculiar faithlessness—his deviation, finally, from the norm of belief in or attachment to something—that marks him as a secularly comic character of a unique kind. So unique or extreme that, unlike the usual comic character, such as Shakespeare's Falstaff, Molière's Orgon, or even O'Neill's own Richard Miller from his only "real" comedy, *Ah, Wilderness* (1932)—who creates havoc or disorder through deviation from reasonable values like common sense, good nature, social intelligence, flexibility, moderation, and tolerance—Yank cannot be reintegrated into his society in the end. (For one filmic version of a conventional comic character in action, see Chaplin's *Gold Rush* [1925] with its gentle, telescoped satire of material greed during the Roaring Twenties.) At the conclusion of *The Hairy Ape*, life does not go on and it certainly does not multiply as it does in traditional comedy, which (derived as the word "comedy" is from the ancient Greek *komos*, meaning "revel," and *aeidein*, meaning "to sing") often ends in festivity and marriage. Yank is all alone and "outside," in death as in life, on earth as in—the earth. And there "perhaps the Hairy Ape at last belongs" (232), unlike the usual comic protagonist, who really belongs from the very beginning and has only to wake up to that fact in the end.

Nonetheless, in his rejection and betrayal by all classes of society, Yank has something of the Christ-figure about him, as does the Cashier in the German Georg Kaiser's play *From Morn to Midnight* (1912)—which O'Neill read before he wrote *The Hairy Ape*, and which uses the station-play (or stations-of-the-cross) structure, borrowed from medieval religious drama, that became characteristic of both German and American expressionism. (O'Neill is quoted as stating that he had read Kaiser's drama before writing *The Hairy Ape* in B. H. Clark, *Eugene O'Neill: The Man and His Plays* [New York: Dover, 1947], 83.) Like *From Morn to Midnight* and Shaw's even earlier *Major Barbara* (1905), *The Hairy Ape* also links capitalism and Christianity in a mutually beneficial political conspiracy to exploit the poverty-stricken masses. (That "conspiracy" takes the form of explicit Salvation Army scenes in the Shaw and Kaiser plays, but the Salvation Army gets only one passing and contemptuous reference from Yank [172].) When, for example, Yank asks Long, on Fifth Avenue in Scene 5, where "*her* [Mildred's] kind" is, his friend replies, "In church, blarst 'em! Arskin' Jesus to give 'em more money" (203). When the wealthy churchgoers come out, they discuss ways to combat radicals (of the working class) and false doctrines (like anti-capitalism). At the same, they refer to their pastor as Doctor Caiaphas (207), an allusion on O'Neill's part to the high priest Caiaphas, who presided at the council that condemned Christ to death and declared that "It was better that one man die for all people" (John 18:14).

The authors of the other three gospels note that when Christ died "the curtain hanging in the temple was torn in two from top to bottom" (Matthew 27:50-51; Luke 23:45-46; Mark 15:37-38). The modern oppressors of humanity, for their part, specify in *The Hairy Ape* that proceeds from their "hundred percent American bazaar" will be used for repairing just such a curtain, i.e., for "rehabilitating the veil of the temple" (207). O'Neill thus suggests in the Fifth-Avenue Scene that the moneyed class, using the pretext of religious zeal, will ruthlessly crush any movement that threatens its economic position and will crucify anew any presumed—and presumptuous—rebel. Yank falls into this category at the end of Scene 5 when he is "clubbed . . . and fallen upon" (210) by the servants of the rich, the police, even as they subdue him at the end of Scene 6 when he tries to break out of jail. Something similar occurs again at the end of Scene 7, when Yank is overpowered by Wobblies, or members of the International Workers of the World, who suspect him of spying for *their* nemesis: the police. With immobilized arms and pinioned legs, as clumsy and artless as an animal, Yank takes on here the traits of a misunderstood savior—or the characteristics of a despised cross-bearer.

Christ-figure though he may be, Yank is meant as well—if only by O'Neill's choice of his first name, together with his melting pot of a "language," Brooklynese—to be the archetypal American, analogous to the archetypal Italian of futurist drama (which was still being produced in Italy at the same time as *The Hairy Ape* was being staged in New York). The central preoccupations of the futurists were speed and technology; like Yank, they were particularly drawn to the intoxicating power of machines, as Yank himself describes it in the following speech from early in the play:

> Sure I'm part of de engines! . . . Dey move, don't dey? Dey're speed, ain't dey? Dey smash trou, don't dey? . . . Dat's new stuff! Dat belongs! . . . I start somep'n and de woild moves! . . . I'm de ting in coal dat makes it boin; I'm steam and oil for de engines; I'm de ting in noise dat makes yuh hear it; I'm smoke and express trains and steamers and factory whistles . . . And I'm what makes iron into steel! Steel, dat stands for de whole ting! And I'm steel—steel—steel! (176-177)

The futurists welcomed steel and all the other products of industrial society—with its electricity, urbanization, and revolution in the means of transport and communication—with an all-embracing optimism, for they saw them as the means by which people would be able to dominate their environment totally. The speed, change, and motion of the industrial age were also fundamental to the futurists' love of the modern and their rejection of the static, lethargic past—the very "natural" past about which Paddy rhapsodizes in Scene 1 of O'Neill's play. As these Italians realized—in such plays as *Genius and Culture* (1915, by Umberto Boccioni), *The Arrest* (1916, by F. T. Marinetti), and *Lights* (1922, by Francesco Cangiullo)—the effects of the speed of transport and communication on modern sensibility were such that people were aware not just of their immediate surroundings but of the whole world.

In essence, then, the limits of time and space had been transcended—as they are, in a sense, in any production of *The Hairy Ape*, which moves from a transatlantic ocean liner bound for Southampton, England, to several locations on the streets of New York, and which takes place over a period of two months. Now it was possible to live through events both distant and near at hand: in fact, to be everywhere at the same time. Accordingly, Marinetti and his followers held that the speed of modern life called for a corresponding speed of communication in contemporary art, which should—unlike the conventional theater—be far briefer and more compressed or synthesized than even *The Hairy Ape*, yet at the same time incorporate simultaneous action occurring in different places or at different times.

Futurism took hold in Italy—and, in somewhat different, more metaphorical, as well as more short-lived, theatrical form, in the former U.S.S.R. (which, unlike soon-to-be Fascist Italy, restricted or completely suppressed the freedom even of those artists, like the Russian futurists, who supported the Communist revolution)—as in no other Western nation partly because this country, like the Soviet Union, underwent industrialization (as well as nationalization or consolidation) much later than, say, the United States. For this reason Italian futurists embraced the machine age and all that it made possible—including war, which they labeled the supreme, health-bestowing activity—to an extent unknown in American artistic circles.

Here, by contrast, playwrights like O'Neill, Elmer Rice (in *The Adding Machine* [1923]), and Sophie Treadwell (in *Machinal* [1928]) were using techniques borrowed from the German expressionists (who themselves rejected or at least vigorously questioned modern technology along with the military-industrial complex it spawned) to question both their country's rise to economic-cum-martial supremacy and its engineering of what amounted, in effect, to a second Industrial Revolution. Hence O'Neill's attempt, in *The Hairy Ape*, to depict the stokers—with the possible exception of Yank, "their most highly developed individual" (166) and consequently the very kind of individual (unsentimental, autonomous, hyper-efficient) championed by the Italian futurists—as soulless automatons who move and work mechanically, look alike, and speak with "a brazen, metallic quality as if their throats were phonograph horns" (170).

But the rich in this play are equally mechanical—and hardly a class to which Yank would (or could) aspire to belong, anyway—from the "incongruous, artificial . . ., inert and disharmonious" (180) Mildred and her aunt, to the "procession of gaudy marionettes" (207) on Fifth Avenue "with something of the relentless horror of Frankenstein monsters in their detached, mechanical unawareness" (207). And one of the reasons O'Neill made them so was less to indict or satirize the wealthy, as a polemical, anti-capitalistic workers' drama of the 1930s might, than to suggest that the rich, too, are victims of modern industrial civilization (which may be why, when Yank swings at them on New York's Fifth Avenue, nothing happens: they are already lifeless victims). Out of tune with the natural world, hardly in communion with any spiritual one, and consequently out of synch with, or unattuned to, themselves, they find their ideal representative in the bloodless, wraithlike Mildred, who has "a pale . . . face, [and] looks fretful, nervous, and discontented, bored by her own anemia" (180). It appears, O'Neill writes further, "as if the vitality of her stock had been sapped before she was conceived, so that she is the expression not of its life energy but merely of the artificialities that energy had won for itself in the spending" (180-181).

Yank Smith, moreover, is symbolic of the wealthy of the world in addition to all its workers, even though he rejects, and is rejected by, both the workers' movement and the uppermost leisure class. He is representative, then, of the displacement of modern humanity in general: of people who, in the Marxist sense, become alienated from themselves because their work is not part of their life; because their work takes over their life entirely, as in the case of Yank; or, in the case of the idle, upper-class Mildred, as opposed to an unemployed member of the underclass, because work is something that they do not even want. As a result, these people find themselves alienated from other human beings as well, with whom they no longer share a social essence or to whose society they no longer feel they belong.

In Yank's case, that alienation translates into a kind of permanent, fatal existentialism—a paralyzing clash, if you will, between Dante's medieval-cum-Renaissance Christianity and Marinetti's twentieth-century, totalitarian godlessness (or elevation of science and technology to godlike status). And the very structure of *The Hairy Ape* reveals this clash, which itself, in a sense, prevents Yank from moving either backward or forward, on to the past or back to the future. For, on the one hand, the episodic form of the play may be conducive to the illustration of a progressive if incremental journey toward spiritual wholeness or organicity; on the other hand, however, that same episodic form, in the rapidity with which it can transcend or condense time and place, suggests the Machine Age of which Yank is a part, with its ease of transport, atomization of human existence, speed of tempo, and even simultaneity of experience.

Looked at another way, the eight scenes of the play break down half and half between modernism in the form of futurism and medievalism in the form of the stations-of-the-cross drama. The first part of *The Hairy Ape*, all on the ship, is "modern." Here, the principles of Marinetti's futurism seem evident in the stokehole as Yank and his cohorts feed the machine at the same time they are, in a way, fed by it. The stokers' language in scene 1, for example, incorporates simultaneous speech during which they "talk over" one another, and actions themselves occur simultaneously when, in scene 2, the men (whom we should be able to see on stage) work below in the stokehole even as Mildred and her aunt are visible on top on the ocean liner's promenade deck.

After Mildred meets the "filthy beast," of course, the play completely changes. Following one more scene aboard ship, scene 4, the underlying structure of *The Hairy Ape* switches to that of a medieval station drama, relying now upon sequence rather than simultaneity. Thus, just as the play's own dramatic journey moves away from the modern and into the past, Yank devolves to see himself ultimately as the Hairy Ape (in both his description and in O'Neill's final stage direction [232]). The fateful meeting with Mildred, one could say, is the end of modernism-cum-futurism for him: "thought" or (self-) reflection kills Yank's forward movement in the present, and then in scenes 5-8 he learns that, although he may call himself a "Hairy Ape," he can't go back in time, either.

Yank, then, doesn't belong in either temporal realm after his brief but deadly encounter with Mildred—a fact brought home all the more by Mildred's disappearance from the plot at the end of Scene 3, and with her any hope for the beautification or beatification of this "beast" through romance. (Improbable as such a romance may be, Paddy hints at it in Scene 4 when he declares, "[Yank's] fallen in love" [195]. When Yank says that he has really "fallen in hate," Paddy retorts, "'Twould take a wise man to tell one from the other" [195].) For examples of ape-like characters who *do* belong in their respective Renaissance and modern "forms" or realms, who have a self-awareness initially denied to Yank, and who themselves have their encounters with beauties (Miranda and Blanche DuBois), one need only turn to Yank's distant ancestor Caliban from *The Tempest* (1611) and his near descendant Stanley Kowalski in *A Streetcar Named Desire* (1947, just three years after the release of the Hollywood film of *The Hairy Ape*, starring William Bendix and Susan Hayward).

Why so lowly a naturalistic character as Yank as symbolic protagonist of this drama? Because, in his utter identification with the machine, he is as close as we can get in a modern character to primitive or prehistoric man's union with nature, on the one hand, and the communion of a Christian saint, martyr, or "mere" true believer with God, on the other hand. He is what Emerson, already in the mid-nineteenth century, was calling the machine man, "Metamorphosed into a thing." And it is precisely because of such utter identification that Yank's eventual alienation from the machine (something not foreseen by the Italian futurists in their attempt to fashion man himself as the most superior of machines)—his fall, as it were—is rendered more dramatic, more effective, than it would be for a character not so closely identified. When Yank loses this identification, he has nothing left to fall back on: certainly not God or nature, nor, obviously, is his mind sophisticated enough to embrace secular humanism. He becomes like a puppet without his deterministic strings—one who can no longer be "yanked," if you will. Moreover, as O'Neill himself points out above, even when Yank tries to commune with his "brother" ape, his evolutionary ancestor, he is rejected. He dies in a cage of steel as night falls on the Central Park Zoo, without a future of either a material or a spiritual kind.

We may feel superior to this "comic" character, as we do to comic characters in general from our objective viewpoint, but we laugh at him at our own peril—unless, that is, our laughter is accompanied by the smile of recognition. For Robert "Yank" Smith is an alienated Everyman—*in nuce*, every Robert Smith in America, then as now—or he is no one. O'Neill's discovery, you see—and the discovery of other American dramatists at this time—was that "small" events in the lives of "small" people like Yank could be presented so that they reflected the wider world outside a ship's boiler room, or a home's living room. A national literature of plays thus set in bourgeois living rooms or proletarian workplaces is a deeply democratic literature, one which assumes that the important subjects are those that manifest themselves in the daily lives of ordinary (not "noble" or "heroic") people like Yank Smith.

And, common man or not, Yank certainly has his stature increased by O'Neill's use of the equivalent of Greek choruses throughout *The Hairy Ape*. In the stokehole scenes, the forecastle scene, the Fifth-Avenue scene, the I.W.W. scene, the jail scene, and the zoo scene—indeed, every scene except the second one between Mildred and her aunt, in which Yank does not appear—O'Neill introduced the clamor and chatter of people or animals to set the tone and milieu of his drama; to indicate the masses from whom Yank stands out, to remind us of the essentially social nature of human experience at the same time as we are supplied with a host of witnesses to Yank's private or individual suffering; and to provide us with a kind of frame or lens through which to view Yank as he undergoes his *agon*.

That frame or lens was heightened in the original New York production during the Fifth-Avenue scene because the actors playing rich people wore Greek-like masks (the first use of masks in a serious play on Broadway, where *The Hairy Ape* was moved from the Provincetown Playhouse, also in New York)—a device that O'Neill later regretted he had not used in the stokehole scene and other scenes as well. Our socio-choral perspective on Yank might thus be derisive or dismissive, depending on the "chorus" and its mask, but then again it could be a combination of the reverential and the fearful (as it is in the case of the stokers in Scenes 1 and 3), or it could be lamentatory (as it is in the case of the "chattering, whimpering wail" [232] of the monkeys at the end of the play, after Yank has expired).

Whether we view Yank as a fully tragic character in the classical sense seems to me less important, however, than the fact that O'Neill has bestowed on so lowly a figure a number of characteristics we traditionally associate with tragedy. To wit: a kind of freedom of action that enables Yank to choose his course without much restriction, at the same time as we sense the tragic irony of his choices; his own crude proletarian idiom, which, like verse, sets him apart and has a peculiar evocativeness, even exaltation; a life lived, not in a home (let alone with a wife and children), but outside in something akin to a public arena (on a "public" ship and in other such places), which publicness itself—like Yank's choral witnesses—confers moral, spiritual, and philosophical significance on his actions; a hubris in his superior physical strength, which is contrasted with Yank's bewilderment (a word used no fewer than four times in the stage directions by O'Neill to describe Yank's perception of his situation: 192, 196, 225, 232) at almost everything that happens to him subsequent to his encounter with Mildred; and, finally, Yank's consciousness or understanding of *what* has happened to him and *why*, which is summed up in a concluding recognition speech that forever removes this character from the realm of the pathetic, the uninitiated, the witless, or the merely animalistic at the same time as it confers on him tragic dignity.

Ironically, Yank's consciousness was "given" to him by his nemesis Mildred, and it is fully expressed, ultimately, not to another human being but only to a gorilla and a chorus of monkeys:

> So yuh're what she seen when she looked at me, de white-faced tart! I was you to her, get me? On'y outa de cage—broke out—free to moider her, see? Sure! Dat's what she tought. She wasn't wise dat I was in a cage, too—worser'n yours—sure—a damn sight—'cause you got some chanct to bust loose—but me—. . . Youse can sit and dope dream in de past, green woods, de jungle and de rest of it. Den yuh belong and dey don't. . . . Sure, you're de best off! Yuh can't tink, can yuh? Yuh can't talk neider. But I kin make a bluff at talkin' and tinkin'—a'most git away wit it—a'most!—and dat's where de joker comes in. (229-230)

It is shortly after he speaks these words of recognition that Yank dies in the gorilla's cage of the Central Park Zoo, never having returned to the security of the stokehole on his ship—an alternative that was open to him but which he bravely did not, could not, or would not take. To the prison-house of self, in life, Yank seems to prefer death in a cage at the hands of a creature not quite of his own kind, yet still very much like him.

It is not by chance that *The Hairy Ape* assimilates such seemingly disparate international influences as late nineteenth-century European naturalism (with its view of man as an animal or even an object for study and control), Italian futurism, German expressionism, Greek tragedy, and a Renaissance work like the *Divine Comedy*. For O'Neill was America's first serious—by which I mean important—dramatist, and he became a serious artist in part because, by the time he came of age, the foundations of an artistic (in contrast to commercial) theater had been laid in the United States. For one thing, the non-profit "little theater" movement, modeled after the independent theaters of Europe, had engendered considerable enthusiasm in places like New York, Chicago, and Detroit; and, combined with the modified, conceptualized realism of the "new stagecraft" of such designers as Cleon Throckmorton and Robert Edmond Jones (who jointly created the set and lights for *The Hairy Ape*'s initial little-theater production at the Provincetown), this movement made possible the production of serious new plays that might not otherwise have had commercial promise.

In addition, selected Americans had observed foreign developments in the performing arts and had returned to write about them in *Theatre Arts*, the first American periodical devoted, as its title indicates, to a consideration of the art of theater; and a number of esteemed foreign troupes and productions themselves had visited the States, if not for the first time then for the first time in large numbers.   Moreover, the study of world theater and drama, contemporary as well as classical, had been introduced into several American colleges and universities, along with playwriting classes such as the one O'Neill himself took at Harvard during 1914-1915 with George Pierce Baker; and prizes like the Pulitzer and the New York Drama Critics' Circle Award began to be given yearly for the "best new American play." Last, but certainly not least, the rise of the cinema (and, by the early 1920s, radio along with it) as the most popular art of the twentieth century—even as the theater had been the most popular form of the nineteenth century (a fact that O'Neill well knew from his own experiences as a young man touring with his matinée-idol father, James O'Neill)—cleared the way for serious American playwrights to think about something other than commercial success, something the drama could accomplish that films could not or that the theater could realize better than any movie could hope to do.

All of this, in some measure, was the result of World War I—the first fully and horrifically mechanized war, let us remember—which marked not only the ascent of the United States as a military and economic superpower, but also the opening up of the American nation to outside intellectual-artistic influence on an unprecedented scale. As I have already suggested, the Great War—as it was and continues to be called by those who recognize that "great" in this case is a pejorative term—also unleashed the first wave of American dramatist-critics, who immediately envisioned the negative side, or psychic cost, of the United States's newly recognized, now unrivaled wealth and power. O'Neill was foremost among these dramatist-critics, and *The Hairy Ape*, like such other early, experimental plays of his as *The Emperor Jones* (1920) and *The Great God Brown* (1926), is evidence both of his newfound dramatic art and of his emergent critical temper.

Work Cited

O'Neill, Eugene.   *Three Plays:* Anna Christie, The Emperor Jones, *and* The Hairy Ape.   New York: Vintage 1972.

CHAPTER TWO

THE FRONT PAGE, FARCE, AND AMERICAN COMEDY

The success of *The Front Page* (1928) made Ben Hecht and Charles MacArthur, both former newspapermen, famous as dramatic collaborators. Together they also wrote *Twentieth Century* (1932), a farcical comedy about flamboyant movie people, and other plays, as well as a number of screenplays for such popular films as *Gunga Din* (1939) and *Wuthering Heights* (1939). Later, they briefly became writer-directors, with one of their pictures, *The Scoundrel* (1935, from Hecht's play *All He Ever Loved*), winning an Oscar for each of them. Hecht in particular is remembered for his labors in Hollywood, where he scripted two of the best Hitchcock movies (*Spellbound*, in 1945, and *Notorious*, in 1946) and helped invent several genres. One of them was the gangster film (with the silent *Underworld* [1927], succeeded by the talkie that Hecht scripted, *Scarface* [1932]), and another the madcap or screwball comedy. The first of these comedies was Howard Hawks's adaptation of *Twentieth Century* in 1934, to be followed in 1940 by Hawks's *His Girl Friday*, a version of *The Front Page* that featured a woman in the role of Hildy Johnson.

The fact that Hecht and McArthur are better known for their screen efforts than their stage work is significant. For, when they were writing, there was comparatively little pure slapstick or physical humor in the theater, that being the specialty from the start of silent film comedians like Keaton, Chaplin, Harry Langdon, and Harold Lloyd; also strikingly absent from the American playwriting tradition, with rare exceptions, was the sex or bedroom farce of the Feydeau school. As a result, there was little exploration of comedy's anarchic or critical potential in American drama during the first three decades of the twentieth century—or, indeed, of any period except briefly in the 1960s. While audiences in the commercial Broadway theatre were surprisingly supportive of challenging serious drama, they came to comedies for relaxation and escape; they also came with the confidence that they would be able to go home with their values and assumptions unshaken. Thus did these audiences confirm the snobbish, perhaps universal, misgiving that comedy is an inferior art—one better suited for the "lowly" screen—despite the achievement in this genre of such dramatists as Aristophanes, Molière, Shakespeare, and Shaw.

Moreover, with the advent of sound in the cinema, a kind of film did indeed explore comedy's anarchic or critical potential: the aforementioned screwball comedy. Socially aware, dramatically structured, and intellectually based, such comedies depended on dialogue for sophisticated, witty humor, though they still contained marvelous sight gags performed by comedians who were as aggressive and ridiculous in speech as in action. The nature of this sound comedy is always zany and often chaotic; indeed, the nonsense is so consistent and pervasive that it seems to operate with a logical non-logic or irrationality of its own in pictures like Hawks's *Bringing Up Baby* (1938), George Cukor's *The Philadelphia Story* (1940), and Preston Sturges's *The Palm Beach Story* (1942) as well as his *Miracle of Morgan's Creek* (1940).

Significant in these films was a very emancipated, taboo-breaking view of womanhood to go along with the liberated spirit of their own scripts; the heroine behaved as independently and aggressively as the male, if not more so, and demonstrated a good deal of intelligence of her own in a brainy, energetic battle of the sexes. Hence the 1940, gender-reversed adaptation of *The Front Page*, in which Hildy becomes a woman reporter who was once married to Walter Burns, and who remarries him together with the newspaper business at the end rather than settling down with a pallid husband and a passel of kids in the provincial backwater of Albany, New York. Ben Hecht even collaborated (though uncredited) with Charles Lederer on the scenario for *His Girl Friday* in addition to being the co-author of the movie's source, and in this case as well as in his and MacArthur's other screen efforts, the theater's loss was certainly the cinema's gain.

As for the action of the play *The Front Page*, all three acts are set in the Press Room of the Chicago Courts Building, which is crowded with journalists covering a hanging that is to take place early the next morning. The execution of Earl Williams, an anarchist in an age of "Red Menace" hysteria and the murderer of a black policeman, has been twice postponed so that it will have maximum effect just before an imminent election. In it the black vote and the law-and-order platform will be pivotal factors—so pivotal that the cynical newspapermen dwell on them expansively during intervals in their card-playing and banter about women. Also on their minds, however, is a rumor that Hildy Johnson is retiring from court reporting after fifteen years to leave town and get married. This rumor is confirmed by Hildy on his arrival, with the additional news that he is going into the comfortable world of advertising in New York City, where his pay will more than double. Hildy is booked on a train with his fiancée, Peggy Grant, and prospective mother-in-law that night, and he takes advantage of the situation to make a last abusive telephone call to Walter Burns, his boss.

The rest of the action involves the hour-by-hour deferral of Hildy's plans, as the mayor and sheriff collude in concealing a reprieve, the condemned man escapes, a hunt takes most of the reporters across the city, and the escapee crashes in through the window of the press room to give himself up to Johnson, who immediately becomes immersed in the best scoop in his career. The resolution contains an element of melodrama, with the release of the handcuffed Hildy and Burns after the general exposure of corruption and blackmail, and with the couple departing to take a later train. In a final wry twist to the plot, however, Burns ensures that Hildy will be arrested during a stop in La Porte, Indiana, and returned to Chicago.

After try-outs in Atlantic City, *The Front Page* opened in New York on August 14, 1928, and since that first night this madcap comedy about Chicago newspaper life has become one of the most frequently produced plays in American theatre. (The play has already enjoyed three movie versions—one of them, as already noted, macerating this hard-nosed farce into a gender-reversed romantic comedy, with Rosalind Russell as a female Hildy Johnson and Cary Grant doing one of his incomparable comic turns as her editor-lover, Walter Burns.) One reason *The Front Page* has remained alive is that it is simultaneously the best-known critique and cliché of American journalism, a work that newspaper people have spent over seventy-five years trying to live up to. There are still editors who enjoy behaving like the play's Walter Burns in front of their young reporters, who in turn delight in perpetuating the myth of Hildy Johnson for their own newsroom audience. This situation has created a kind of ethical schizophrenia whereby journalists are expected to talk like cynical scoundrels while behaving with the exaggerated conscientiousness of seminarians.

As early as 1934, one nationally known newspaper editor, Stanley Walker, counseled young hopefuls to ignore everything *The Front Page* told them about journalism. Such warnings have only increased, as changes in the news business have made the milieu of this play look more and more antique. Yet homage persists to the tradition that it created. And that tradition is bolstered by all the later plays, films, and novels about the press that somehow entrench rather than debunk the stereotypes Hecht and MacArthur created. *The Front Page* and its progeny have thus generated healthy suspicions about journalism and its servants in the minds of millions of people who otherwise would have no knowledge of either. In at least a couple of ways, then, *The Front Page*, in its effect on popular culture, is one of the most powerful and lasting works in American literature.

What most people don't know, however, is that the play is a *pièce à clef*. Not only is its whole flavor actually that of a frantic and long-vanished age of American journalism, but some of the names of characters and institutions, some situations, even some bits of dialogue, were taken from real life, even though the co-authors felt that they had to tone down what they knew to be the truth. For one thing, the language of the streets was diluted, to be restored to something like its original vulgarity only in Billy Wilder's 1974 film version (the third movie adaptation). Still, the famous curtain-closer of cunning editor Walter Burns ("The son of a bitch stole my *watch*!") created a stir, much more than the sprinkling of goddamns and such in the rest of the play. Indeed, the New York police wanted to arrest the cast; and even in the first movie version, released in 1931, a well-placed clatter from a typewriter obscured the coarsest part of the closing line. As late as 1970, when the second Broadway revival was adapted for television, one critic felt obliged to comment that "this particular production marks a break-through for TV profanity because the play's classic last line, which is the essence of the character of Walter Burns, is intact."

To address now the real-life counterparts of the characters in *The Front Page*, Earl Williams, the condemned prisoner, is a composite of various radicals, but his escape from the Cook County Jail derives from the case of Terrible Tommy O'Connor, a thirty-five-year-old Irish immigrant convicted in 1921 of killing a night watchman during the robbery of the Illinois Central Railroad's downtown station. He broke out days before he was sentenced to hang but, unlike Williams, was never recaptured; one rumor had it that he returned to Ireland and perished fighting the British. For decades, the gallows in Chicago remained intact in the event he should ever be caught. The year before *The Front Page* appeared, Hecht had used the O'Connor escape in his script for Josef von Sternberg's *Underworld*—which, it's worth repeating, was the first of the Hollywood gangster films.

Where the reporters are concerned, the Canadian writer Vincent Starrett, who knew Hecht and MacArthur when he worked on the Chicago dailies, recalled years later, "There was no newspaper slave in Chicago but swore he recognized every figure on the boards." Certainly the most obvious of the shanghai victims is the ace reporter Hildy Johnson. He's based on a Swedish immigrant named Hilding Johnson, who once broke into a jury room with a deadline pressing, learned of the verdict by going through old ballots in the waste-paper basket, then left phony evidence for a competitor he knew would be breaking in later. "Poor Hildy!" wrote Starrett. "He died a few years after the play was produced (in 1931, at age forty-five)—I saw him laughing in his box opening night—and it was said that his determined effort to approximate his reckless counterpart on the stage had hastened his untimely end."

In fact, the eccentricity of *The Front Page*'s characters was considerably de-emphasized in the paste-pot process by which Hecht and MacArthur fashioned their finished product. As Hecht was said to have remarked, no one in the audience would have believed the real thing. The character of Walter Burns is a case in point. It was based on Walter Crawford Howey, for whom MacArthur had worked on both the *Tribune* and the *Herald-Examiner* and who possessed one of the most robust personal legends in Chicago journalism. One of his early triumphs was a series of muckracking articles that drove Mayor Fred Busse (according to notes in *The Front Page* script, the original owner of Bensinger's rolltop desk) out of office. As city editor of the *Tribune*, Howey became notorious for a style of news-gathering that included intimidating witnesses and blackmailing municipal, county, and state authorities, whose signed but undated resignations he kept in his desk for use in emergencies. He and a few of his rivals came to symbolize daily journalism in the 1920s, a time when each big story was a melodrama.

In 1910, Howey blew up at the owners of the *Tribune* and transferred his allegiance to Hearst's *Herald-Examiner*, the "Madhouse on Madison Street." Dion O'Bannion, the notorious gangster later shot down in his flower shop by Al Capone's henchmen, was the *Her-Ex* circulation manager. His job (not unlike Diamond Louie's in the play) was to persuade vendors to carry the Hearst paper in preference to the *Tribune*. Soon full-blown circulation wars developed. Howey had only one eye, and some said he lost the other one fighting in such wars. Others contended that he lost it by falling on a copy spike while sitting drunkenly at his desk. Whatever the case, Hecht remarked that he could tell the glass eye from the natural one: the glass eye, he said, had warmth. The *Herald-Examiner* folded in 1939, and thereafter Howey's career declined steadily. He died in 1955 at age seventy-three. In a last tribute to his old boss, MacArthur visited him in the hospital during his final illness and gave him a watch engraved "To the Best Newspaperman I Know"—just like the one in *The Front Page*.

Initially, the authors had intended to reflect their "intellectual disdain of and superiority to the Newspaper," but in writing the play they found they were "not so much dramatists or intellectuals as two reporters in exile." Thus, despite its "oaths and realisms," the work became for them "a Valentine thrown to the past, a Ballad full of *Heimweh* and Love." The managing editor Walter Burns is emphatically excluded from the Valentine, however, when he is described in a stage direction as

that product of thoughtless, pointless, nerve-drumming unmorality [sic] that is the Boss Journalist—the licensed eavesdropper, trouble-maker, bombinator and Town Snitch, misnamed The Press.

Inasmuch as other factors of disdain remain in the play, they are directed at local government, which unfolds as a maze of nepotism, self-advancement, and other corruption. A secondary—and much lighter—filament of dramatic satire focuses on the emergent vogue for popular psychoanalysis, picking as targets a policeman who analyzes Williams as a "dual personality," a reporter who has a phobic obsession with dirt, and a psychiatrist who, assessing Williams's sanity, gets him to re-enact the crime with the gun he used to escape.

Though *The Front Page* has often been termed a "comic melodrama," it is closer to a farcical or physical comedy, with a complicated and implausible pattern of intrigue, concealment, coincidence, and situational absurdity, maximizing the resource value of every door, window, desk, and even watch on stage. In fact, one could argue that action leads to objects in farce of this kind, and objects are always defeating the characters, no matter how single-minded they have been in their fervent, fast-paced pursuit of a short-range goal or immediate gratification. Where real-life characters think, such farcical ones—caught as they are in the thick of things—use instinct to get what they want. And though they may finally be defeated in a high-stakes game, even a life-and-death situation, there are no real consequences for them, because there is no visible or irreparable harm.

Thus, despite all the (offstage) shooting and (onstage) brandishing of weapons in *The Front Page*, no one gets killed—not the psychiatrist Dr. Eglehofer, whom Earl Williams shoots in the stomach; not the deputy who gets shot in the buttocks during the city-wide manhunt for Williams; not Mollie Malloy after she jumps out of the window of the press room; not Mrs. Grant after the car in which Louie is kidnapping her crashes into a police patrol; and not even Earl himself, who is reprieved instead of executed. The one person who does die, the black policeman whom Earl murders, gets shot well before the play begins—accidentally, claims the killer whose cause is "all humanity."

Yet, for all the physical or corporeal survival of *The Front Page*'s characters, they become as objectified, mechanized, or dehumanized—as spiritually extinct—as the things that are always getting in their way or frustrating their plans, from Hildy's cane to the sheriff's gun to Bensinger's desk to Walter's watch. Without the time to think or reflect, with only the time to move and shout and do, these figures are placed on the same level as the antagonistic, inanimate objects, or props that not only get deployed against them, but also seem to take on a life of their own. In this way *The Front Page* transcends the "mere" funniness of all farce to become a serious comment on the unthinking, or animalistic, side of human life—particularly as it is lived at such fast pace by these opportunists.

What also takes the play beyond pure farce is the depth of its societal and characterological portraiture, as the characters' capacity for childishness, callousness, and even sadism provides a subtext to every laugh. The studied insensitivity of most of the journalists is tested through the catalyst of minor characters such as Mollie Malloy, the prostitute who comforted Williams when she found him in a disturbed state the day before the murder and thus became a key witness on his behalf. The reporters, however, have sensationalized her connection with the condemned man well beyond the point of exaggeration, and their brutal baiting of her, which will result in her attempt at suicide in the second act, emphatically registers how out of touch with her humanism they are. When, with "*a scream of terror and exultation*," she throws herself through the third-story window, the journalists are mostly "*awed and astonished*," and even Hildy seems to have forgotten her a little later; such reaction contrasts strongly with the response of the sole policeman present, who is "*sick at heart*," his body "*doubled up with pain.*" Emotional cauterization seems an essential precondition for journalism, and in the first act this condition is registered through the regular sound of the gallows being exercised, with a "*whirr and crash,*" indicating that sandbags are being used to test the machinery of death.

That journalism is an arena in which manhood is proven, is asserted throughout *The Front Page*. When a reporter's wife appears, we are told,

> If she is a bit acidulated, tight-lipped and sharp-spoken, no one can blame her, least of all these bravos of the press room, who have small respect for themselves or each other as husbands, fathers and lovers.

This woman expresses her reservations about Hildy's marriage, to which another reporter retorts: "If I was married to that dame I'd kick her humpbacked." At the end of the second act, Hildy's "*tortured male spirit takes refuge in hysteria*," and he rejects his fiancée, declaiming, "God damn it—I'm a newspaper man," which throws Peggy into retreat, "*her sobs filling the room and corridor.*" Hildy's remorse consists in observing that he treated her "like she was some waitress," but Walter Burns consoles him by telling him that he "acted like a man for the first time in [his] life!"

Burns's belief that women are murderers or "Borgias" is scarcely substantiated by the conduct of Mollie or Peggy, but the fundamental misogyny of the play's tribute to the newspaper world echoes throughout the play. "I was in love once," Walter tells us in an uncharacteristic moment of Sir Andrew Aguecheek tenderness, only to add, ". . . with my third wife." To an ailing reporter, Burns misanthropically shouts, "To hell with your diabetes, this is important." His passion for his newspaper thus leaves him indifferent to any weaknesses, male or female, that aren't exploitable. Like the play itself, he has a cartilaginous heart, and by the time he barks the play's famous final line, Walter Burns has created a comic scoundrel unique in the annals of deception.

The Front Page, then, doesn't have a soft bone in its body. Though its co-authors may originally have conceived the work as a satire on ruthless reporters and sensationalistic journalism, only to end up in their view with a valentine to the whole newspaper profession, the adduced evidence does not support their claim. (Nor would the casting of an actor who could make Walter ruthless, not just rambunctious as were Adolphe Menjou and Walter Matthau in the 1931 and 1974 film versions, respectively.) These reporters certainly have their engaging side—so do the hack politicians and corrupt cops who serve as foils for their banter. But for all the double crosses, competitive dodges, sardonic backbiting, good-natured chicanery, and idiomatic wisecracks (expressed in that special urban argot that Eugene O'Neill kept trying, with varying success, to create), the play provides a glimpse of the seamy side of American politics and press practices that is ferociously contemporary.

When the governor, for example, sends a reprieve for Earl Williams on the last day of the campaign—his motive, as a Democrat, being to undercut his party's Republican rivals in the persons of the sheriff and the mayor—the latter bribes the messenger to say he never delivered it. When the prisoner escapes, the mayor orders him shot on sight. (Indeed, in the way that it takes a beady look at human corruption, *The Front Page* suggests how soft we have since become as a democratic republic and an artistic culture.) The truth is, nobody gives a damn about Earl Williams—not Walter Burns, who only wants an exclusive for the *Examiner*; not the reporters, who tailor the facts to suit their purposes; not even Hildy Johnson, who helps to hide him in a rival reporter's desk but has no intention of saving Earl's life.

As a matter of fact, aside from Mollie Malloy, that sentimental hooker who jumps out of a window rather than testify—and who, along with the condemned man, is ironically the person in the play with the biggest heart, if not the only heart—Earl Williams has no value for anyone except as an opportunity for greed, ambition, vanity, or worse. For the press, the highest premium is "the great big Scoop": the reporters want Williams hanged not at seven in the morning but at five, in time for the city edition. For the politicians, whose only motive is perpetuating themselves in office, ideology, conscience, and even human life itself are hostages to expediency. *The Front Page*, one might say, dramatizes Darwin's survival theory with a breezy sangfroid equaled before only by Ben Jonson and John Gay, and only by Bertolt Brecht and David Mamet in our own time. Not only in its effect on popular culture, then, but also in its dramatic artistry, this is one of the most incisive and enduring works in the history of American theater.

Works Cited

Hecht, Ben. Charlie: The Improbable Life and Times of Charles MacArthur. New York: Harper and Brothers, 1957.

—. *Lettters from Bohemia*. Garden City, New York: Doubleday & Co., 1964.

Hecht, Ben and Charles MacArthur. *The Front Page*. New York: Samuel French, 1950.

Murray, George. *The Madhouse on Madison Street*. Chicago: Follett Publishing Co., 1965.

Starrett, Vincent. *Born in a Bookshop: Chapters from the Chicago Renaissance*. Norman: Univ. of Oklahoma Press, 1965.

CHAPTER THREE

ON THE ROAD TO TRAGEDY: MICE, LAND, AND CANDY IN *OF MICE AND MEN*

It has often been suggested that the Candy-and-his-dog subplot in *Of Mice and Men* (1937) is a typical example of Steinbeck's heavyhandedness and overfondness for parallels. For example, Robert Murray Davis has written that "When structural patterns in Steinbeck's novels are clear, they are almost blindingly obvious" (4). This reasoning lies behind the decision to omit the dog entirely from some student and workshop productions of the play. But Candy and the dog are very important to the action. The point of Carlson's shooting of the dog—who is old and blind and smells—is not to make an easy parallel with George's shooting of Lennie. It is not so much the dog who is in the same position as the imbecilic Lennie; it is the shooting of the dog that places Candy in the same position. Once he does not have his dog to look after anymore, Candy realizes the precariousness of his own position on the ranch: he is without one hand and therefore only able to "swamp out" bunkhouses, and he is fast approaching senility.

This point has escaped several fine critics. In an otherwise highly laudatory reading of the "play-novelette," as he calls it, as a Biblical allegory (George=Cain and Lennie=Abel), Peter Lisca writes:

> Less subtle, perhaps too obvious, is the relationship of Candy and his dog, which is made parallel to that of George and Lennie . . . Thus the mounting threats to the dog and his eventual shooting foreshadow the destruction of George's "dog," Lennie, which eventually takes place, shot by the same gun in the same way—"right in the back of the head . . . why he'd never know what hit him." (Lisca 84-85)

Harry T. Moore has gone so far as to say that "one of the most noticeable of the many little tricks [that] have been used throughout the story to prepare us for Lennie's death is the obvious comparison of Lennie with a worthless old dog that must be shot, as Lennie must be at the last" (52).

As I am arguing, however, Steinbeck stresses the similarity between Candy's position and Lennie's. Candy, like no other character in the play, treats

Lennie as his mental equal. Furthermore, George never explains Lennie's condition to Candy as he does, say, to Slim. Not accidentally, it is to Lennie that Candy describes the "figuring" he has been doing, describes how, if they go about it right, they can make some money on the rabbits they propose to have on their farm (even if Lennie, for his part, can think of nothing except petting the rabbits). Candy *sounds* like Lennie when he says, "We gonna have a room to ourselves. We gonna have a dog and chickens. We gonna have green corn and maybe a cow" (129). And he acts like Lennie when he comes into Crooks's room in the barn, saying only, "This is the first time I ever been in [Crooks's] room"; he seems honestly not to realize that the reason for this is that, as Crooks declares, "Guys don't come in a colored man's room" (128). Yet Candy has been on the ranch for a long time, just as Crooks has.

So, like Lennie, Candy needs someone to run his affairs, to make the rest of his life easier and more congenial. He needs George. Slim promises Candy a puppy from his bitch Lulu's litter to compensate for the shooting of his sheep dog, but Candy never gets that puppy, and he never asks for it. Lennie can attempt to look after a pup, because he has George to look after him. Candy is in search of a home for *himself*; he cannot afford, at this point, to give one to a dog. But Candy, finally, is not Lennie, and George will not team up with him after Lennie is gone. Candy does not accompany the men in their hunt for Lennie, after Curley's wife is found dead in the barn. He stays all alone on the ranch, deserted, at it were, by everyone, even as he will be by George after Lennie has been shot. Candy's "Poor bastard" (161), spoken to Curley's dead wife, lying in the hay, once the men have left, could just as well be applied to himself as to Lennie or Curley's wife.

The failure to appreciate Candy's true position in the drama has led to underappreciation of the tragic dimensions of Steinbeck's novella. In a review of the 1975 New York production of *Of Mice and Men* (directed by Edwin Sherin), for example, Stanley Kauffmann of *The New Republic* wrote that

> The tragic inevitability at which Steinbeck aimed is dimmed by the creakiness of the arrangements. We know with somewhat pleasant ironical foreknowledge in the first scene, when the two friends discuss their plans to have a place of their own, that they will never get it; but Steinbeck ensures the grim ending with the nervous young husband at the ranch and his arbitrarily restless wife. Besides, Lennie's feeble-mindedness mitigates the tragedy. He is a "case" on the loose, not a man susceptible to trouble. If he were only slow-witted, instead of defective, there would be some hint of what his life might have been. With the idiot Lennie there are no alternatives. (158)

But *Of Mice and Men* is not Lennie's tragedy; Kauffmann seems to forget that there is a character named George Milton in the play.

Harry T. Moore is more illuminating on the subject of *Of Mice and Men* as tragedy, but his view of George as no more than a pathetic character is the opposite of mine:

> Violence without tragedy: that is the weakness of this book. . . . There is no tragedy as we understand the word in reference to literature. . . . There is no authentic tragedy, which comes out of character. Even if we slur over the criticism that Lennie is a poor choice for a central figure in the story because from the start the odds against him are too great—even if we get beyond this and admit George as the true protagonist, we still don't find tragedy. George is no more than pathetic. He attracts sympathy because he has to lose his friend Lennie, to whom he has been so loyal, and whom he has to kill at the last in order to save him from the others. But because this isn't genuine tragedy, it gives the reader a brutal shock when George kills Lennie, and it cannot be anything else . . . (50-52)

In a related argument, Howard Levant, criticizes *Of Mice and Men* for what he believes to be a split focus that diminishes its emotional impact (i.e., its tragic weight):

> The secondary hero is subordinate in Steinbeck's fiction—except in *Of Mice and Men*. There, Lennie's murder propels George into a sudden prominence that has no structural basis. Is the novel concerned with Lennie's innocence or George's guilt? The formal requirements of a play-novelette mandate a structural refocus. Steinbeck needs a high point to ring down the curtain. With Lennie dead, Steinbeck must use and emphasize George's guilt. The close is formulated—the result of a hasty switch—not structured from preceding events, so it produces an inconclusive ending in view of what has happened previously. And the ideal of the farm vanishes with Lennie's death, when George tells Candy the plan is off. (143)

There is tragedy in *Of Mice and Men*, then, Levant, Kauffmann, and Moore to the contrary. That is why Candy is in the play.

The tragedy is so understated, however, that one barely notices it. And this tragedy really has nothing to do with George's shooting of Lennie, per se. As the film critic Otis Ferguson once remarked, "I have never been quite sure that George shouldn't have shot [Lennie] before the story began" (285). Ferguson was not trying to be funny. His meaning was that Lennie is a "case" on the loose, and that his killing of Curley's wife, and being shot for it by George, could just as easily have happened before the play or after it as during it. Steinbeck arranges for it to happen during the play, after the two men meet Candy. Does he do this just so that we can feel sorry for poor Lennie, as many believe? No, I don't think so. His point was that George deeply loved this "idiot," with the result that he always wanted Lennie to be with him in his travels and in his work. Once he shoots Lennie, George can still get the farm with Candy if he wants to. (Recall that it is largely Candy's money that will buy the farm, and Candy is still more than willing to put up that money.) But he declines, which proves that being in one safe place with *Lennie* was more important to him than simply being in one safe place. He elects to continue living the hard life of a ranchhand rather than settle down to life on a small farm with Candy. George can have a better life, yet he turns it down. Unquestionably, he will suffer more on the road, without Lennie, than on the farm, without Lennie. He never gives himself a chance to, in his words, "get used to" Candy.

This is not simple pathos. It approximates tragedy because it suggests not simply that *George loved Lennie too much*, that he was unnaturally attached to him, but also that only by developing an unnatural attachment to Lennie could he ever have put up with (and done so much for) someone like him in the first place. The implication of George's rejection of Candy's offer is that he is sentencing himself to the same fate as other "guys that go round on the ranches alone" (77): he will not have any fun, and after a while he will get mean. He will live out the fate predicted for him by Crooks: this is the accompaniment to, or extension of, the tragic inevitability of the play. Crooks says, "I seen hundreds of men come by on the road and on the ranches, bindles on their back and that same damn thing in their head. Hundreds of 'em. They come and they quit and they go on. And every damn one of 'em is got a little piece of land in his head. And never a goddamn one of 'em gets it" (126). The implication is that George will have that little piece of land in his head once again, after months of working hard and blowing his money in "cathouses" and pool rooms, and that is when he will become tragically aware of how he really lost his land—not by losing Lennie, but by rejecting Candy—and how he will never be given the chance to get it again. Like Othello, he will have loved not wisely, but too well. Like any other tragic hero's, his awareness will be one of self-acceptance more than self-reproach.

So while the play underlines the bond of friendship—and loneliness—that exists between George and Lennie (a bond difficult for some in today's audiences to accept on any but homosexual grounds), it also makes that bond responsible for George's rash decision not to buy the small farm with Candy's financial assistance. We are in full sympathy with George when he makes this decision, still we cannot help but feel at the same time that he is making a mistake, that he is doing something noble yet horrible and wasteful (of Candy's life as well as his own). Candy's "Poor bastard" this time applies to George, whom we leave alone, with the dead Lennie, at the end of the play.

George, it must be said, is not especially articulate or self-examining. He has never married: Lennie is his emotional attachment. He does not make many friends or ask many questions. Candy is his only "attachment" to the ranch: Candy first fills him in about the Boss, then about Curley and his wife, Crooks, and Slim. And Candy, with his life savings, becomes George's way out of the ranch life. With Lennie dead, he potentially becomes George's emotional attachment. He is, in the end, the embodiment or articulation of all the aims and emotions that George in his sorrow is oblivious to, but which will live to haunt him again. That is why Steinbeck ends scenes one and two of Act III with Candy and George in the same position: hunching over dead bodies. They are in the same position, in need of each other, but inalterably separated. And finally they are silent, one seemingly in memory of the other.

Like George, the play's tragedy is quiet. Like George, the play seems to focus more on Lennie than its own life, or on any wider artistic avenues it might have pursued. That, more than anything else, is its identification with George. The play sacrifices attention to him for attention to Lennie. That is the way George would have wanted it, and that is why, unfairly, *Of Mice and Men* has too often been called nothing more than a work of sentiment (See Moore, 51; Kauffmann, 157; and Kazin, 398). Now sentimentality is usually accounted a vice, because it bespeaks a propensity to express a greater degree of feeling than a specific situation warrants. But sentimentality need not be a vital flaw; it isn't in *Of Mice and Men*, where Steinbeck controls it. Such sentimentality is often the characteristic of a young and vigorous people whose experience of life is, so to speak, still new and uncontaminated by too frequent disillusionment. In this sense our history makes us a sentimental people and it is only natural that our arts, particularly our folk or popular arts, should reveal this quality.

But popular or not, *Of Mice and Men* is much more than a work of sentiment. We come to George's tragedy the long way around, through Candy. Lennie is not diminished by this; rather, George and Candy are elevated. And one of the ways in which George in particular is elevated is through Steinbeck's thorough weaving of the seemingly throwaway, sentimental symbol of the mouse into the fabric of the play's action. We see that symbol first in the play's title, which Steinbeck took from the Robert Burns poem ("To a Mouse," 1786) containing the line "The best-laid schemes o' mice and men, / Gang aft agley [go oft astray]." It is clear why the dramatist so borrowed the phrase "of mice and men," for George and Lennie's plan to get a small place of their own goes astray once Lennie kills Curley's Wife. But there is another, less immediately apparent reason, for Steinbeck uses the dead mouse to symbolize the past and to foreshadow the future.

To wit, Lennie always killed the mice that his Aunt Clara gave him to play with by pinching their heads; he could have killed the girl in Weed when he tried to feel her dress, as if she were a mouse, and she strongly resisted. He and George were chased out of the town of Weed because of this incident, and, at the start of the play, they are on their way to a ranch job in the Salinas Valley when they stop for the night in a small clearing. George throws into the brush the dead mouse that Lennie has been secretly petting during their journey, but Lennie retrieves it when he goes for firewood. Then George takes it from him again and tosses it as far away as he can.

George's action is symbolic, for he is removing from his sight an omen of the future. After they go to work, Lennie kills first the puppy Slim gives him by handling it too often and too roughly; then he kills Curley's Wife by accidentally breaking her neck when she tries to stop him from stroking her hair so hard. He flees the ranch and returns to the small clearing to wait for George, who has told him to go there if he gets into trouble. Lennie returns, that is, to the place where his past and his future converged in the symbol of the mouse, and where he, as a kind of pet to George, will await at George's hands the fate of the mice, the puppy, and Curley's Wife: death.

The play is thus the story of two men and the symbolic mice that surround them and contribute to their doom—a doom whose seed lay, in the first place, in the very nature of their relationship: Lennie's dimwitted "mouse" to George's thoughtful man. Even as Lennie "loved" the mice, the puppy, and Curley's Wife so much that he inadvertently killed them, so too, as I have argued, George loved Lennie so much that he wound up having to kill him. He wanted to remain with Lennie and lead a normal life eventually on a small farm, whereas the best place for his friend would have been in a home or hospital or even in the wild. Just when they are able to get the farm with the help of Candy's money, the inevitable happens in Lennie's killing of Curley's Wife. George then shoots Lennie as one would an animal, as he does not want him to suffer a savage death at Curley's hands, or, if he escaped death, to waste away in jail. It is no accident, then, that in the opening scene of *Of Mice and Men* Lennie is likened to an animal: George angrily proclaims that he should be in a cage with lots of mice, where they can pet *him*, and Lennie retaliates by saying that perhaps he would be better off alone, living in the hills or in a cave.

Although Steinbeck first wrote *Of Mice and Men* in the form of a novel, of course, I think that the story of Lennie and George, and Candy, is better suited to the drama into which he eventually turned it, as do both Alfred Kazin and Harry T. Moore. Kazin claims that *Of Mice and Men* is "openly written for the stage" (399), and Moore elaborates his point:

> Structurally, the novel was from the first a play: it is divided into six parts, each part a scene—the reader may observe that the action never moves away from a central point in each of these units. Steinbeck's manner of writing was coming over quite firmly to the dramatic. . . . After *Of Mice and Men* was published and the suggestion was made that it be prepared for the stage, Steinbeck said it could be produced directly from the book, as the earliest moving pictures had been produced. It was staged in almost exactly this way in the spring of 1937 by a

labor-theater group in San Francisco . . . When Steinbeck transferred the story into final dramatic form for the New York stage he took 85% of his lines bodily from the novel. A few incidents needed juggling, one or two minor new ones were introduced, and some (such as Lennie's imaginary speech with his Aunt Clara at the end of the novel) were omitted. A Hollywood studio bought the film rights to *Of Mice and Men*, but the picture has not been made yet. (48-49. Moore was writing in 1939; the Lewis Milestone-directed film of *Of Mice and Men* was released in 1940, to be followed over half a century later by Gary Sinise's film of the play, with a screenplay by the dramatist Horton Foote.)

George, as I have suggested, is a more or less mute protagonist, and in the story *as novel* we expect Steinbeck, as the narrator, to speak for him, to explain his reasoning and his feelings. But Steinbeck doesn't. That, more specifically, is why the novel, together with its extension, the play, has often struck readers overwhelmingly as a work of sentiment. The novel, I would argue, by documenting the story of George and Lennie without fully accounting for George's role in events, *the full effect of events on him*, seems, if not thereby to glorify George's suffering, then to martyr Lennie.

The play doesn't have this problem, or shouldn't to the attentive reader or spectator, Levant's argument notwithstanding that *because* Steinbeck structured the novel of *Of Mice and Men* as a play, he restricted his narrative to visible action and thus was unable fully to explore complex human motives and relationships (134-135). The drama has no narrator, obviously, so we don't expect anyone to speak for George. We therefore accept his muteness more easily, and we look for the materials of the drama itself to speak for him. Because of the necessary condensation of the dramatic form, we see more distinctly the choice he has, after Lennie's death, between life alone on the road and life on a farm with Candy. We see all the more powerfully, because they are embodied on stage, the love and compassion George has for Lennie. Hence the drama is ideally suited to the portrayal of George Milton's tragedy, because, even as his actions speak for themselves, so too does the drama's action—or imitation of an action—speak for itself. This drama, like most drama, has no narrator, and George is unable, or unwilling, to "narrate" his deepest feelings and sorrows. Quietly, above all through the strategic placement of Candy in the action, *Of Mice and Men* dramatizes George's tragedy. Quietly, above all through his automatic rejection of life on the farm with Candy, George conveys to us, perhaps better than the words of a more articulate man ever could, the depth of his love for Lennie and the extent to which he is willing to—can do nothing but—suffer for that love.

In the end, Steinbeck touched some deep American themes in *Of Mice and Men*: the great myth of the road and two male companions, of our hunger for "brotherhood"—a feeling enhanced by the seeming loneliness of all Americans during the Great Depression. For this reason, perhaps, the thirties were years when the theater, along with the other arts, rediscovered America. *Green Grow the Lilacs* (1931), one of several of Lynn Riggs's Oklahoma plays, Erskine Caldwell's *Tobacco Road* (1933), and Paul Osborn's *Morning's at Seven* (1939) are among the works that in one way or another perform a function similar to that of Steinbeck's play. *Of Mice and Men*, unlike the many (New York) city plays from the 1930s, for its part naturalistically concentrates on the unemployed of the farm lands, the itinerants and ranch workers, while it alludes to the bus and truck drivers whose travels through the country permitted them to observe the state of the nation in its broad horizon.

Thus there is a strong residue of nineteenth-century feeling about the land in *Of Mice and Men*—that working on the land is the basic good, while owning some of it is salvation. I can't think of another successful American drama since the mid-to-late thirties with that feeling (except perhaps Sam Shepard's *Curse of the Starving Class* [1976], and, peripherally, *Long Day's Journey into Night* [1941] in its depiction of the itinerant actor James Tyrone's obsession with land-ownership), or even one centered on rural work. Steinbeck knows our erstwhile longing for a home on the range, not a mere feeding place. And he has the same genuine sympathy for the lonesome devil whose sole companion is a mangy old dog as for the black American cut off from his fellow workers because of his skin color. Indeed, Steinbeck suggests with something like an austere sorrow, as opposed to the radical politics of a John Howard Lawson, a Clifford Odets, or his own novels *In Dubious Battle* (1936) and *The Grapes of Wrath* (1939), that none of America's "underprivileged" will ever reach the home *they* crave until they arrive at a greater social consciousness. Because of what has happened since it was written, then—the rapid decline of family farming, the relentless burgeoning of mechanized agribusiness—*Of Mice and Men* has come to be a play about the end not only of George and Lennie, but also of something in America, in American drama, and in the American dream.

Works Cited

Davis, Robert Murray. Introduction to *Steinbeck: A Collection of Critical Essays.* Englewood Cliffs, NJ: Prentice-Hall, 1972.

Ferguson, Otis. *The Film Criticism of Otis Ferguson.* Philadelphia: Temple UP, 1971.

Kauffmann, Stanley. *Persons of the Drama.* New York: Harper and Row, 1976.

Kazin, Alfred. *On Native Grounds: An Interpretation of Modern American Prose Literature.* New York: Harcourt, Brace, 1942.

Levant, Howard. *The Novels of John Steinbeck: A Critical Study.* Columbia: U f Missouri P, 1974.

Lisca, Peter. *John Steinbeck: Nature and Myth.* New York: Thomas Y. Crowell, 1978.

Moore, Harry T. *The Novels of John Steinbeck: A First Critical Study,* 2nd ed. (1939); rpt. Port Washington, New York: Kennikat P, 1968.

Steinbeck, John. *Of Mice and Men: A Play in Three Acts.* New York: Covici-Friede, 1937.

CHAPTER FOUR

WHOSE TOWN IS IT, AND WHITHER GOES IT? AN HISTORICO-AESTHETIC COMPARATIVE-INFLUENTIAL INQUIRY INTO *OUR TOWN*

It has long seemed to me that Thornton Wilder's *Our Town* (1938) has two flaws at its center that have never been adequately addressed by critics, if addressed at all. The first has to do with the play's implicit argument that the cause of man's unhappiness is not his failure to achieve or sustain greatness or wealth, but rather his failure "to find a value above all price for the smallest events in our daily life," his inability to delight in the beauty of ordinary, "undramatic" existence. The quoted words are Wilder's own, from the preface to his *Three Plays* (xi), and over the years critics like Malcolm Goldstein (96-108), Rex Burbank (75-83), Hermann Stresau (60-61), Eugene Current-Garcia (581), Gerald Berkowitz (61-63), Donald Haberman (*Plays*, 15-16, 57-59, 63-64; *American Play*, 16, 18, 38, 73-74), and Diane Almeida (20) have taken his word as gospel in their own discussions of *Our Town*.

In the play itself Emily Webb acts as the spokesman for the playwright's view when, after her death, she returns to life simultaneously to observe and relive her twelfth birthday. Here is what she concludes:

> [Life] goes so fast. We don't have time to look at one another. I didn't realize. So all that was going on and we never noticed. [. . .] Good-by, Good-by, world. Good-by, Grover's Corners . . . Mama and Papa. Good-by to clocks ticking . . . and Mama's sunflowers. And food and coffee. And new-ironed dresses and hot baths . . . and sleeping and waking up. Oh, earth, you're too wonderful for anybody to realize you. Do any human beings ever realize life while they live it?—every, every minute?
>
> [. . .] That's all human beings are! Just blind people. (100-101; bracketed ellipses are mine, here and throughout)

The problem with this view, as applied to the characters in *Our Town*, is that they are not particularly blind, or unhappy, or troubled, with the exception of the town malcontent, Simon Stimson. Indeed, more than most *dramatis personae*, the characters in this play *do* take the time to appreciate the dailiness of human existence, to bear witness to the wonder of God's creation, and that perhaps explains why they are so clear-eyed and uncomplicated. David Castronovo seems to realize this when he writes that "Wilder's people in *Our Town* are rarely allowed to move out of their mysterious innocence and become hokey figures who are too sophisticated for their setting and the terms of their dramatic existence" (91). But then Castronovo goes on blithely and unconvincingly to declare that "Emily—the young girl who poses the greatest threat to the play by her speechmaking about blindness and the fact that we never 'look at one another'—is not allowed to spoil the play" (91), which is to say the side of the play that reveals characters who, for all their innocence, are not so blind and do take the time, in Emily's words, to "look at one another" (99).

One reason these characters bear such witness to the wonder of God's creation is that they have the time to do so, since, unlike conventional theatrical figures, they are not caught up in suspenseful conflicts or the carrying out of momentous dramatic actions. (Act I is prosaically called "Daily Life," Act II "Love and Marriage," and Act III "Death and Dying" [47].) Another reason is that they live in an isolated place—they small town of Grover's Corners, New Hampshire (population 2,642 [22])—where they are *able* to appreciate the dailiness of human existence, undeterred by the masses of people, mass transportation, and massive buildings common to big cities. The whole point of *Our Town*, Emily's criticisms of her family and friends notwithstanding, is to document not only the pleasurable anti-drama of everyday life, but also the pleasure the ordinary or unremarkable townspeople take in enacting it: in portraying "the way [people] were in the provinces north of New York at the beginning of the twentieth century [. . .] in [their] growing up and in [their] marrying and in [their] living and in [their] dying" (32). As Mr. Webb, the editor of the local newspaper and Emily's father, puts it in Act I:

> No [. . .] there isn't much culture [in Grover's Corners]; but maybe this is the place to tell you that we've got a lot of pleasures of a kind here: we like the sun comin' up over the mountain in the morning, and we all notice a good deal about the birds. We pay a lot of attention to them. And we watch the change of the seasons; yes, everybody knows about them. But those other things [. . .] there ain't much. (25)

Among the "we" of Editor Webb's statement, we may include Emily Webb, Mr. Webb himself, Constable Warren, Mrs. Gibbs, Mrs. Soames, and Mrs. Webb, all of whom take the time to notice the moon in Act I, as the following lines of dialogue and stage directions make clear:

George. Hello!
Emily. I can't work at all. The moonlight's so *terrible.* (33)

Mrs. Gibbs. Myrtle Webb! Look at that moon, will you! Tsk-tsk-tsk. Potato weather, for sure.
[Mrs. Soames, Mrs. Webb, and Mrs. Gibbs] are silent a moment, gazing up at the moon. (38)

Mrs. Gibbs. Now, Frank, don't be grouchy. Come out and smell the heliotrope in the moonlight. *They stroll out arm in arm along the footlights.* Isn't that wonderful? (39)

Mr. Webb. Good evening, Bill.
Constable Warren. Evenin', Mr. Webb.
Mr. Webb. Quite a moon!
Constable Warren. Yepp. (42)

Mr. Webb. Why aren't you in bed?
Emily. I don't know. I just can't sleep yet, Papa. The moonlight's so *wonderful.* And the smell of Mrs. Gibbs' heliotrope. Can you smell it?
Mr. Webb. Hm . . . Yes. (44)

Above all we must number among the "we" of Editor Webb's statement the Stage/Town Manager, who at the very start of the play observes that "the sky is beginning to show some streaks of light over in the East there, behind our mount'in. The morning star always gets wonderful bright the minute before it has to go—doesn't it? (*He stares at it for a moment* [. . .])" (6); who at the top of Act II notes that "the sun's come up over a thousand times. Summers and winters have cracked the mountains a little bit more and the rains have brought down some of the dirt" (46), in addition to arguing, as Emily does in Act III, that "You've got to love life to have life, and you've got to have life to love life" (47); and who at the opening of Act III pays a lot of attention to the natural surroundings of the cemetery in Grover's Corners:

[This cemetery's] on a hilltop—a windy hilltop—lots of sky, lots of clouds—often lots of sun and moon and stars. You come up here on a fine afternoon and you can see range on range of hills—awful blue they are—up there by Lake Sunapee and Lake Winnipesaukee . . . and way up, if you've got a glass, you can see the White Mountains and Mt. Washington—where North Conway and Conway is. And, of course, our favorite mountain, Mt. Monadnock, 's right here—and all these towns that lie around it: Jaffrey, 'n East Jaffrey, 'n Peterborough, 'n Dublin; and there, quite a ways down, is Grover's Corners. Yes, beautiful spot up here. Mountain laurel and li-lacks. (80)

So the inhabitants of Grover's Corners, New Hampshire, have the time and space to pay attention to the rising sun and the flight of birds, to observe the change of seasons and the growth of children, to savor the roses blooming and the coffee brewing. But they have the time and space to do these things because they live in a time and place when and where there apparently were more time and space to devote to the "small pleasures" of living: the United States of 1901-1913, before World Wars I and II established this country as an industrial-military superpower the job of whose workers—living in larger and larger, as well as more and more, cities—was to keep America ahead of all the other nations of the world in addition to competing with their fellow citizens for a fair share of the American Dream.

Our Town was first published and produced in 1938 for a Depression-weary and war-wary American public; thus it seems to me no accident that the play looks back to an earlier, almost innocent or idyllic era, before the events of 1914-1938 changed forever the way Americans would regard the world and each other. (By 1938 the New Deal was over, and the Roosevelt administration was turning its attention from domestic reform to the gathering storm in Europe and the Far East.) In this sense, the play is not simply a nostalgic tribute to the "good old days" of the late nineteenth and early twentieth centuries, a generalized instance of the American tendency to idealize the past, as Francis Fergusson (52-53), George D. Stephens (262, 264), and Thomas E. Porter (219) maintain. Rather, *Our Town* is in fact nearly a piece of isolationist propaganda that promotes the virtues of a simple, unhurried, unthreatened life in the isolated small towns of America—where for one place the virtues of such a life need no such promoting, despite Emily's criticisms of her fellow townspeople and to the detriment of the play's artistic wholeness or thematic unity.

It may seem folksy, for example, that Dr. Gibbs would rather remain at home in Grover's Corners than visit so cosmopolitan a city as Paris, France, but Mrs. Gibbs's explanation of her husband's desire to stay put rings of isolationism-cum-chauvinism:

> No, he said, it might make him discontented with Grover's Corners to go traipsin' about Europe; better to let well enough alone, he says. Every two years he makes a trip to the battlefields of the Civil War [on which Dr. Gibbs is an expert] and that's enough treat for anybody, he says. (20)

In apparent contradistinction to her husband, it occurs to Mrs. Gibbs "that once in your life before you die you ought to see a country where they don't talk in English and *don't even want to*" (20; emphasis mine). Emily Webb might have responded, based on her speech to her classmates about the Louisiana Purchase (27, 29-30), that with the addition of this Southern state Mrs. Gibbs already had a little bit of France in America. (Recall that Emily's alternate speech topic was the Monroe Doctrine [27], which tellingly proclaimed that the United States would not brook any political or economic interference in the Western hemisphere by European powers.)

Like the Gibbses' remarks and Emily's American history assignment, the following, seemingly innocuous lines by the Stage Manager in Act I also smack of isolationism-cum-chauvinism. He implies here that America's participation in World War I—which ended in the winter of 1919 with the signing of five treaties, one of them in the Parisian suburb of Versailles—served no purpose whatsoever; and that the first nonstop, solo airplane flight from New York to Paris, made by Charles Lindbergh in 1927, was and is no more important than the daily life of any small, New England town:

> [Joe Crowell] got a scholarship to Massachusetts Tech. Graduated head of his class there [. . .] Goin' to be a great engineer, Joe was. But the war broke out and he died in France.—*All that education for nothing.* (10, emphasis mine; see the Stage Manager's opposite remark, in Act III, about Union soldiers from New Hampshire who died during the Civil War [80-81])

> I'm going to have a copy of this play put in the cornerstone [together with a Bible and the Constitution of the United States, so that] people a thousand years from now'll know a few simple facts about us—*more than the Treaty of Versailles and the Lindbergh flight.* (32; emphasis mine)

Among those few simple facts about what the Stage Manager calls "the *real* life of the people [. . .] in the provinces north of New York at the beginning of the twentieth century" (32), by which he means the quotidian activities of citizens as opposed to the public pronouncements and pursuits of princes or their martial equivalents, one should not ignore our country's internal isolationism of two kinds. First, there is the comic regionalism, indeed "state-ism," championed by the Stage Manager when he remarks that "the Cartwright interests have just begun building a new bank in Grover's Corners—had to go to Vermont for the marble, sorry to say" (31-32); by Emily when she declares that "Grover's Corners isn't a very important place when you think of all—New Hampshire; but I think it's a very nice town" (66); then by George when he responds to her later in the same conversation, "I guess new people aren't any better than old ones. [. . .] I don't need to go [away to State Agriculture College] and meet the people in other towns" (67); and finally by Sam Craig when he reveals, upon returning to Grover's Corners for Emily's funeral, that he's now in business out West—which is where Buffalo, New York, is located as far as he is concerned (82).

Second, and most important, there is our internal isolationism of a tragic kind: that is, the segregation of American towns according to race and ethnicity, which we began to remedy only after World War II, when veterans from minority groups demanded equal treatment in housing along with other areas of civilian life in return for their military service to the nation. The pre-Great War world of the Gibbses and the Webbs, then, is decidedly *not* "an anti-elitist vision of human existence," as David Castronovo believes (93). In Grover's Corners, for instance, "Polish Town's across the tracks, [along with] some Canuck families" (6), and the "Catholic Church is over beyond the tracks" (6) as well. Such segregation, of course, was the result as well as the cause of what the Belligerent Man in *Our Town* calls "social injustice" and "industrial inequality" (24). When asked by this "belligerent" man what the citizens of Grover's Corners are going to do about poverty and discrimination in their town, Mr. Webb lamely—and peremptorily—responds,

> Well, I dunno. . . . I guess we're all hunting like everybody else for a way the diligent and sensible can rise to the top and the lazy and quarrelsome can sink to the bottom. But it ain't easy to find. Meanwhile, we do all we can to help those that can't help themselves and those that can we leave alone.—Are there any other questions? (25)

Mr. Webb's statement that "we do all we can to help those that can't help themselves" may appear to be charitable, but in fact it is obfuscatory, for it assumes that the racially and ethnically segregated are *unable to* help themselves as opposed to being *prevented from* doing so. Similarly, when he declares that "we're all hunting [. . .] for a way the diligent and sensible can rise to the top and the lazy and quarrelsome can sink to the bottom," Mr. Webb seems to be in favor of equal treatment for everybody, but in reality he is playing to his audience's prejudice that blacks and newly-arrived European immigrants belong at the bottom of the socioeconomic ladder.

That prejudice is confirmed early in the play by Dr. Gibbs's report that he is returning home from the birth of "*just* some twins [. . .] over in Polish Town" (9; emphasis mine); by the State Manager's remark that "the earliest tombstones in the cemetery [belong to] Grovers and Cartwrights and Gibbses and Herseys—*same names as are around here now*" [with the exception, that is, of those belongings to Poles and "Canucks"] (7; emphasis mine); and by the Stage Manger's ominous interruption of Professor Willard's anthropological survey of Grover's Corners—a survey that itself avoids mention of the program of genocide we conducted against the Indians—at the moment this "rural savant" comes to the Slavic and Mediterranean migration to America:

> *Professor Willard.* Yes . . . anthropological data: Early Amerindian stock. Cotahatchee tribes . . . no evidence before the tenth century of this era . . . hm . . . now entirely disappeared . . . possible traces in three families. Migration toward the end of the seventeenth century of English brachiocephalic blue-eyed stock . . . for the most part. Since then some Slav and Mediterranean—

Stage Manager. And the population, Professor Willard? (22)

This same ethnic prejudice is confirmed later in the play by Constable Warren's report that he has been out "rescuin' a party; darn near froze to death, down by Polish town thar. Got drunk and lay out in the snowdrifts" (94). When Mr. Webb tells the constable that "We must get [this story] in the paper" (96), Warren quickly avers, "'Twan't much" (96). And that's the end of the matter, because the drunk is naturally a "dumb Polack," one of the ten per cent of the town's illiterate laborers (23), not a member of the Anglo-Saxon Protestant majority.

This fellow must not be as dumb as the women of Grover's Corners, however, for at least he got to vote if he was twenty-one (and a citizen), whereas "women vote indirect" (23), which is to say only by influencing their husbands' votes. The women of the United States did not gain suffrage until 1920. Nor, of course, did they achieve equal educational or professional opportunity until quite some time after that, as *Our Town* inadvertently makes clear when it portrays Emily Webb as "naturally bright" (28), indeed "the brightest girl in school" (15), and in any event brighter than the dimwitted if kindhearted George Gibbs (whom she must help with his math homework in Act I); yet Wilder makes *George* President of the high-school Senior Class to Emily's Secretary-Treasurer, and gives him the chance to go away to college but not her. Young Joe Crowell, Jr., sums up the thinking in Grover's Corners on the status of women when, in response to Dr. Gibbs's question, "How do you boys feel about [the upcoming marriage of your schoolteacher, Miss Foster]?" he innocently but revealingly declares that "if a person starts out to be a teacher, she ought to stay one" (9). In other words, women cannot or should not combine family with career; and Miss Foster's choices, or the limitations thereon, are clear: either remain the teacher she was trained to be and become a spinster, or give up teaching for the life of a wife and mother. Moreover, as a mother she should teach her own daughter not to waste taxpayers' money on a higher education that in the end she will not use!

I have gone to the trouble in the preceding paragraphs of documenting the historicity of *Our Town* because this historicity works against the play's universalizing tendency, and is thus its second major flaw. *Our Town* would be a play for all people of all time—in deliberate contrast to the drama of sociopolitical consciousness, even left-wing propaganda, produced by such writers as Clifford Odets, John Howard Lawson, and Elmer Rice during the 1930s—but in its own time it is not even a play for all the ethnic and racial groups of Grover's Corners, let alone all the nationalities of the world. The Stage Manager relates Grover's Corners to the past civilizations of Greece and Rome as well as to future ones, to the surrounding countryside and to evolution (21-22, 32, 71, 80); Wilder eliminates scenery almost completely in order to avoid the suggestion that the meaning of the play's action relates only to Grover's Corners, New Hampshire; and Rebecca Gibbs connects the individual to town, county, state, country, world, universe, and God when she quotes the address on Jane Crofut's letter in Act I (45). Yet for all these attempts to link the Grover's Corners of 1901-1913 to the great world beyond as well as to other historical periods—perhaps partly as a *result* of these attempts—*Our Town* remains time- and place-bound.   It is the conservative record or dramatic preservation of a conservative, even reactionary, attitude toward life, and it hides behind what appears to be radical, self-searching dramaturgy but is in fact little more than contrived, self-serving theatricalism.

To wit, on the surface *Our Town* has the trappings of an avant-garde play, or of such a play as influenced by the anti-illusionistic conventions of the Asian theatre (Sang-Kyong, 288-299): a narrator, the Stage Manager, who disrupts the illusion of present-tense reality and attempts to work against the rule of sentiment onstage; "No curtain [to conceal the 'fourth wall'].   No scenery" (5), no props to speak of, which necessitates the miming of actions such as eating and drinking, as well as delivering milk or newspapers; characters who address the audience (like Professor Willard, Editor Webb, and Mrs. Webb) and acknowledge the existence of the Stage Manager, as well as dead characters who speak in the last act; an episodic dramatic form stretching over twelve years (Act I takes place in 1901, Act II in 1904, and Act II in 1913) that allows for flashbacks (the courtship of George and Emily in Act II, Emily's twelfth birthday in Act III) and flash-forwards (the Stage Manager's foretelling, in Act I, of the invention of the automobile and the deaths of Dr. Gibbs, Mrs. Gibbs, and Joe Crowell), and that necessitates the building, dismantling, and rebuilding of the town in various configurations upon the same site, such that there is the sensation of movement through time and space within a framework that is ultimately static, in the manner of a cubist collage; and a lyric mood rather than a dramatic conflict in the conventional sense of protagonist-versus-antagonist.

In fact, each time there is the possibility of dramatic conflict in *Our Town*, it quickly dissolves into the clean and clear New Hampshire air.   For instance, when Dr. Gibbs confronts his son with failing to perform the chore of chopping wood for Mrs. Gibbs's kitchen stove, George offers no excuse for his behavior; indeed, he sheds tears instead of uttering angry words of self-justification and tacitly agrees to give his mother all the help she needs in the future (36).   When Constable Warren and Editor Webb encounter the drunken Simon Stimson on the street at night in Act I, the one man looks the other way, the other says "Good evening" twice, while Simon himself "pauses a moment and stares . . . [then] continues on his way without a word and disappears at the right" (43).   And when Emily criticizes George's "conceited and stuck-up" behavior during their courtship scene, George offers no defense of himself whatsoever; instead he embraces her remarks with the following words: "I'm glad you said it, Emily. I never thought that such a thing was happening to me. I guess it's hard for a fella not to have faults creep into his character" (63). Moreover, despite the fact that Emily and George both get cold feet immediately before they are to be married (George declares "All I want to do is to be [single] fella—" [74], while Emily cries out, "I *hate* [George]. . . . I don't want to get married" [75]), nothing comes of their panic and aversion. Instead of having an argument and canceling the wedding, they quickly come to their senses and unite, as planned, in holy matrimony.

Characters like these are typed or familiar, however—the town malcontent, the folksy sheriff, the steady milkman, the knowing newspaper editor, the boy-and-girl next door, all flat figures from the primitive world of folk art—not psychologically complex or "conflicted," let alone inscrutable, and they certainly are not figures who call into question the whole idea of unified character or integrated personality, like those of Pirandello. Indeed, when Editor Webb fields questions from the audience in Act I, he neither drops out of character nor steps out from the play, in character, in order to do so: instead he answers "plants" in the audience—not real audience members asking improvised questions—whose queries manage to keep him firmly within the world of *Our Town*. And nothing is made, either by Wilder or the citizens of Grover's Corners, of the fact that the State Manager plays or metamorphoses into multiple roles in *Our Town*: Mrs. Forrest, an old lady into whom George bumps while playing baseball on Main Street (27); Mr. Morgan, the owner of the local drugstore and soda fountain (64); the minister presiding at George and Emily's wedding (71); the literal manager of the stage who belongs to the "real" world of the theatre, about which he immediately tells us: "This play is called *Our Town*. It was written by Thornton Wilder; produced and directed by A. . . . In it you will see Miss C. . . . ; Miss D. . . . ; Miss E. . . .; and Mr. F. . . .; Mr. G. . . .; Mr. H. . . .; and many others" (5); as well as the town's native son, natural leader, and documentary biographer, historical chronicler, or choral spokesman, who speaks of "our" town (5-7) in the same accent as every other citizen of Grover's Corners—every other white Anglo-Saxon citizen, that is (e.g., "holla'" for "holler" or "hollow" [6], "'twan't" for "it wasn't" [72], "hull" for "whole" [6]).

Just as Wilder's *dramatis personae* are not designed either to plumb the depths of character, on the one hand, or to deconstruct it, on the other, neither is his interruption of the linear progression of time designed to probe the nature of time—to suggest its relativistic quality—or to question the principle of inexorable, deterministic causality. Rather, *Our Town* flashes back from 1938 to 1901-1913, then from 1913 to 1899 (the year of Emily's twelfth birthday), for the purpose of chauvinistic nostalgia, even as it flashes forward for the sake of cosmic wonder (although, tellingly, it never really goes beyond the present of 1938); and it does so through the offices of an omniscient, omnipotent, and omnipresent State Manager who creates the play's lyric atmosphere, not because he wishes to emphasize the subjectivity of his own voice or to stress the essential "plotlessness" of human existence, but rather out of a desire to banish all dramatic confrontation to the wings, which is to say subsume it within his own quiescent oneness.

In this he is, of course, a godlike figure, if not a spokesman for God himself in such speeches as the following, which more than suggest that human beings are created in the image of the divine and are thus superior to the rest of creation:

> The real hero of this scene [George and Emily's wedding] isn't on stage at all, and you know who that is. It's like what one of those European fellas said: every child born into the world is nature's attempt to make a perfect human being. Well, we've seen nature pushing and contriving for some time now. We all know that nature's interested in quantity; but I think she's interested in quality, too—that's why I'm in the ministry. (71)

> We all know that *something* is eternal. And it ain't houses and it ain't names, and it ain't earth, and it ain't even the stars . . . everybody knows in their bones that *something* is eternal, and that something has to do with human beings. All the greatest people ever lived have been telling us that for five thousand years and yet you'd be surprised how people are always losing hold of it. There's something way down deep that's eternal about every human being. (*Pause.*) You know as well as I do that the dead [like Emily] don't stay interested in us living people for very long. [. . .] They're waitin'. They're waitin' for something that they feel is coming'. Something important, and great. Aren't they waitin' for the eternal part in them to come out clear? (81-82)

> Yes, it's clearing up. There are the stars—doing their old, old crisscross journeys in the sky. Scholars haven't settled the matter yet, but they seem to think there are no living beings up there. Just chalk . . . or fire. Only this one is straining away, straining away all the time to make something of itself. (103)

In the second speech above, the Stage Manager is clearly referring to the immortality of the human soul, but he—or Wilder—does so without the realization that in modern, not to speak of avant-garde, drama, the patriarchal relationship between God and the individual soul has been replaced by the adversarial relationship between man and his own psychology, his will to comprehend himself, even as the patriarchal relationship between ruler and subject has been replaced by the adversarial relationship between man and society, in the form of society's drive to marginalize all those that it cannot or will not homogenize.

In the third speech, quoted from the very end of the play, the Stage Manager seems to want to vanquish any uncertainty the audience might have about the significant of the human species in God's eye. He seems also to anticipate, as well as to relieve, the nationwide panic created by Orson Welles's pseudo-documentary radio broadcast based on H. G. Wells's science-fiction tale of an invasion from Mars, *The War of the Worlds* (1898), which aired on CBS on Halloween night in 1938, about nine months after *Our Town*'s New York opening. In peremptorily concluding that there are no living beings "up there," the Stage Manager sounds rather like the would-be debunkers of Copernicus and Galileo in the sixteenth and seventeenth centuries (even later, of course, especially where Catholic dogma is concerned). These charlatans insisted that the sun revolved around the earth, for to accept the reverse findings of the two scientists—and, likewise, the theory that intelligent life can be found in outer space—was to admit that our planet and its human inhabitants were not at the center of a divinely ordered universe.

The moon naturally does revolve around the earth, and Wilder does not miss the chance to underline the stability of its orbit or the competence of those who keep a watchful eye on it, as the following exchange reveals:

> *Rebecca.* George, . . . I think maybe the moon's getting nearer and nearer and there'll be a big 'splosion.
> *George.* Rebecca, you don't know anything. If the moon were getting nearer, the guys that sit up all night with telescopes would see it first and they'd tell about it, and it'd be in all the newspapers. (41-42)

The reliable "guys that sit up all night with telescopes" are ironically the same ones who, a few centuries back, incontrovertibly relegated the planet earth to third position in order from the sun, which they now understood to be the central body of the solar system. Along with thinkers like Montaigne and Machiavelli, and later Marx, Freud, Darwin, Compte, Nietzsche, and Einstein—whose theory of relativity itself is questioned by "A Man From Among the Dead" in Act III (102)—they thus initiated the slow death of God in literature as well as life, or at the very least the idea that, if there is a God, He did and does not conceive of lowly man as the greatest, noblest, or worthiest of all His creations.

Our Town to the contrary, the fundamental subject matter of almost all serious plays of the nineteenth and twentieth centuries is the attempt to resurrect fundamental ethical or philosophical certainties *without* resurrecting the fundamental spiritual certainty of a judgmental or mindful God—the very God Mrs. Gibbs appears to invoke when she advises the deceased Emily to "think only of what's ahead, and be ready for what's ahead" (92). Contrary to the evidence I have already adduced from the play showing average human beings who are perfectly aware of the Platonic essence or eternal dimension of reality, as well as contrary to the evidence from Wilder's own non-fiction of his belief that human beings can find their relationship to God or the transcendental in a conscious appreciation of the natural life around them (*American Characteristics*, 207-208; *Journals*, 125), the Stage Manager implies that it is only this God who, in the person of "saints and poets" (like the Stage Manager, whom Wilder himself once played?), can realize the wonder of life while it is being lived or appreciate the extraordinary beauty of ordinary, unremarkable human existence (100). He thereby implies that this God is the providential designer or moral center of a conventional dramatic triad whose two other components are psychology and causality—a triad that governs the traditional narrative of the eighteenth and nineteenth centuries as well.

Yet modern drama (for my purposes, the realism and naturalism of the social-problem play) banished theology as well as autocracy from its triadic paradigm of human action, as I indicate above, thus deepening the dramatic role played by psychology, sociology, and linearity or linkage, while avant-garde drama (all the –isms that react against realism and naturalism, such as symbolism, expressionism, surrealism, and futurism) demonstrated that a play's movement can be governed by something completely outside the triad that links motive to act, act to logical sequence of events, and logical outcome to divine or regal judgment. For the avant-garde, beginning in the late nineteenth century with Jarry if not earlier with such German visionaries as Tieck, Büchner, and Grabbe, the nature of reality itself becomes the prime subject of plays because of a loss of confidence in the assumed model for dramatizing human behavior and thinking about human existence. Wilder writes as if no such revolution in the writing of drama had occurred, though we know that he was well aware of it (if only through his intimate friendship with, professional admiration for, and professed artistic debt to Gertrude Stein, who, in her rejection of the cogency of plot and idea for the sensuality or pure form of language, gesture, and space, was probably the first thoroughgoing American avant-garde dramatist [Haberman, *Plays*, 37-38, 70; Burns, *Letters*, 175]). Or rather he borrows from that revolution its "designer fashions" while continuing to wear the emperor's old clothes underneath.

Those "old clothes" include the realistic, period clothing that characters normally wear in productions of *Our Town* in the absence of specific costuming direction from Wilder, as well as the realistic sound effects of a rooster (5), a train whistle (7), clinking milk bottles (11), a factory whistle (15), cackling chickens (18), chirping crickets (42), and a clock striking the hour (103). The "old clothes" even include an essential observance of the (neo)classical unities, since there is certainly no subplot (one might even argue that there is no plot);

the entire action takes place in one location, the town of Grover's Corners; and, even though years pass, the morning-to-evening, birth-to-death structure of the play's three acts suggests a kind of unity of time. Wilder eliminates most scenery, it is true, including some only "for those who think they have to have scenery" (7), in the Stage Manager's condescending words, but this elimination strikes me more as a convenient way to get around the need for multiple settings in this superficially episodic play (Main Street, the Webb and Gibbs homes, Morgan's drugstore, the Congregational Church, the town cemetery) than as a genuine if misguided-misconceived attempt to give the drama universal significance or symbolic resonance, let alone suggest that the stage is the unencumbered mind of God or bald reflection of infinity itself.

Surely Wilder was not subscribing to Jarry's anti-realistic, quasi-Absurd theories of theatre and drama, as Donald Haberman maintains (*Plays*, 65-68), when he took it upon himself to kill the use of a box set for any production of *Our Town*. And if Pirandello had attempted, in M. C. Kuner's words, "to liberate the conventional stage from its physical limitations by centering much of the action in the minds of the characters and by juggling such opposites as madness and sanity, falsehood and truth, illusion and reality, always asking which was which" (137-138), then, Kuner to the contrary, Wilder's theatre surely is the opposite of the Pirandellian one where nothing is absolute or fixed, where everything is relative and fluid. Wilder is interested above all in *Our Town* in confirming, indeed glorifying, the eternal verities of family, country, and God, not in questioning or undercutting them. And he does so in a manner middlebrows can appreciate most: the conventionally unconventional, or the traditionally experimental. Namely, he tells bourgeois audiences exactly what they want to hear, but in a way that makes them think they are discovering something new or startling.

Wilder thus makes the familiar strange or striking in a way consonant with the Brechtian theory of *Verfremdung*, but certainly not to an end of which the politically revolutionary Brecht would approve. (The Brechtian theory of *Verfremdung* itself was influenced even earlier than Wilder by the anti-illusionistic, suspense-diminishing conventions of the Asian theatre, prominent among them the use of a narrator.) This is the same Brecht who, at about the time *Our Town* was being produced, was writing his two greatest epic "Schaustücke," *Mother Courage and Her Children* (1939) and *The Life of Galileo* (1939), in an effort to bridge the gap between the numbering prosaism of the modern problem play and the indulgent ethereality of avant-garde drama, not to retreat from it.

And this is the same Thornton Wilder who wrote *Our Town* at about the time that the American cinema was producing "screwball comedies" such as *My Man Godfrey* (1936) and *His Girl Friday* (1940)—the romantic subgenre that, like Wilder's play, was really affirming the traditional values that propel capitalist enterprise (hard work, happy family, hierarchical State) while it appeared to be doing something boldly experimental, even revolutionary, from a thematic if not a formal point of view. In the case of screwball comedy, this was the promotion of social as well as gender equality for all Americans. It is no coincidence that, with the Depression at their backs and the Second World War staring them in the face, Americans warmed to such entertainment in the theater as well as the cinema. For this entertainment helped them to affirm their own long-held beliefs, ideals, and aims at the same time as it cleverly made them feel that they were progressively preparing themselves to enter, if not positivistically embrace, the mid-to-latter part of the twentieth century.

Wilder himself tried his hand at romantic comedy in *The Merchant of Yonkers* (based on the Austrian Johann Nestroy's century-old *He Intends to Have a Fling* [1842], itself based on *A Day Well Spent* [1835], by the English dramatist John Oxenford), written at the same time as *Our Town*, interestingly enough; later rewritten as *The Matchmaker* (1954, filmed 1958); and then tellingly adapted into the enormously successful musical *Hello, Dolly!* in 1963 (filmed 1969). The film version of *Our Town*, made in 1940 only two years after the play's world première, did not turn the work into a loving screwball comedy, it is true. But, among other elements, it did add homespun, realistic scenery (while retaining the narrative device of the State Manager in this medium whose camera is already an omniscient narrator) and, most important, it made Emily's death-cum-funeral scene merely her dream, so that the heroine could live to be happily reunited at the end with her husband, George, and their two children. Which is another way of saying that the film of *Our Town*, despite such superficial divergence from the play, may be truer to the core of Wilder's dramatic vision than many critics have been willing to believe—may in fact expose that core for the rotten apple, the patriotic gore, or the sentimental essence that it is and always has been.

Wilder's chief rival in the late 1930s in the spreading of metaphysical as well as mundane euphoria was William Saroyan, whose message was that the earth was a good, not an evil, place and that people should simply have a wonderful time—like Jasper MacGregor, who in *My Hearts in the Highlands* (1939) gladdens the hearts of everyone with his melodious bugle-playing. In *The Time of Your Life* (1939), set in Nick's waterfront bar in San Francisco, everyone contentedly "does his own thing" in a dramatic world where, as in Wilder's, plot has almost become unnecessary. A typical stage direction from this play, Saroyan's best-known one, reads:

Each person belongs to the environment, in his own person, as himself: Wesley is playing better than ever. Harry is hoofing better than ever. Nick is behind the bar shining glasses. Joe is smiling at the toy and studying it. Dudley, although

still troubled, is at least calm now and full of melancholy poise. Willit, at the
marble-game, is happy. The Arab is deep in his memories where he wants to be.
(60-61)

In other words, with so much going for them toward the end of the thirties, why
would people want to make trouble and go out on strike? They could take in a
movie, take a Sunday drive, or just take their time instead!

A few years later in 1942 with Wilder's *Skin of Our Teeth*, the saga of
the passage of a universal family, the Antrobuses, through ice ages, military
conflicts, and numerous catastrophes of world history—and thus a testimonial to
humanity's ability to survive all disasters—the facile optimism or sunny
complacency exhibited by this playwright in *Our Town* remained unshaken in
the middle of a war the likes of whose horrors the planet had not yet seen or
even imagined. Similarly, when the United States was in the throes of the Great
Depression, Thornton Wilder was writing such one-acts as *The Long Christmas
Dinner* (1931), *Pullman Car Hiawatha* (1931), and *The Happy Journey to
Trenton and Camden* (1931), each of which was dedicated, like the rest of his
oeuvre, both to a celebration of the marvels of human existence and to the
proposition that no matter how lousy any situation may look, all will turn out
well in the end.

Introduced in these short plays, collected under the title *"The Long
Christmas Dinner" and Other Plays in One Act* (1931), are the pseudo-
experimental elements that were to surface again in *Our Town* and *The Skin of
Our Teeth*: chiefly, movement back and forth in time in an apparent attempt to
achieve a "double vision" that sees the past at work in the shaping of the
present; the use of a bare stage and pantomime in order to universalize rather
than localize the action; and the employment of a quasi-omniscient stage
manager who interrupts events to supply sociological information together with
the wisdom of the great philosophers, ostensibly providing the audience in the
process with perspective on or critical distance from the events of the drama.
(We even see something like this last device in *The Matchmaker* when, just
before the final curtain falls, Barnaby addresses the audience with the message
that this play is all about getting the right amount of "adventure" into one's life.)

As far as negative influence goes, *Our Town* probably has not had
much on American, not to speak of British, drama: paradoxically, the play is *sui
generis* at the same time as it itself combines (if not completely digests) the
sundry influences of Asian theatre, Greek drama, folk art, Gertrude Stein, and
Bertolt Brecht. *The Glass Menagerie* (1944) uses a narrator, it is true, but Tom
Wingfield's narration in that intimate memory play dates back to Tennessee
Williams' original conception of it as a short story titled "Portrait of a Girl in
Glass" (1941), not to any genuine desire to reconceive the structure of drama or
to question the reliability of memory. For its part, Arthur Miller's intermittent

use of a retrospective tribunal—in the person of the lawyer, Alfieri—in *A View From the Bridge* (1955) is an explicit if ultimately strained attempt to evoke the chorus of Graeco-Roman tragedy (just like Wilder's Stage Manager), and thereby to draw parallels between ancient fatefulness and the inevitable logic of Sicilian justice as opposed to American law. Despite their use of narrative or choral devices, then, both these works are fundamentally realistic, just like most American plays—including *Our Town*.

Thus, in David Savran's words, "[Thornton] Wilder's [deluded] hope [that he had helped to prepare the way for a new drama which would replace or at least rival realism-cum-naturalism] has been fulfilled less conspicuously by new dramaturgy than new performance, and most powerfully, perhaps, by a work that uses his own script [of *Our Town*] as a starting point" (18). The work to which Savran refers is the Wooster Group's controversial performance piece titled *The Road to Immortality: Part One (Route 1 & 9 [The Last Act])*, first produced in 1981 and revived in 1987.

Here is a description of the Wooster Group's deconstruction of *Our Town*, a production that points to the Group's perception of the play's reactionary conservatism far in advance of traditional critics and even of a non-traditional critic like myself:

> *Our Town* shows up first indirectly [in *The Road to Immortality*] in a parody of Clifton Fadiman delivering an *Encyclopedia Britannica* lecture on the meaning of the play in a film strip that is played on television monitors. It is awkward, with sound distortion, and clearly shows its age. The scenes from *Our Town* are full of heavy music and close-ups of the actors' faces, all of it inappropriate. The tone is pedantic and condescending, and it is clearly directed to a high school audience.
>
> Scenes from *Our Town* are played on the monitors, too, not as part of the lecture, but in the general style of television soap opera. At the same time white actors in blackface . . . are performing a routine of the black vaudeville comedian Pigmeat Markham and generally mirroring the action of *Our Town* in the guise of black ghetto life, as well. Often the action was crude, sometimes sexual, sometimes overt, sometimes furtive. (Haberman, *"Our Town,"* 103)

If there is any work that resembles *Our Town* in form as well as content, it is oddly enough Dylan Thomas' "play for voices" written for radio, *Under Milk Wood* (1954). There is no evidence of which I am aware that the poet Thomas knew *Our Town*, let alone consciously modeled his only drama—if in fact *Under Milk Wood* can be called one—after it. Nonetheless, not only are the resemblances there, but Thomas's play, like Wilder's, may also be his best-known work. Certainly, along with his lilting poems about childhood like "Fern Hill" and his story "A Child's Christmas in Wales" (which has come to rival Dickens' *Christmas Carol*), it helped him to become a popular, selling author late in his relatively short life through its attempt in poetic, alliterative prose to imagine a world that is completely good, to recapture the enchantment of original innocence. So much so that Dylan Thomas has been called the J. M. Barrie of our time.

His *Under Milk Wood* is the portrait of a small Welsh, seaside village named Llareggub (Laugharne in reality), whose inhabitants are heard in vocal self-revelation during the course of a single day, from early morning to the dark of night, and in the process evoke a magical, golden age of Celtic peasantry expressing themselves in lyrical cadences. Like *Our Town*, *Under Milk Wood* contains no dramatic conflict, no development of character or even encounters between characters, no action in the usual theatrical sense of that word. There is, however, a surprising amount of "movement," from one part of the village to another; from character to character among the play's cast of around seventy "voices," for whom Thomas provides rich verbal textures or colors for the ear; and, as in the case of Wilder's piece, there is movement from the present to the past and back again.

Moreover, like the Stage Manager of *Our Town*, the "First Voice" of *Under Milk Wood* serves as a kind of narrator or choral figure (assisted by the "Second Voice"), a vocal guide who opens, accompanies, and closes the "action" and so seemingly fulfills the idea from which the work sprang in Thomas's mind in 1939: that of a mad village visited by a kindly inspector from the outside, certified by him as collectively insane, and sealed off so as not to infect the rest of the world. In the end, however, the village of Llareggub turns out to be the only sane and happy place surviving in a mad, mad world that had given us, during the genesis and gestation of *Under Milk Wood*, the Second World War, the neutron bomb, the Holocaust, and the long Cold War to come between the Soviet Union and the United States.

In its retreat to the idyllic rusticity of the Welsh seaside, *Under Milk Wood* thus resembles *Our Town* with its look back in protectionist nostalgia to one of the many small towns bedecking the vast landscape of pre-World War I America. The difference, however, is that Thomas's wistfully compassionate vision is leavened by a rollicking sense of humor, a fair sprinkling of songs, poems, and ballads, and a joyful expression of bawdy (e.g., the name of the Welsh village, which should be read backwards), not to say realized in brilliantly imagistic-atmosphere language that is sometimes self-consciously poetic in the same way that Wilder's language is self-consciously unpoetic, even pedestrian or homely. The difference also is that Thomas's almost expressionist technique of mental projection in his radio play—with its cheerful blend of romance, sentiment (if not sentimentality), saltiness, and comedy—owes something to the "Circe" episode in *Ulysses* (1922), whereas the Wilder of *Our*

Town (and of *The Skin of Our Teeth* as well, whose cosmic point of view suffers from a certain cuteness) seems able to absorb only the universal dimension or generalizing function from Joyce's work. Moreover, the characters of *Under Milk Wood* are a bunch of eccentrics who vigorously express their individuality and freedom—a town full of accommodated Simon Stimsons, as it were—in contrast to the stick figures of *Our Town* who conform in every way to their era's notions of normality and decency.

The very title of the play poetically suggests the uniqueness of the village of Llareggub, not the idea that it belongs to us or is at one with us. The wood, named as "Milk Wood" only briefly during the play, is of no special significance to the "action." It is a haunt of courting couples and it probably is filled with milkwood trees: more than that we cannot say of the wood, yet Thomas takes his title from it, a title that first went through several prosaic incarnations from *The Town that Was Mad* to *Quite Early One Morning* to *Llareggub, a Piece for Radio Perhaps*. The poetry of the title *Under Milk Wood* is in its juxtaposition of two such incongruous nouns, wood and milk, whose contrast between solidity and fluidity evokes the selfsame contrast between the solidity or fleshliness of the play's characters, whom we nonetheless do not see, and the fluidity or the mellifluousness of their voices, which is all that we hear.

Lastly, *Under Milk Wood* could be said to allude poetically to the title and content of Thomas Hardy's third novel, *Under the Greenwood Tree* (1872), a delicately ironic, humorously romantic idyll without the ominous undertones of its author's later work. This novel was the first of Hardy's to indicate the area of life in which he was to find his greatest inspiration: literally, the region where he lived, the county of Dorset in the south of England, and which he used as a setting for almost all his fiction. Hardy tried to express in *Under the Greenwood Tree*, as he did in his collective work, the physical atmosphere of southern England as it had been in the first half of the nineteenth century— almost elevating this landscape to the level of a character. He tried as well to create human figures that he had heard of or known in his youth, but who already belonged, when he was writing, to a past age.

Similarly, *Under Milk Wood* is an attempt to memorialize the little Welsh town by the sea, Laugharne, where Dylan Thomas spent his happiest and most fruitful times, and of whose communal life he therefore had intimate knowledge. This perhaps spells the real difference between Thomas's play and Wilder's *Our Town*: that the one springs from deeply felt, affectionate experience, whereas the other derives from Wilder's *idea* of what life in an American small town was like. It is his version of pastoral, as it were, for this was a man who grew up in China, graduated from both Yale and Princeton, and studied archeology in Rome. For a more credible rendering of small-town life in the United States in the first two decades of the twentieth century, one would

do better to turn to the stories of Sherwood Anderson's *Winesburg, Ohio*
(1919)—whose own recurrent figure, the young newspaper reporter George
Willard, finally rejects the town and sets out in search of the freedom and
vitality that such a place can but dimly offer—or even to the poetry of Edgar
Lee Masters' *Spoon River Anthology* (1915), whose free-verse epitaphs by
citizens buried in an Illinois cemetery can compete with anything the deceased
inhabitants of Grover's Corners say in Act III of *Our Town*.

Like Masters' work, *Under Milk Wood* could itself be called a kind of
narrative poem, whose narrative "Voices" for this reason seem less obtrusive,
artificial, or spuriously folksy, in their existence on the page, than does Wilder's
Stage Manager (as those "Voices" do in staged readings as well as on the radio
for which the play was designed, where they are invisible like everyone or
everything else). Moreover, even as George Willard abandoned Winesburg for
the wide world, Dylan Thomas tragically left Laugharne for the fame and
funding of London and New York. Thornton Wilder, for his part, never
departed from Grover's Corners because he had never been there. And his
experiment in dramatic form summarily fails not only because he is so
concerned with its universality that he neglects to reconcile the particulars of
time, place, and person with that universality, but also because, paradoxically,
Our Town is too particular—too isolatedly historical, politically tendentious, or
socially unresponsive—ever to rise to the level of the universal. *"Our" Town*,
indeed.

Works Cited

Almeida, Diane. "Four Saints in Our Town: A Comparative Analysis of Works
    by Gertrude Stein and Thornton Wilder." *Journal of American Drama and
    Theatre*, 9 (Fall 1997): 1-23.
Berkowitz, Gerald. *American Drama of the Twentieth Century*. New York:
    Longman, 1992.
Burbank, Rex. *Thornton Wilder*. 2nd ed. Boston: Twayne, 1978.
Burns, Edward, and Ulla E. Dydo, ed. *The Letters of Gertrude Stein and
    Thornton Wilder*. New Haven: Yale University Press, 1996.
Castronovo, David. *Thornton Wilder*. New York: Ungar, 1986.
Current-Garcia, Eugene. Entry on *Our Town*. *International Dictionary of
    Theatre—1: Plays*. Ed. Mark Hawkins-Dady. Chicago: St. James Press,
    1992. 581.
Fergusson, Francis. "Three Allegorists: Brecht, Wilder, and Eliot." *The Human
    Image in Dramatic Literature*. New York: Doubleday, 1957. 41-71.
Ferris, Paul. *Dylan Thomas*. London: Hodder and Stoughton, 1977.

Goldstein, Malcolm. *The Art of Thornton Wilder*. Lincoln: University of Nebraska Press, 1965.

Haberman, Donald. *The Plays of Thornton Wilder*. Middletown: Wesleyan University Press, 1967.

—. *"Our Town": An American Play*. Boston: Twayne, 1989.

Kuner, M. C. *Thornton Wilder: The Bright and the Dark*. New York: Crowell, 1972.

Porter, Thomas E. "A Green Corner of the Universe: *Our Town*." In his *Myth and Modern American Drama*. Detroit: Wayne State University Press, 1969. 200-224.

Sang-Kyong, Lee. "Zur Rezeption ostasiatischer Theatertradition in Thornton Wilders *Our Town*." *Arcadia* 22.3 (1987): 284-300.

Saroyan, William. *The Time of Your Life*. New York: Harcourt, Brace, 1939.

Savran, David. *The Wooster Group, 1975-1985: Breaking the Rules*. Ann Arbor: UMI Research Press, 1986.

Stephens, George D. "*Our Town*—Great American Tragedy?" *Modern Drama* 1.4 (Feb. 1959): 258-264. (A response to Ballet, Arthur. "In Our Living and in Our Dying." *The English Journal* 45.5 [May 1956]: 243-249.)

Stresau, Hermann. *Thornton Wilder*. Trans. Frieda Schutze. New York: Ungar, 1971.

Thomas, Dylan. *"Under Milk Wood": A Play for Voices*. London: J. M. Dent, 1954.

Wilder, Thornton. *Our Town*. 1938. New York: HaperCollins, 1985.

—. Preface. *Three Plays*. New York: Bantam, 1961. vii-xii.

—. *American Characteristics and Other Essays*. Ed. Donald Gallup. New York: Harper and Row, 1979.

—. *The Journals of Thornton Wilder: 1938-1961*. Ed. Donald Gallup. New Haven: Yale University Press, 1985.

CHAPTER FIVE

THE UNBEARABLE LİGHT-NESS OF BEİNG: GERTRUDE STEİN'S *DOCTOR FAUSTUS LİGHTS THE LİGHTS* İN THE LİGHT OF THE TWENTİETH CENTURY

Attempting to categorize or classify the theatrical avant-garde of the early twentieth century is at best problematic. No guaranteed criterion exists that, cutting across misleading chronological boundaries, would permit us to classify this play as being of unquestionable Dada inspiration and that play as being of purely surrealist derivation. Considering that most avant-garde movements, both in drama and the plastic arts, sought to explode conventional ideas, labels, and categories—in style as well as genre and form—it seems rather unfair to impose rigid limits on the artistic products of such movements.

However, despite the radical differences among various texts of the period, every avant-garde play can be identified by its disruption of three conventional or traditional dramatic elements: faith in the providential designs of an omnipotent, omniscient, and omnipresent God as well as a divine monarch; confidence in a psychology of the individual that can cogently link human motives to human acts; and belief in a causality of events, in the idea that people's actions over time can be closely connected in a logical, almost inevitable sequence. In effect, avant-garde plays replace each of these three elements with its antithesis. If in modern realistic and naturalistic drama, the patriarchal relationship between God and the individual soul was replaced by the adversarial relationship between man and his own psychology, his will to comprehend himself, even as the patriarchal relationship between ruler and subject was replaced by the adversarial relationship between man and society, in avant-garde drama the action can be governed by something completely outside the triad that links motive to act, act to logical sequence of events, and logical outcome to divine or regal judgment. In other words, God is dead, the King has been deposed, and moral authority as well as metaphysical truth has consequently become relative; psychology itself has been replaced by illogical if not incomprehensible human motivation; and causality has been superseded by the non-linear, sometimes even static, plot.

As I shall attempt to show through an examination of Gertrude Stein's *Doctor Faustus Lights the Lights* (1938), Stein's drama provides ample evidence of these three disruptions of conventional drama, as well as exhibiting similarities to the Dadaist and Surrealist drama being written and produced in early twentieth-century Paris. Stein's plays evidence not only formal similarities with the products of these artistic movements, they also adopt their modernist world-view—which for Stein included feminism, a fascination with cinema, concerns about total or mechanized war, and questions regarding the role of art in the new era. Beyond these interests she shares with her male contemporaries, Stein demonstrates great concern for women as they are represented in art and repeatedly exhibits feminist themes in her work. This feminist focus, presented in the form of avant-garde art, is remarkably similar to that of Hannah Höch, whose visual art used the same fragmentation and montage techniques as other Dadaists, but for the purpose (among others) of criticizing typical representations of women.

In Stein's writing in general and in her drama in particular, the dominant artistic and cultural trends of the twentieth century thus emerge. Though she is perhaps the least well known of America's twentieth-century playwrights, she is the first genuine avant-garde dramatist of her country. As such, the history of experimental theater and drama in America is virtually inconceivable without her influence. One of America's earliest avant-garde theater groups, for example—the Living Theater—began production in 1951 with Stein's curtainraiser "Ladies' Voices" (1916). Robert Wilson produced her play *Doctor Faustus Lights the Lights* in 1992 and, in 1998, the Wooster Group performed its adaptation of Stein's *Doctor Faustus,* titled *House/Lights.* Richard Foreman, for one, has credited Stein as the most significant influence on his work. Anne Bogart's theater and Stan Brakhage's films have built their respective aesthetics upon Stein's principles, and further parallels can be made between Stein and such contemporary, experimental dramatists as Suzan-Lori Parks and María Irene Fornés, not to speak of Adrienne Kennedy before them.

Yet despite her dramatic influence, Stein's plays are rarely studied, even among Stein scholars; similarly, the field of theater studies to date has largely ignored her dramatic output. It is my contention, however, that Gertrude Stein's drama deserves consideration on its own terms, as drama and as theater. These plays have an interior logic as well as a dramatic progression in which Stein continually works out her vision of modernity and modernism, culminating in her greatest dramatic work, *Doctor Faustus Lights the Lights.* At its core, Stein's drama is even prophetic, an artistic herald for the latter half of the twentieth century. Through her use of non-linear language, fragmented characters, and non-narrative "plot," Stein seemingly predicts the rise of non-linear communication (as found on the Internet), even as her art itself was influenced by the horror of weapons of mass destruction and the increasingly technological landscape of the "developed" West. That she has never completely disappeared from our collective theatrical and cultural imagination is only one testament to her enduring influence and artistic significance. The other is her work itself, which continues to excite the imagination, challenge the conventions of language as well as thought, and reflect the state of humanity more than half a century later.

Although Stein clearly played a critical role in the development of experimental playwriting, it is in performance that Stein's influence is most visible and most enduring. Nearly every year for the past decade, another new Stein play or adaptation has appeared on American stages. The operas *Four Saints in Three Acts* (1927) and *The Mother of Us All* (1945-1946) are regularly performed and her non-dramatic work has been consistently adapted for performance. Indeed, as the American avant-garde moves into the twenty-first century, Stein is an integral part of its theater. Since Robert Wilson's production of *Doctor Faustus Lights the Lights* in 1992, for example, he has directed two other works by Stein: *Four Saints in Three Acts* in 1996, and *Saints and Singing* (1922) in 1998. And in 1998 the Wooster Group's adaptation of *Doctor Faustus Lights the Lights, House/Lights*, combined Stein's text with Joseph Mawra's 1964 sexploitation film *Olga's House of Shame,* in a production directed by Elizabeth LeCompte.

Thus, despite the argument that American avant-garde performance has been and continues to be largely anti-textual, Stein's literary influence has been an enduring presence. In fact, it is precisely this apparent incongruity that makes Stein's presence in avant-garde performance so compelling. One might question how a director such as Robert Wilson can baldly state that "You don't have to listen to the words, because words don't mean anything," and yet still claim the word-fixated Stein as a major influence; or why a theater ensemble as visceral and revolutionary as the Living Theater would begin its inaugural season with a playwright as cerebral as Gertrude Stein. Or one could ask how two artists as radically different as Judith Malina and Wilson could both find their origins in Gertrude Stein; while the work of two others, Meredith Monk and Lee Breuer, is almost always placed in context through reference to Stein. It is in response to such testaments that Stein emerges as more than a great playwright. Stein's writing not only transformed dramatic literature, but her sense of theatricality, expressed both in her drama and in lectures, also profoundly affected American avant-garde performance. It affected criticism as well, changing not only the theater that critics watch, but also the *way* they watch.

But it is primarily with Stein's writing that I am concerned here, as it exhibits its artistry in *Doctor Faustus Lights the Lights*. More intellectually accessible than much of her early work, *Doctor Faustus Lights the Lights* blends her unique approach to language and structure with universal themes, which for her included feminist ones. The play represents a transition between the two periods in Stein's enormous dramatic *oeuvre* (over seventy-five works), which Donald Sutherland has described as "The Play as Movement and Landscape, 1922-1932" and "The Melodic Drama, Melodrama, and Opera, 1932-1946" (207). In *Doctor Faustus Lights the Lights* Stein uses identifiable characters and attributes specific dialogue to them, but the language exhibits all the idiosyncrasies of her earlier work—lack of punctuation, multiple identities for major   characters, disembodied voices, punning, non-sequiturs, and repetition.   Stein's language now focuses on something other than its own structure; she shifts from a concern with it to such philosophical or metaphysical problems as those of moral value and human identity. Still, she maintains throughout the play a style readily identifiable as her own.

Despite numerous essays that have been published on Stein's drama in general, and on *Doctor Faustus Lights the Lights* in particular, few attempts have been made to connect her plays with other avant-garde drama of the period. (It should be noted here that I refer exclusively to the theatrical avant-garde. There is a wide range of essays connecting Stein's poetry, fiction, and drama with Cubist and other avant-garde painting and visual art, most especially that of Picasso. However, few of these studies discuss Stein's drama in the context of Dada or Surrealist performance or any of the numerous theoretical writings of fellow avant-garde writers.) There are a number of possible reasons for this, not the least of which is her rather isolated position as an affluent Jewish-American lesbian living among the financially struggling European men who constituted the vast majority of avant-garde writers. Furthermore, Stein's plays are often considered to be more literary than dramatic. Indeed, Stein is more often respected not for her own *oeuvre* but for her influence on other artists: avant-garde painters such as Picasso, Matisse, and Braque; young American writers like Ernest Hemingway and F. Scott Fitzgerald; and non-traditional American theatre figures and movements of the 1960s and 1970s, including not only Richard Foreman's Ontological-Hysteric Theater and Robert Wilson's Theatre of Silence-and-Images, but also Richard Schechner and his Performance Group.

Interestingly, Stein is most often thought to have been influenced by, and to have been a part of, the painterly avant-garde more than the dramatic one. While it is true that the programmatic and frequently disruptive Stein text is not unlike the strategy of a collage, for example—in which the symbolic decoding is left to the respective observer—the technique of disruption-through-fragmentation was not limited to the visual art of Dada, but could be found in their performances as well. Moreover, the disruption of audience expectations was an essential component of avant-garde theatre beginning with Alfred Jarry's *Ubu Roi* (1896), and simultaneity was pioneered by the Futurists. It is no coincidence that Stein's plays reflect techniques and attitudes common among both the Dadaists and the Surrealists, since many of them were her close friends and associates.

To be fair, a few critics have acknowledged the connection between Stein and the drama of Jarry, Guillaume Apollinaire's *The Breasts of Tiresias* (1917), and Tristan Tzara's *The Gas Heart* (1920). These critics have perceived that, like her contemporaries, Stein advocated anti-naturalism in the performing arts: no plot; directionless happenings; no characters; non-referential, and therefore self-contained, movement; no logic in the sequence of events; no transitions; no connections; no sense of progress. But they have also gone on to claim that, unlike the Surrealists, she had no interest in the unconscious. Yet, given Stein's study of psychology at Radcliffe and Johns Hopkins Medical School, it seems unlikely that she would have had absolutely no interest in the unconscious, especially since Surrealism sought to unify the unconscious and conscious minds. In addition, both Stein and André Breton, the founder of the Surrealist movement, experimented with automatic writing. Indeed, as a psychology student, Stein used herself and others as subjects for experiments in automatic writing.

Stein claimed to have used automatic writing in her early work, and critics have cited evidence of it throughout her career. As late as 1936, only two years before *Doctor Faustus Lights the Lights* was published, Stein gave a lecture, "What Are Master-Pieces and why are there so few of them," in which she described automatic writing (or "secondary writing," as she refers to it):

> If you do not remember while you are writing, it may seem confused to others but actually it is clear and eventually that clarity will be clear, that is what a master-piece is, but if you remember while you are writing it will seem clear at the time to any one but the clarity will go out of it that is what a master-piece is not. (150)

Breton, for his part, considered it the aim of Surrealism to promote automatic writing to "the exclusion of all other" arts.   In his essay "The Automatic Message," he wrote:

> If the surrealist effort has tended above all to restore inspiration to favor, and if, in order to do so, we have extolled automatic forms of expression to the exclusion of all others, and if in addition psychoanalysis, beyond every expectation, has charged with penetrable meaning the kinds of improvisation

previously too easily held to be gratuitous and has conferred upon them, outside
all aesthetic considerations, every significant value as human documents, it is
nevertheless necessary to admit that sufficient light is far from having been cast
on the conditions in which an "automatic" text or drawing must be obtained in
order to be fully valid. (100)

Certainly passages in *Doctor Faustus Lights the Lights* reflect the
kind of stream of consciousness that Breton called "automatic writing." In
his opening monologue, for example, Doctor Faustus "automatically" tells
the story of Faust up to the turning point of almost every other Faust
version. Whereas the turning point of Goethe's and Marlowe's Faustian
dramas is Faust's decision to sell his soul to the devil, Stein begins her
play *after* Faustus has made his decision:

> What do I care there is no here nor there. What am I. I am Doctor Faustus who
> knows everything can do everything and you say it was through you but not at
> all, if 1 had not been in a hurry and if I had taken my time I would have known
> how to make white electric light and day-light and night light and what did I do I
> saw you miserable devil I saw you and I was deceived and I believed miserable
> devil I thought I needed you, and I thought I was tempted by the devil and I
> know no temptation is tempting unless the devil tells you so. (89)

Considering the absence of syntax in the above speech and the free association
implied by such shifts as "can do everything and you say it was through you, "
as well as by "and night light and what did I do I saw you miserable devil," one
can deduce that Stein wrote this either without consciously "thinking out" the
speech of her character, or else by consciously attempting to have Faustus speak
as if he were not thinking in a logical and orderly manner. Doctor Faustus
speaks in such cycles throughout the play, repeating phrases or words and
frequently rhyming.

Critics have interpreted this style of speech in a variety of
psychological ways: Jungian and autobiographical, to name only two. What
these interpretations ignore, however, are the blatant similarities between Stein's
response to twentieth-century experience and the responses of the Dadaists and
Surrealists. Rather than being merely an extension of her psyche, Stein's Faust
exhibits the same frustrations, desires, and creative impulses as her fellow
avant-garde artists in Europe. To wit, Doctor Faustus had been enchanted
enough with electric light to agree to sell his soul for it, yet when he first
appears in Stein's text, he has nothing but contempt for the light he has created:

> I keep on having so much light that light is not bright and what after all is the use
> of light, you can see just as well without it, you can go around just as well
> without it, you can get up and go to bed just as well without it, and I I wanted to
> make it and the devil take it yes devil you do not even want it and I sold my soul

to make it. (90)

This sentiment is remarkably similar to that of the Dada artists, who, while they rejected what they saw as the banality of naturalism and the anthropomorphic arrogance of romanticism, also came in time to distrust the very modernism from which they had emerged. Like the Dadaists, Faustus exhibits an early fascination with the technology of the modern world, but he eventually rejects the light he has created. Written several years after the demise of Dada and on the eve of Hitler's invasion of France, Stein's *Doctor Faustus* incorporates not only the Surrealists' interest in the unconscious, then, but also both the Dadaists' fascination with technology—particularly the technological art of cinema—and their distrust of technology clearly warranted by the horrors of mechanized warfare already exhibited during World War 1.

Stein even uses formal techniques similar to those employed by the Dadaists. In her lecture "Composition as Explanation" (1926), for example, she describes the "continuous present" as "a beginning again and again and again, it was a list it was a similarity and everything different it was a similarity and everything different it was a distribution and an equilibration" (29). Often referred to as repetition, this "continuous present" might also be understood as a form of simultaneity, originally a performance technique borrowed from the Italian Futurists by Dada. Francis Picabia's Dadaist play, *Relâche* (*No Performance* or *Relax*, 1924), for instance, began on stage with a film prologue by the young René Clair and music by Erik Satie. After one minute, hundreds of lights in photographic metallic reflectors blinded the audience. These formed the backdrop. On the stage, dozens of disconnected activities were then enacted. A fireman for the theatre smoked cigarettes and poured water from one pail to another. Man Ray, the American artist, sat on the side of the stage, occasionally marking off space with his shoes. Figures from Lucas Cranach's painting *Adam and Eve* appeared. Tuxedoed playboys disrobed. And an automobile brought on a young couple in evening clothes.

While *Doctor Faustus Lights the Lights* does not contain such simultaneous, layered activity, the lack of progression in the plot does create a kind of "continuous present." There is no cause-and-effect, no evolving plot line. Rather, the events that occur in *Doctor Faustus Lights the Lights* embody the simultaneous present that one can associate with twentieth-century life. It has been, in a way, the mission of the twentieth century (and beyond) to destroy progressive history and create a single time in which everything in the past and possibly the future would be simultaneous. As Gertrude Stein herself writes in her 1934 lecture "Plays," "The business of Art as I have tried to explain in 'Composition as Explanation' is to live in the actual present, that is the complete and actual present, and to completely express that complete actual present." By opening her play after Faust's fatal decision has been made, Stein creates that "complete actual" or continuous present, for she has effectively robbed the drama of its potential suspense. Without it, the tempo of the play is flattened, for suspense by its very nature is dependent on time. Anything but taut with anticipation, the audience has most of its questions answered from the opening moment. There is no question as to whether Faustus will or will not sell his soul, or as to whether he made the right decision; from the start, Doctor Faustus both acknowledges his decision to sell his soul—indeed, the fact that he has already sold it—and admits his dissatisfaction with that decision. By so diffusing the suspense of *Doctor Faustus Lights the Lights*, Stein disrupts not only her drama's time-line, but also its causal progression.

Similarly, Stein uses rapid shifts of location to create a sense that various activities are taking place in simultaneous time, even if they do not actually do so. This "editing" or "montage" is quite possibly a technique Stein borrowed from the cinema, for we know she believed that film had fundamentally changed people's ways of viewing and hearing. In "Plays" she writes,

> I suppose one might have gotten to know a good deal about these things from cinema and how it changed from sight to sound, and how much before there was real sound how much of the sight was sound or how much it was not. In other words the cinema undoubtedly had a new way of understanding sight and sound in relation to emotion and time. (64)

Like Stein, the Dadaists and Surrealists considered film a major artistic innovation. And film provides an essential link between the European avant-garde and American art of all forms in the twentieth century. While Dada was growing up in America, that is, so were moving pictures (and like Dada they were primarily an American phenomenon rather than a British one). The use of collage and montage, the representation of unconscious desire, for example—all to be found in Dada and Surrealism—find their roots in cinematic technique.

Indeed, in the dream and in film one sees the image of something that is not really there, in an illusion similar to that of a mirror. In his avant-garde play *Him* (1927), another American writer, e.e. cummings—whose poetic experiments with language in poetry were related to Stein's in prose—explicitly plays with the illusion of the mirror and its reflection of unconscious dreams and desires. Cummings' two main characters, Him and Me, take their names from their images in a mirror. In addition to exploring the role of characters-as-mirrors, cummings creates the structure of his play as the literal mirror of a play:

Him:	This play of mine is all about mirrors.
Me:	But who's the hero?
Him:	*(To her)* The hero of this play of mine?
	(Hesitates) A man . . .
Me:	Naturally. What sort of man?
Him:	The sort of man—who is writing a play about a man who is writing a sort of play.
Me:	That's a queer hero, isn't it?
Him:	Isn't it?
Me:	And what is this hero called?
Him:	*(Very slowly)* This hero is called 'Mr. O.Him, the Man in the Mirror.'
Me:	O.Him.
	(Smiles) And the heroine?
	(Quickly) Or isn't there any?
Him:	On the contrary. My heroine lives over there—.
	(Points to the Mirror)
Me:	*(Turning at the invisible window)* Me?
Him:	Me, the beautiful mistress of the extraordinary Mr. O.Him.
Me:	—Extraordinary because he thinks she's beautiful?
Him:	Extraordinary because I need a shave because he needs a shave. (29-30)

Aside from its formal similarities to the European avant-garde and that avant-garde's much smaller dramatic offshoot in the United States, *Doctor Faustus Lights the Lights* is important, as I noted earlier, for its explicit violations of the three fundamental elements of conventional or traditional drama: in brief, psychology, causality, and morality or providentially. Rather than merely mimic the techniques of the Dadaists or Surrealists, Stein disrupts this triad even further than either cummings in *Him* or Wilder in his allegedly avant-garde play *Our Town* (1938), thereby establishing herself as the foremost dramatist of the American avant-garde.

It is noteworthy that *Our Town,* published in the same year as *Doctor Faustus Lights the Lights,* deals with the same issues as Stein's play—namely, the individual's place in the world, humanity's relationship to a higher power, and the longing, if not for a better world, then for a greater appreciation of the world-in-itself, in all its mundane dailiness. Considering that both Stein and Wilder were writing in Europe (she in Paris and he in Switzerland) on the eve of World War II, it is not surprising that each was preoccupied with the question of where the world was headed. Yet, though the two were friends and corresponded during this time, their dramatic results could hardly be more different. Whereas Wilder, amid the trappings of the avant-garde (as I have described that avant-garde), clearly advocates in his play a retreat from modernist technology and a return to simple living in the small towns of late nineteenth-to-early-twentieth-century America, Stein seems to believe that there can be no retreat and that the consequences of this technology must be faced in the present as well as in the future.

To repeat, Doctor Faustus begins his journey not before or even *with* the decision to sell his soul, but after its sale. And, like Faust, the Dadaists themselves emerged into a world that had already lost its secure faith in absolutes. Confronted with mechanical processes and biological determinism, the individual saw less and less scope for self-determined action. So too did Gertrude Stein emerge into such a world, and so too was she confronted, with the result that a patriarchal God had to disappear from her drama—to be replaced by a humanity in conflict with itself and with an industrial-technological environment of humankind's own creation.

The Faust legend itself stems from another kind of creation, for it is something of a retelling of the Biblical myth of the Garden of Eden as it appears in Genesis 2-3. There Eve is tempted by the devil, in the form of a serpent, to taste fruit from the tree of knowledge and to share that fruit with Adam—an action that banishes all humanity from paradise. Similarly, the Faust of legend is tempted to sell his soul to the devil (and, consequently, his right to a place in the paradise of heaven—the only Eden humankind can ever know) in exchange for omniscience, even omnipotence. Throughout Stein's play, major characters themselves usurp or reject power typically associated with God. Faustus claims the power to create light, as does Marguerite Ida-Helena Annabel, although she seems less interested in this power than Faust. (This female character's dual names and fluctuating identity mark her as a kind of conflated womankind, which complicates the use of verb tenses throughout the play. Marguerite Ida-Helena Annabel's names themselves derive from various recountings or dramatizations of the Faust legend by Christopher Marlowe [1588], Karl von Holtei; [1829], George Sand [1869], Ida Hahn-Hahn [1840], and Stephen Vincent Benét [1937].) Instead, Marguerite Ida-Helena Annabel rejects all deities, turning her back on both the sun (which could be interpreted as a natural god) and the electric light (the new technological god).

Like the Biblical Eve, Marguerite Ida-Helena Annabel is bitten by a viper. Initially, however, Marguerite Ida-Helena Annabel appears to triumph over the bite. Faustus cures her, despite his repeated assertions that he cannot see her, and thereafter Marguerite Ida-Helena Annabel becomes immune to the viper's poison. As Stein's Chorus intones, "See the viper there, / Cannot hurt her" (106). At first glance, this seems to be a triumph of science over God, but Marguerite Ida-Helena Annabel rejects not only the natural light of the sun but also the science of Faust. And for the first time in the play she gains a unity of identity: "With her back to the sun / One sun / And she is one / Marguerite Ida and Helena Annabel as well" (107).

With both unity and duality thus present in her main female character, Stein focuses attention on the multiple identities of women. Like the Dadaists, who expressed skepticism about the unity of character in any dramatic or theatrical presentation, Stein creates a character who in name alone evokes both the good and evil depictions of women in history and literature. Half of the four-part name, Marguerite Ida, contains positive connotations of motherhood—Margaret the faithful wife and mother of multiple Faust legends, and Ida the mother of the gods—while the second half, Helena Annabel, suggests images of sexual temptation and demonic, anti-familial sentiment, aside from its possible (ironic?) reference to the mother of the Virgin Mary. (Annabel suggests the name Hannah, which in Hebrew refers to the Anna Perenna of Italian tradition and also to the mother of the Virgin Mary.) In creating such a fractured, complex identity for this figure, Stein, in my view, is contradicting one-dimensional representations of women and illuminating the absurdity of the longstanding Madonna-Whore dichotomy. A reader or viewer must constantly reconcile the manifold nature of Marguerite Ida-Helena Annabel with the singular pronoun "she." The stubbornness of Stein's technique, moreover, is evident in criticism of the play, where scholars almost always shorten the character's name to "Marguerite Ida" or her initials, MIHA, rather than confuse their own readers' sense of grammar and logic.

The duality of Marguerite Ida-Helena Annabel's character is visible not only in her name, but also in the events that surround her. She is at once an agent of action and the passive victim or recipient of others' actions. As an embodiment of Eve, she survives the bite of the snake, to become as powerful as Doctor Faustus in her ability to create light—candlelight in this case. Nevertheless, she still succumbs to "the man from the sea" (107), who appears as another embodiment of the same viper she had earlier eluded and seduces her, exclaiming that "I am the only he and you are the only she and we are the only we" (108). His language, of course, recalls Adam and Eve, the first he and she. But through Marguerite Ida-Helena Annabel, Stein inverts the story of Adam and Eve in the Garden of Eden.

For this Eve is not only not responsible for her own temptation (she is unwittingly bitten by the serpent and even fails to realize it was a serpent that was responsible for the bite), she is also relieved of the responsibility for the fall of humanity. It is the Adam figure, in fact ("the only he"), who is linked to both the devil *and* the serpent: "And indeed behind the man of the seas is Mephistopheles . . ." (108). This Adam is born from the sea, an image often equated with female sexuality, whereas the Eve of the Bible is born from Adam's rib. When the man from the seas arrives with Mephistopheles, moreover, two children repeatedly call this seemingly maternal man "Mr. Viper." Indeed, the only figure from Genesis who does not appear here is God himself.

Despite the inversion of the Eve character and the absence of a Judeo-Christian God from *Doctor Faustus Lights the Lights,* humanity nonetheless suffers a spiritual fate equivalent to Adam and Eve's banishment from the Garden of Eden. Even as Stein subverts or dismisses traditional theology, humans in the play seem to impose a similar fate on themselves as they choose to reject God and face their difficult lives alone. This rejection of God by humanity culminates in Faust's damnation, not as the result of an act of God or seduction by a woman, but rather of his own free will. Considering her dismissal of traditional theology, it should not be surprising, then, that Stein opens the play after the central religious crisis—Faust's decision to sell his soul to the devil for knowledge—which in other dramatizations of the Faust legend serves as the turning point. For Stein, like the Dadaists and Surrealists, the religious crisis—whether to believe in or turn away from a higher being, whether to accept or reject organized religion—is past history and no longer relevant to her "continuous present."

Rather than concern himself with his relationship to, or the repercussions of the existence of, a godlike figure, Stein's Doctor Faustus begins the play by lamenting his own foolishness at allowing someone else (the devil) to wield influence over him. Like the egotism of previous Fausts, his own egotism is central to his character, as when this Faustus vents his frustration on Mephistopheles. While Faust immediately regrets his decision to sell his soul for electric light, his regret—or, better, his remorse—is motivated not by fear of an almighty creator or a crisis of conscience, but rather by his immediate *physical* discomfort—caused by the relentless glare of the lights. "I keep on having so much light that light is not bright" (89), he complains. As I have implied, the spiritual wrath of God is thus systematically replaced by the secular wrath of technology, as represented by electric light, in *Doctor Faustus Lights the Lights.*

That God is replaced by the modern technology of electricity may be Stein's punning reference to Goethe's criticism of the Enlightenment in his *Faust.* Despite its centrality to the theme, however, the "spirituality" of the electric lights has so far been ignored in criticism of *Doctor Faustus Lights the Lights.* In recent scholarship about the play, in fact, Faust is frequently compared to so secular a figure as Thomas Edison. What this interpretation ignores, though, is the tremendous theological or ontological weight placed on the electric lights in the absence of a god figure in the drama. Faust is not an inventor grown tired of his invention. Rather, he has ceased to be able to control it; he cannot escape the very lights he has created and they torment him. Furthermore, these electric lights communicate with Faustus, an issue not addressed by the Edison analogy. Early in the play, for example, Faust sings a duet with his dog—and the lights—about the electric lights:

Bathe me
says Doctor Faustus
Bathe me
In the electric lights
During this time the electric lights come and go
What is it
says Doctor Faustus
Thank you
says the dog.
Just this moment the electric lights get
brighter and nothing comes
Was it it
says Doctor Faustus
Faustus meditates he does not see the dog.
Will it
Will it
Will it be
Will it be it.
Faustus sighs and repeats
Will it be it.
A duet between the dog and Faustus
Will it be it.
Just it.
At that moment the electric light gets pale again and in that moment Faustus
shocked says
It is it . . . (92)

The above "duet" between Faust, the dog, and the lights clearly
indicates a superior role for the lights, as well as their ability to convey
information to Faustus. Indeed, just before his repetitious questioning of the
lights, Faust meditates so deeply that he seems to forget the dog, with whom
he has sung the duet until now. This meditation then culminates in an
unnamed or undecipherable revelation by the lights: "It is it . . ." Certainly,
this relationship is more complicated than that between an inventor and his
object, and, although Faustus does usurp a godlike power in creating the light,
it is the light that ultimately controls him.

Further articulated through this relationship between Doctor Faustus
and the lights is the play's singular moral design. For Faust may have been able
to create electric light, but he cannot control it; he has produced a never-ending
day, but no corresponding night. Stein has thus returned, via Faust's creation, to
a godless and disordered world by undoing, as it were, God's first act of
creation. As the first book of Genesis reads,

And God said, "Let there be light"; and there was light. And God saw that the light was good; and God separated the light from the darkness. God called the light Day, and the darkness he called Night. And there was evening and morning, one day. (Genesis 1.3-5)

God's first act is to separate light from darkness, thereby creating day and night, evening and morning. But Faust's creation of the electric light does away with this distinction, and Stein equates this merging of day and night, light and dark, with the disappearance of moral order from the universe. And it is after Doctor Faustus has acknowledged that he foolishly traded his soul for the lights that he articulates the new "moral order" of the play:

Who cares if you lie if you steal, there is no snake to grind under one's heel, there is no hope there is no death there is no life there is no breath, there just is every day all day and when there is no day there is no clay. (90)

The cycle of day into night has been broken and with it the moral certainty of the separation of light from dark, good from evil. When Faustus rhetorically asks, "Who cares if you lie if you steal," it is clear that God might have cared, but He is now absent. And in the absence of God, the natural world suffers, as do all living beings who are dependent upon it. Not only is Faust tormented by the unrelenting lights, for example, but so is his dog:

I am a dog and I bay at the moon, I did yes I used to do it I used to bay at the moon I always used to do it and now now not any more, I cannot, of course I cannot, the electric lights they make it be that there is no night and if there is no night then there is no moon and if there is no moon I do not see it and if I do not see it I cannot bay at all. (111)

From the human as opposed to the canine angle, Faust's boy companion notes that, without a moon, "no one is crazy any more" (111). Given the events of the play, however, the boy's observation begs the question, what is "crazy" in the context of this play? Given the talking dog who says "thank you," multiple identities, a day without end, a devil who appears to have little direct power over humanity, and a universe without moral order, it seems that the lack of a moon has actually made the world crazier. Of course what Stein implies, through her dismantling of a theological framework for the play's action, is that the craziness of humanity is the result neither of a natural aberration nor of the absence of God. Humanity is *innately* prone to maddening self-destructiveness, and the lifting of moral sanctions merely reveals the true nature of the beings underneath.

Stein posits the inability of humanity to advance or improve itself in her essay "What Are Master-Pieces and why are there so few of them." In a piece that seems to be a gloss on *Doctor Faustus Lights the Lights,* she questions *anyone's* ability to create art—to create timeless *master*pieces—in a world where human development seems less to support Charles Darwin's theory of evolution than to be trapped in its own vicious cycle or re-volution:

> What is the use of being a boy if you are going to grow up to be a man. And what is the use there is no use from the standpoint of master-pieces there is no use. Anybody can really know that.

> There is really no use in being a boy if you are going to grow up to be a man and boy you can be certain that that is continuing and a master-piece does not continue it is as it is but it does not continue. It is very interesting that no one is content with being a man and boy but he must also be a son and a father and the fact that they all die has something to do with time but it has nothing to do with a master-piece. (153)

Written in 1936, just two years before *Doctor Faustus Lights the Lights,* the above text finds its way into Faust's musing about himself and his role in the universe: "I go where I go, where is there there is where and all the day and all the night too it grew and grew and there is no way to say I and a dog and a boy, if a boy is to grow to be a man am I a boy am I a dog is a dog a boy is a boy a dog and what am I I cannot cry what am I oh what am I" (98). This might be construed as a dream sequence—"Doctor Faustus the dog and the boy all sleeping" (98)—for Faustus repeatedly sees himself here as interchangeable with the dog and the boy and consequently lacking a definite identity of his own:

> Man and dog dog and man each one can tell it all like a ball with a caress no tenderness, man and dog just the same each one can take the blame each one can well as well tell it all as—they can, man and dog, well well man and dog what is the difference between a man and a dog when I say none. (98)

Towards the end of the play, Faust even responds to his dog with the very same line that has been repeated by the animal itself throughout the play: "Yes thank you" (111).

Stein may create multiple identities for Marguerite Ida-Helena Annabel, but Faust's ongoing questioning of himself does not result in even a temporary unity or oneness of identity. Doctor Faustus thus appears to be incapable of spiritual fulfillment through God or even the devil, who is unable to convince Faustus that he has, or had, a soul. Faust's self-querying actually begins with this question posed to the devil: "I have made it but have I a soul to pay for it" (90). Moreover, his question "what am I" (89), made to appear a declaration, is repeated frequently throughout the play—yet Faustus does not find an answer. In fact, after his final action, the killing of the boy and the dog so as to gain entrance into hell, Marguerite Ida-Helena Annabel's failure to recognize him denies Faust his identity. Before falling helplessly into the arms of the man from the seas, Marguerite Ida-Helena Annabel says, "you are not Doctor Faustus no not ever never never" (118). Faust's quest to understand himself may be as unrelenting as the glare of the electric lights, but it is also just as unfulfilling. As the circularity of Faust's musings suggests, the attempt to know oneself—in the hope of bettering, renewing, or redeeming oneself—is essentially futile.

If the fundamental subject matter of almost all serious plays of the nineteenth through twenty-first centuries is the attempt to resurrect fundamental ethical and philosophical certainties *without* resurrecting the fundamental spiritual certainty of a judgmental or mindful God, then not only has Gertrude Stein replaced the spiritual certainty of God with the secular amorality of modern technology, she has also replaced the psycho-scientific certainty of integrated yet developing personality with the inability of humanity either to comprehend itself or to evolve. In this play, all the characters are reduced to the same frustrating inability not only to understand themselves, but also to understand the world and to act upon it. Marguerite Ida-Helena Annabel cannot defend herself against the man from the seas; the devil cannot control Doctor Faustus (not even long enough to convince him that he once had a soul); Faust cannot regulate the lights once he has created them, and at the end of the play he fails to convince Marguerite Ida-Helena Annabel to accompany him to hell; and both the boy and the dog have no power over their own lives, manipulated as they are by Faust—and ultimately killed by him.

Like Wilder's *Our Town,* again, *Doctor Faustus Lights the Lights* investigates the triumph of modern technology and the role of God in contemporary life. But rather than offer romantic nostalgia and spiritual redemption to a Depression-weary and war-wary American public, through isolation—and isolationism—in a quaint New Hampshire town of the turn of the twentieth century, Stein accepts the impotence of humanity without a god, without morals, and without a real sense of itself. Indeed, in an almost Absurdist fashion, Stein's characters revel in their own frustration and ignorance. As a final gesture to this frustration, or frustrated knowledge, Stein ends the play with a little boy and little girl futilely calling for the man from the sea, or Mr. Viper as they address him: "Please Mr. Viper listen to me he is he and she is she and we are we please Mr. Viper listen to me" (118).

The end for Doctor Faustus is a similarly fruitless gesture. Faust's frustration with the world culminates in his desire to "go to hell," which neatly returns the play to its theological question—does Doctor Faustus have a soul? Ironically, Mephistopheles informs Faustus that he cannot enter hell without a soul, which Faust has sold. In order to enter hell, Doctor Faustus is therefore told, he must commit a sin. When he asks, "What sin, how can I without a soul commit a sin," Mephisto peremptorily replies, "Kill anything" (116). Faust then kills his companions, the boy and the dog, and descends into hell.

In light of Faust's damnation, we may usefully consider the doctrinal distinction between venial sin and mortal sin as articulated by the Catholic Church. Damnation occurs where the sin is mortal, not venial. For sin to be mortal the act must be of grave matter and involve a deliberate turning away from God. This, say the catechisms, asks for as full a knowledge of the consequences as the sinner is able to embrace. Such a distinction may explain why Doctor Faustus can turn away from God initially (through the pact he makes with Mephisto before Stein's play begins) with no obvious consequences, but turn from God at the conclusion of the play, through murder, and enter hell. Significantly, the word "sin" is used only in this final scene. Faust's initial turning away from God is motivated by his desire for knowledge, not by any desire to repudiate or "kill" the deity. For this reason we may regard his first sin as venial. At the end of the play, however, Faustus consciously turns from God by committing the mortal sin of murder—i.e., by killing a human being made in God's image.

I believe that Stein uses the majority of the play as a build, undramatic as it may seem, to this final moment. Faust desires to go to hell to escape the reality that he himself has created through his rejection of God in favor of technology. But, for Stein in *Doctor Faustus Lights the Lights*, the term "hell" describes this very technological reality (or nightmare): "Any light is just a light and now there is nothing more either by day or by night just a light" (91). The unrelenting light can be read as a modern analogue to the eternal fires of hell. This technological light has the capacity, with its heat and radiance (neither warm and nourishing like the sun, nor gently haloed like candlelight), to overwhelm all other forms of light and, like the hell of theology, every type of faith.

Living in Europe during the 1930s, Stein thus reflects the anxiety of a continent only recently recovered from the first mechanized world war, yet now poised on the brink of a second one—a war whose technological devastation and human waste would beggar the imagination. Unlike the retrogressive Emily in *Our Town,* Stein could not advocate that humans simply and happily "realize life while they live it—every, every minute" (100). Rather she suggests, like other avant-garde writers of her time, that life cannot be totally realized or understood, and she avers, unlike the comforting Stage Manager in Wilder's *Our Town,* that no God exists to create moral order or to prevent humankind from technological self-extinction.

The question remains, did Gertrude Stein herself reject faith in God, or is she warning others against the abandonment of such faith? Clearly, Stein demonstrated during her life a fascination with religion, Catholicism in particular. Though Stein herself was Jewish, Catholicism seems always to have held a fascination for her. Yet in her early writings, such as the Radcliffe Themes (written 1894-1895), *The Making of Americans* (written 1903-1911) and *Quod Erat Demonstrandum* (written 1903), Stein challenged institutional or organized religion with its patriarchal and hierarchical structure. Her objections to such religion thus tempered her enthusiasm for the Catholic Church. While Stein's religious ideas owe much to Catholicism, then, even her earliest writings are openly critical of some Catholic beliefs and practices.

    In their place, Stein advocated an individualized, woman-identified religion in which first-hand spiritual experience becomes the individual's goal. If one compares her characterization of Marguerite Ida-Helena Annabel as a self-contained, candlelit entity to her essentialization of the electrically lit Faust in the amorphous "what am I," Stein clearly argues for a feminine version of spirituality. And yet, Marguerite Ida-Helena Annabel falls helplessly into the arms of Mr. Viper at the conclusion of the play, a final action that indicates nihilistic hopelessness for humanity rather than religious salvation. Like the Dadaists, to name only one avant-garde group, Stein lost faith in the traditional patriarchal God, but she also lost faith both in unconventional feminine spirituality and, paradoxically, in the human potential of any individual *without* absolute faith. Faust's "individual quest," after all, ends in murder, despair, and chaos. And the grim attitude that permeates *Doctor Faustus Lights the Lights* continues after World War II, in the works of such writers as Jean-Paul Sartre, Albert Camus, Samuel Beckett, and Eugène Ionesco, who saw humankind's trust in a higher power betrayed by the human folly—the hellfire of the Holocaust and atomic obliteration—of the last great war.

Works Cited

Breton, André. "The Automatic Message." In *What Is Surrealism?* Ed. Franklin Rosemont. London: Pluto Press, 1978.
cummings, e.e. *Him.* New York: Boni and Liveright, 1927.
Stein, Gertrude. *Doctor Faustus Lights the Lights.* In her *Last Operas and Plays.* New York: Rinehart and Co., 1949.
—. "What are Master-Pieces and why are there so few of them." In her *Writings and Lectures, 1911-1945.* Ed. Patricia Meyerowitz. London: Peter Owen, 1967.
—. "Plays." In her *Writings and Lectures, 1911-1945.* Ed Patricia Meyerowitz. London: Peter Owen, 1967.

—. "Composition as Explanation." In her *Writings and Lectures, 1911-1945.* Ed. Patricia Meyerowitz. London: Peter Owen, 1967.

Sutherland, Donald. *Gertrude Stein: A Biography of Her Work.* New Haven, Conn.: Yale University Press, 1951.

Wilder, Thornton. *Our Town.* 1938. New York: HarperPerennial, 1992.

CHAPTER SIX

THE BLUE ROSE OF ST. LOUIS: LAURA, ROMANTICISM, AND *THE GLASS MENAGERIE*

Laura Wingfield of *The Glass Menagerie* (1944) hardly qualifies as a Romantic superwoman, a majestic ego eager to transcend the "mereness" of mundane human existence. In his narration of the drama at the same time as he plays a part in it, together with his final, self-centered leave-taking from the domestic misery/ménage[rie] of his mother and sister for oceangoing as well as artistic adventure, Tom owns that role. (See Harold Bloom's discussion of Tom as a Romantic figure in his Introduction to *Tennessee Williams*, pp. 3-5.) But Laura does represent the kind of person for whom the Romantics of the early nineteenth century felt increasing sympathy: the fragile, almost unearthly ego brutalized by life in the industrialized, overpopulated, depersonalized cities of the Western world.

This physically as well as emotionally fragile woman of almost twenty-four escapes from her mid-twentieth-century urban predicament (in St. Louis, to which her family has migrated from the rural-pastoral South of Tennessee and Mississippi), as someone of Romantic temperament would, through art and music—through the beauty of her glass menagerie and of the records she plays on her Victrola. Moreover, although she failed to graduate from high school, Laura fondly remembers a choral class she took with Gentleman Jim O'Connor and the three performances of *The Pirates of Penzance, or The Slave of Duty* (1879) in which he not only sang the baritone lead, but also married the heroine in the end. And instead of attending Rubicam's Business College, as her mother had planned she do, this high-school dropout went daily to "the art museum and the bird houses at the Zoo. I visited the penguins every day! Sometimes I did without lunch and went to the movies. Lately I've been spending most of my afternoons in the Jewel Box, that big glass house where they raise tropical flowers" (33).

Like a Romantic, then, Laura has a love for Nature in addition to Art—a nature that is artfully memorialized in her collection of little animals made out of glass, and that is painfully absent from the area surrounding the Wingfield apartment, which Williams describes as "one of those vast hive-like conglomerations of cellular living-units that flower as warty growths in overcrowded urban centers of lower middle-class population and are symptomatic of the impulse of this largest and fundamentally enslaved section of American society to avoid fluidity and differentiation and to exist and function as one interfused mass of automatism" (21). Indeed, even Laura's name signifies her affinity for the natural together with the transcendent: "Laura" is somewhat ironically derived from the laurel shrub or tree (as is the name of Blanche DuBois's hometown of Laurel, Mississippi, in *A Streetcar Names Desire* [1947]), a wreath of which was conferred as a mark of honor in ancient times upon dramatic poets, military heroes, and athletic victors; and "Wingfield" brings to mind the flight of birds across a meadow of, let us say, dandelions (in Scene 7, Jim offers Laura a glass of "dandelion wine" [89]), on up into the sky. In addition, in Christian antiquity a "laura" was an aggregation of detached cells tenanted by recluse monks under a superior, in Egypt and the desert country near Jordan—that is, by a group of natural beings attempting to achieve divine transcendence.

Perhaps most important, Laura was the name of the mysterious woman who inspired the (unrequited) love poetry of Petrarch, after he saw her while attending church services on Good Friday, 6 April 1327. In these lyrics (most commonly referred to as the *Canzoniere* [1349]), Petrarch does not seem so much to want sensually to possess Laura as spiritually to contemplate her, and he always contemplates her against the background of nature. This Italian poet sees Laura precisely as his countryman Dante saw Beatrice: as an inspiration, a consolation, and a guide, indeed ultimately as a saint whose glorious virtue will point him the way to Heaven. Hence, Petrarch's Laura, like Williams's heroine, is the epitome of earthly or natural beauty at the same time as she is the model of otherworldly or transcendent beatitude:

> And one whom sight of her on earth entranced
> Will call himself more blessed than ever now,
> Seeing her loveliness in Heaven enhanced!
> (lines 143-145 of the "Triumph of Eternity" in Petrarch's *Triumphs* [1338-1374; p. 278, my trans.)

Jim's nickname for Laura, "Blue Roses," itself signifies her affinity for the natural—flowers—together with the transcendent—*blue* flowers, which do not occur naturally and thus come to symbolize her yearning for both ideal or mystical beauty and spiritual or romantic love. ("Blue Mountain," by contrast— the place down South where the youthful Amanda purportedly met her seventeen gentlemen callers one Sunday afternoon [26]—is the appropriate symbol for Laura's mother in its combining of the hardness of nature and the softness or airiness of the color blue. As Williams describes her in his list of characters, Amanda has "great . . . vitality . . . she has endurance and a kind of heroism" [5], at the same time that she is or once was almost as tender and dreamy as her daughter.) That beauty is also symbolized by Laura's favorite among the animals in her glass menagerie, the fabled, otherworldly unicorn, as well as by the place where Laura has spent many of her afternoons, the big "glass house" called the Jewel Box, and by what she saw there: tropical flowers—flowers from another world, as it were, that can survive in St. Louis only by being placed in the artificial environment of a hothouse. And that love comes to her, however fleetingly, in the person of her namer, Jim O'Connor, who beatifies Laura by emphasizing what is special, even divine, about her and downplaying the physical disability or deformity she shares in reverse, if you will, with the unicorn (since one of Laura's legs is "shorter than the other" [5]):

> You don't have the proper amount of faith in yourself. I'm basing that fact on a number of your remarks and also on certain observations I've made. For instance that clumping you thought was so awful in high school. You say that you even dreaded to walk into class. You see what you did? You dropped out of school, you gave up an education because of a clump, which as far as I know was practically non-existent! A little physical defect is what you have. Hardly noticeable even! Magnified thousands of times by imagination! You know what my strong advice to you is? Think of yourself as superior in some way! . . . Why, man alive, Laura! Just look about you a little. What do you see? A world full of common people! All of 'em born and all of 'em going to die! Which of them has one-tenth of your good points! Or mine! Or anyone else's, as far as that goes—gosh! Everybody excels in some one thing. Some in many! (99)

In this speech from the climactic Scene 7, Jim adopts a Romantic-subjective view of human creation as opposed to a naturalistic, deterministic, objective one—ironically so, because he himself appears to be one of the common people with his freckle face, flat or scant nose (64), and mundane job in the same shoe factory where Tom works, and also because, in his aspiration to become a radio or television engineer, he identifies himself with the utilitarian world of mathematics and machines. Nonetheless, Jim echoes here the same Romantic sentiment expressed by Amanda when she misunderstands Tom's own rather Romantic notion of instinct (according to him, "Man is by instinct a lover, a hunter, a fighter" [52]) and declares that Christian adults, like her own "*unusual* children" (49), want "Superior things! Things of the mind and the spirit! Only animals have to satisfy instincts! Surely your aims are somewhat higher than theirs!" (32) Just as surely, Amanda wanted the same "superior things" when she was a debutante in the Mississippi Delta being courted by the sons of plantation owners, but this Daughter of the American Revolution settled instead for marriage to a "commoner" who worked for the telephone company.

Such a union between a woman of superior if by then effete heritage and a man of lower social status yet vital animalism, or let us say the psycho-sexual conquest of the former by the latter, was the seminal subject of Strindberg's naturalistic tragedy *Miss Julie* (1888)—which, incidentally, Robert Brustein once described as the original version of *A Streetcar Named Desire* (29). It is the subject as well of the book of Tom's that his mother returns against his will to the library, D. H. Lawrence's *Lady Chatterley's Lover* (1928). Amanda dismisses its heady, equal mixture of Freud and Darwin as the filthy output of a diseased mind, but one can surmise that its obscenity is not the only aspect of this novel that troubles her. Her stated idea of a good read (38) is naturally *Gone with the Wind* (1936), Margaret Mitchell's mythic romance of the Old South, the Civil War, and Reconstruction, in which at one point the willful, wellborn Scarlett O'Hara kills a vulgar Yankee intruder who would rape her.

The workaday Jim O'Connor, of course, has no intention of sexually subjugating or psychologically dominating Laura Wingfield. On the contrary, he idealizes rather than reifies her by placing her on a pedestal and equating this young woman with a blue rose. In so identifying Laura, Jim unwittingly recalls that widely recognized Romantic symbol of longing for the infinite, of unrequited yearning for absolute emotional and artistic fulfillment: *die blaue Blume*, or the blue flower, drawn from the representative novel of early (German) Romanticism, Novalis's *Heinrich von Ofterdingen* (1802). This prose romance in two books ("Anticipation" and "Fulfillment") is about the evolution of a young poet of great potentiality—in this case, the legendary medieval poet and master singer Heinrich von Ofterdingen. It chronicles his apprenticeship to his art and search (in the company of his mother, no less) for the archetypal symbol, the blue flower, which had appeared to him in a dream:

> The moon's glimmer lit up the room. The youth lay restless on his bed . . . A kind of sweet slumber fell upon [Heinrich] in which he dreamed of indescribable events . . . But what attracted him with the most force was a tall, pale blue flower . . . He gazed upon it for a long time with inexpressible tenderness. Finally, when he wanted to approach the flower, it all at once began to move and change . . . His sweet amazement increased with this strange transformation, until suddenly the voice of his mother woke him and he found himself in his parents' living room. (15, 17)

For Heinrich, this flower comes to represent not only his artistic longing but also his loving fiancée, Mathilde, who has mysteriously died by the time the second book of the novel begins; this book, never finished by Novalis, was to have shown Heinrich's transformation into a poet, even as the first book depicted his preparation for the artistic vocation. Similarly, *The Glass Menagerie* is about the evolution (if not the aesthetic maturation) of the poet

Tom—a man in his early twenties who is not by accident given by Jim the nickname of "Shakespeare," one of the heroes of the Romantic movement in Germany, England, and France—and his effort, through the art of this play, both to find himself and to rediscover or memorialize his beloved sister, a blue flower in human form. The character of Tom, of course, is based in part on Tennessee Williams himself, whose given name was Thomas, even as Laura is modeled after Williams's only sister—Rose.

Laura herself happens to think that "blue is wrong for—roses" (106), but Jim insists that it is right for her because she's pretty "in a very different way from anyone else. . . . The different people are not like other people, but . . . other people are not [so] wonderful. They're one hundred times one thousand. You're one times one! They walk all over the earth. You just stay here. They're common as—weeds, but—you—well, you're—*Blue Roses!*" (105). As her gentleman caller speaks, Laura is aptly bathed in the soft light coming from the new floor lamp her mother has especially purchased for the occasion—a lamp covered by a shade of rose-colored silk that helps to bring out her "fragile, unearthly prettiness" (85)—and she stands before the living-room sofa, suitably framed by its equally new pair of pale blue pillows. Moreover, Jim's words are reinforced by the image of blue roses projected onto a screen or section of wall between the living-room and dining-room areas of the Wingfield apartment, an image that appeared for the first time in Scene 2, both at the start (29) and as Laura later explained to her mother the origin of her nickname (35). The picture of blue roses is itself reinforced in Scene 3 by the image of a "young man at the door of a house with flowers" (37), and in Scene 5 by the image on the screen of a "caller with a bouquet" (59), both of these gentlemen naturally being stand-ins for Jim.

Laura is indeed different, as Jim maintains, but her difference stems from her physical frailty in addition to her fragile prettiness—both of which are symbolized not only by the figurines of her glass menagerie, but also by the "delicate ivory chair" (29) with which Williams identifies Laura in Scene 2. By physical frailty, I am referring not only to the "childhood illness [that] has left her crippled, one leg . . . held in a brace" (5), but also to her frequent faintness, nausea, and colds (see the references thereto on 32-33, 72, 75-76, and 83) together with her bout with pleurosis as a teenager (mentioned on 35 and 93). Even as the nurse of his character Frederic in *The Pirates of Penzance* misunderstood the word "pirates" for "pilots" and unwittingly apprenticed her charge to a band of them as a result, Jim misheard "Blue Roses" when Laura told him, back in high school, that she had had pleurosis, an inflammation of the thin membrane covering the lungs that causes difficult, painful breathing. (Note a breathless Laura or Laura's catching her breath on 32, 74, 76, 88, 92, and 102-103.)

His oxymoronic mishearing is similar to Williams's own "incorrect" hearing of "glass menagerie" for "grass menagerie" (the enclosure where a collection of *live* wild animals is kept)—a "mishearing" underlined by the dramatist's assertion in the "Production Notes" that the "single recurring tune [of the play in production] is . . . like circus music . . . [which paradoxically should be] the lightest, most delicate music in the world and perhaps the saddest. It expresses the surface vivacity of life with the underlying strain of immutable and inexpressible sorrow" (9). (The "glass" in the title *Glass Menagerie* may also be an ironic reference to a wine, beer, or whiskey glass, the very kind of glass that Tom, like his father before him, has been hoisting in order to insulate himself—to protect his own fragility or vulnerability—from the harsh realities of his domestically dutiful life, as well as to stimulate his creative, visionary powers.) Jim's mishearing for its part suggests the oxymoronic existence of Laura Wingfield, a young woman of this world who simultaneously, like the lovely but easily broken creatures of her glass menagerie, seems physically unfit for or unadapted to an earthly life. She is too good for this world, the Romantics might say, and for this reason she could be said to be sadly beautiful or bluely roseate, like the soft-violet color of her kimono (29) in the first scene where the screen-image of blue roses appears.

***

Indeed, Laura's physical as well as emotional frailty betokens an early demise, if not a death-wish on her part—a death that would bestow upon her the ultimate *Einheit mit der Natur*, or union with Nature, so prized by the Romantics and so elusive or unattainable in life. Death imagery may not pervade the surface of *The Glass Menagerie*, but it is surely contained in Jim's nickname for Laura, "Blue Roses," which, as I have already shown, emblematizes an ideal, mystical, or spiritual realm that can only be attained by dying. In fact, the image of blue roses is used in precisely this way in the poem "The Far Away Country," by the British writer Nora Hopper-Chesson—a Celtic revivalist influenced by the example of German Romanticism, like Yeats, and therefore someone with a franker trust in passion and in beauty, in "natural magic" and life's sense of mystery, than was possible to those poets who put their trust in the external world and its laws. This particular lyric out of Hopper-Chesson's several collections of poetry was written just before her death in 1906 at the age of thirty-five, but not published in the United States until 1920, when it appeared as the preface to an anthology of ghost poems edited by an author whose fiction we know Tennessee Williams read: Margaret Widdemer, particularly her novel *The Rose-Garden Husband* (1915), which finds echoes in *The Glass Menagerie* as well as in *A Streetcar Named Desire* (see Mann). So

Williams may have also read Widdemer's compilation of what she calls "ghostly poetry" (vii), particularly Hopper-Chesson's featured prefatory poem (xiv), from which he could have got the idea for Laura Wingfield's strikingly ethereal—and therefore strikingly appropriate—nickname. (Additional circumstantial evidence that Williams may have read Hopper-Chesson's "The Far Away Country" is contained in Amanda's references to a fiction writer named Bessie Mae *Hopper* in Scenes 3 and 4 of *The Glass Menagerie* [38, 55]—Hopper being the surname by which Nora Hopper-Chesson was known until her comparatively late marriage to the author and critic Wilfred Hugh Chesson in 1901, and fiction being an art that she had just begun to take up in addition to poetry with the publication of her novel *The Bell and the Arrow* in 1905, a year before her death.) Here is all of "The Far Away Country," with its recurring image of ineffably blue roses, its expression of a death-wish, and its evocation of an enervatingly long journey through strange lands and over perilous seas, at twilight or pre-dawn, be it taken by a grown man or a newly christened child:

> Far away's the country where I desire to go,
> Far away's the country where the blue roses grow,
> Far away's the country and very far away,
> And who would travel thither must go 'twixt night and day.
>
> Far away's the country, and the seas are wild
> That you must voyage over, grown man or chrisom child,
> O'er leagues of land and water a weary way you'll go
> Before you'll find the country where the blue roses grow.
>
> But O, and O, the roses are very strange and fair,
> You'd travel far to see them, and one might die to wear,
> Yet, far away's the country, and perilous the sea,
> And some may think far fairer the red rose on her tree.
>
> Far away's the country, and strange the way to fare,
> Far away's the country—O would that I were there!
> It's on and on past Whinny Muir and over Brig o' Dread
> And you shall pluck blue roses the day that you are dead.

Death imagery is not only contained in Laura's nickname of "Blue Roses," but it is also at the heart of two poems quoted or invoked by Williams on the screen device included in the authoritative or reading version of the play. The first is "The Ballad of Dead Ladies" (1450), from a collection of ballads on death and love titled *The Testament* (1461), by the medieval poet François Villon (whose macabre imagery as well as intimation of the divine was to influence French Romantics and Symbolists alike, among them Gautier,

Verlaine, and Rimbaud). The following, recurring line from this poem is projected onto the screen as Amanda and Laura appear onstage for the first time in Scene 1 (24), in addition to being projected later in the same scene when Amanda reminisces about the gentlemen callers she once entertained and would now like her daughter to receive (27): Où sont les neiges [d'antan]?", or "Where are the snows of yesteryear?"

Villion uses snow here as a symbol of worldly life's evanescence as well as its natural provenance-cum-dissolution (cf., "ashes to ashes, dust to dust"), its inevitably lost innocence or tarnished purity; and Williams ironically connects the humble Laura and her humbled Southern belle of a mother with the great but departed women of Villon's part historical, part legendary ballad. The first two of these ladies also appear in the long, French allegorical love poem of the thirteenth century titled the *Roman de la Rose* (as well as in Chaucer's fourteenth-century adaptation of it, *The Romaunt of the Rose*), in which, like Heinrich von Ofterdingen, a poet falls in love—while dreaming—with a rosebud and variously attempts to possess this flower of his heart and his mind:

> Tell me where, in what country, is
> Flora, the lovely lady of Rome?
> Where's Alcibiades, or Thaïs,
> Her cousin who was just as fair?
> Echo speaking back every sound
> That's made upon a lake or pond,
> The fairest of them all, where's she?
> But where are the snows of yesteryear?
>
> Where's Héloïse, the learned nun,
> For whose sake alone Abélard
> Lost manhood and became a priest?
> Such misfortune and all for love!
> And furthermore, where is the queen
> Who commanded that Buridan
> Be bagged and thrown into the Seine?
> But where are the snows of yesteryear?
>
> Queen Blanche, as white as a lily
> And with a voice like a songbird's—
> Bertha Broadfoot, Beatrice, Alice,
> Ermengarde, the lady of the Maine—
> Plus good Joan of Arc, whom Englishmen
> Doomed and burned to death at Rouen:
> Where are they, where, oh Mother of God?
> But where are the snows of yesteryear?

Nay, ours is not to ask, dear Lord—
Be it now or in the time to come—
Where they've gone. Ours is but to ask again:
Where are the snows of yesteryear? (117-119); my trans.)

Like much of Villon's work, this poem elevates death to the status of a supreme law that ineluctably ends all earthly life yet ushers in the eternity of the Christian afterlife—an afterlife unironically intimated, embraced, or augured in so modern a drama as *The Glass Menagerie* by the title of Scene 5, "Annunciation" (56); by the winter-to-spring time frame of the action (Scene 2 takes place in mid-to-late February, six weeks after Laura began classes in early January at Rubicam's Business College [31]; Scene 3 occurs in either late winter or early spring [37]; Scene 5 on "a spring evening" [56], possibly March 25th, the day on which the religious Annunciation—or the angel Gabriel's announcement of the Incarnation—is celebrated; and Scenes 6 and 7 on a Friday, if not Good Friday, in "late spring" [69]); and by verbal references in the play to God the Father (62, 84), the Virgin Mary (33, 48), Christian martyrs (38, 55), resurrection (41, 71), baptism (110), paradise (57, 102), grace (24, 83-84), the spirit (52), transubstantiation (45), the erstwhile Catholic practice of eating fish every Friday (61), angels (82), and an Episcopalian house of worship called the Church of Heavenly Rest (87-88). There are aural references to resurrection as well in the early-morning church bells at the start of Scene 4 (44), and we find a musical reference to Christ's rising from the dead in the song "The World Is Waiting for the Sunrise!" from Scene 5 (57). There is no direct reference to Easter in the play, but certainly such allusions to resurrection as Amanda's calls to her son to "Rise and Shine!" in Scene 4 (46), together with Tom's own blasphemous tale to Laura in the same scene (45) of Malvolio the Magician's escape from a nailed-up coffin without removing a single nail, suggest that *The Glass Menagerie* takes place around the time of this annual Christian commemoration of Jesus's return to worldly life and ultimate ascension into heaven, held on the first Sunday after the date of the first full moon that occurs on or after March 21st.

The second poem quoted by Williams is less obviously associated with death, since the playwright uses two lines from it—which, again, appear on the screen between the living and dining rooms of the Wingfield apartment—to anticipate, then announce, the arrival of the Gentleman Caller, James Delaney O'Connor, for dinner in Scene 6. The poem is Emily Dickinson's "The Accent of a Coming Foot" (published as "Suspense" in 1890), which I quote in full:

Elysium is as far as to
The very nearest Room
If in that Room a Friend await

Felicity or Doom—

What fortitude the Soul contains,
That it can so endure
The accent of a coming Foot—
The opening of a Door— (1180, Vol. 3, 1963)

Williams cites the penultimate line of the poem first, then the final line as Tom brings Jim home to meet his sister (69, 74).

Now we know that all of Dickinson's transcendentalist-inspired work was composed within the characteristically American, late nineteenth-century range of relationships among God, man, and nature—with a healthy dose of skepticism, in her case, about the coming age of science. Furthermore, she was preoccupied in her poetry with the idea of death as the gateway to the next existence, as a special glory that has something in common with the conventional paradises offered in hymns and sermons of her day, or with the Book of Revelation that was among her favorite reading. Death for Dickinson means leisure, grandeur, recognition; it means being with the few, rare people whom it was not possible to know fully upon earth: "Death is potential to that Man / Who dies—and to his friend—" (420, Vol. 2, 1955); "A Death blow is a Life blow to some / Who till they died, did not alive become—" (617, Vol. 2, 1955). Much of life for her is anguish endured in an anteroom to death, which is but a prelude to immortality. In the poem "Just lost, when I was saved!" (published in 1891), for example—which bears a topographical resemblance to Nora Hopper-Chesson's "The Far Away Country"—an illness from which the poet has recovered appears as an auspicious as well as inauspicious exploration:

Therefore, as One returned, I feel,
Odd secrets of the line to tell!
Some Sailor, skirting foreign shores—
Some pale Reporter, from the awful doors
Before the Seal! (116-117, Vol. 1, 1963)

Although Emily Dickinson thus speaks again and again of transitoriness and isolation in this world, she is not a mystic like St. Teresa of Avila, or a religious poet like St. John of the Cross. Rather, from the whimsical, domestic, even rococo cast or base of her mind, she flirts with eternity and is coquettish with God, forgiving Him for his "duplicity" and sometimes going so far as to be brash with Him. God is indeed a puzzling figure in her work, the Creator who perhaps does not know why He has created. Dickinson's poems in this way give voice to her unorthodox faith; they are the poetess's reckoning with God, with death, with immortality, infinity, and eternity, as manifested through daily experiences of nature, of human emotions, of spiritual seekings by her own analytical intellect.   To Dickinson, God is burglar, banker, father; gentleman, duke, king: a being apparently personified at times as Death, at other times as a sort of lover.

So too is Jim O'Connor of *The Glass Menagerie* a kind of gentleman, just as he was a champion high-school debater and baritone lead, if he will probably never be a captain of industry.   For his part, Laura's absconding father—whose presence as a fifth character of sorts hovers over the play through his larger-than-life-size, beatifically smiling photograph above the mantel (22-23)—can be called a burglar but not a banker; a lover of other women if no longer of Amanda, whom he has figuratively destroyed along with his two children; a telephone lineman yet not a telepathic being with a direct line to God.   Jim certainly never becomes Laura's lover, even though she secretly loves him, since he is engaged to be married to another (Irish Catholic) woman and remains true to her; he does, however, adumbrate the death of Laura, her release from this life and return to nature, together with her rebirth in heaven.

In this sense, Jim is indeed, as Tom describes him in his narration, "the long-delayed but always expected something that we live for" (23).   The anticipated arrival of someone or something that will provide a form of religious, political, or existential salvation and release to those who await him or it is a familiar subject of modern drama, from Maeterlinck's *The Intruder* (1890) to Odet's *Waiting for Lefty* (1935) to Beckett's *Waiting for Godot* (1954). Although, ironically, the "expected something" usually does not arrive, the Gentleman Caller does make an appearance in *The Glass Menagerie*—one that is tellingly heralded by Tom's "annunciation" of his upcoming visit (59); by Jim's association with a traditional symbol of Christ, the fish (61), as well as with another such symbol, the unicorn, which Laura gives him as a souvenir after he accidentally breaks off its horn, thus in a sense joining herself as feminine flower to the gently masculine, sunnily disposed Jim in a platonic or heavenly marriage removed forever from any possibility of adultery or the cuckold's horn; and by Laura's mentioning of Jim's high-school yearbook picture right after she refers to the picture of Jesus' mother in the local art museum (33-34).   Yet it is the Gentleman Caller's departure rather than his arrival that provides a final solution to Laura's problems, for in intensifying her desperation and isolation, Jim's permanent disappearance after Scene 7 (in combination with the subsequent disappearance of Tom, the Wingfield family's chief means of financial support) could be said to hasten her physical and mental deterioration to the point of death.

"The accent of a coming foot" is, of course, Jim's, but it is also that of the Grim Reaper, who awaits Laura, his "friend," in "the very nearest room." Death will spell her *felicitous* doom, however, for it is identified in Dickinson's poem with Elysium, which in classical mythology represents the paradisiacal abode of the virtuous and blessed after they die. It is there that Laura may finally know fully Mr. James Delaney O'Connor, a man who on earth remained for the most part a figment of her imagination. It is on earth as well that Laura's soul may have had the fortitude to endure the accent of Jim's coming foot, his opening of her apartment door, because that accent and that opening would mean not only momentary escape from the prison-house of her imagination along with her shyness, but also ultimate, perpetual release from the cellblock of her physically crippled body, the wasteland of her emotionally crippled mind, and the enslavement of urbanized subsistence.

Certainly it is not by accident that Williams gives Laura a June birthday (96), when she will turn twenty-four, at the same time as he makes Jim's wedding day the second Sunday in June (111). Through her birth, Laura is thus associated with Juno, the ancient Roman queen of heaven, in whose honor the month was named; the goddess of marriage and childbirth, i.e., the original June bride; and the wife of Jupiter, the supreme deity of the ancient Romans, whose weapon was the thunderbolt that can be heard toward the end of Scene 6 (83)—and the explosive sound of which following an electrical charge of lightning may have inspired the aggressively ambitious Jim to pursue his interest in electrodynamics! Laura may not marry and bear children on earth, but the implication is that in death she will become, or after death she will be resurrected as, the celestial bride of Jesus if not of James-Jupiter.

And surely her death will paradoxically be hastened by the celebration of her birth, for on that day or near that day the man of Laura's dreams, Gentleman Jim O'Connor, will marry someone else, the unseen and prosaically named "Betty." Since *The Glass Menagerie* takes place around Easter, with Easter being celebrated at some time in the course of the play's episodic action, Laura's birthday occurs near Pentecost, or is closer to Pentecost than any other major Christian festival: the seventh Sunday (fifty days) after Easter, that is; the religious holiday marking the descent of the Holy Spirit on the Apostles; and therefore the ideal day to signify or encapsulate the earthly yet transcendent life that chaste Laura Wingfield has led among the lowliest as well as the most noble creatures of God's menagerie.

As further evidence that Williams conceived of Laura as someone experiencing life-in-death or death-in-life, I offer a third poem from which he quotes—this time in the stage directions accompanying the screen title "The accent of a coming foot" in Scene 6. "It is about five on a Friday evening of late spring which comes 'scattering poems in the sky'" (69), the dramatist writes. His direct quotation is slightly inaccurate, but he clearly has in mind "Impressions, IX" (1923; sometimes published as IV instead of IX), by that romantic anarchist of American poetry named E. E. Cummings. I must quote this work in its entirety, for its dominant images—of life-in-death or death-in-life, ascent and descent, of dawn's early light and the candlelight of dusk, the dreams of sleep or the dreaminess of poetry, of harsh city life and the starry, songful life of the mind—recapitulate those of *The Glass Menagerie*:

> the hours rise up putting off stars and it is
> dawn
> into the street of the sky light walks scattering poems
> on earth a candle is
> extinguished   the city
> wakes
> with a song upon her
> mouth having death in her eyes
>
> and it is dawn
> the world
> goes forth to murder dreams . . .
> i see in the street where strong
> men are digging bread
> and i see the brutal face of
> people contented hideous hopeless cruel happy
>
> and it is day,
>
> in the mirror
> i see a frail
> man
> dreaming
> dreams
> dreams in the mirror
>
> and it
> is dusk   on earth
>
> a candle is lighted
> and it is dark.
> the people are in their houses
> the frail man is in his bed
> the city
>
> sleeps with death upon her mouth having a song in her eyes
> the hours descend,
> putting on stars . . .
>
> in the street of the sky walks scattering poems (67, 1991)

The epigraph to *The Glass Menagerie* is itself from a poem by E. E. Cummings, "somewhere i have never travelled" (1931): "nobody, not even the rain, has such small hands." Like Cummings' "Impressions, IX," Dickinson's "Accent of a Coming Foot," Villon's "Ballad of Dead Ladies," and Hopper-Chesson's "The Far Away Country," this poem contains death imagery, or, better, it romantically equates the ecstasy of love with the sublimity of death, as in its first two lines ("somewhere i have never travelled,gladly beyond / any experience,your eyes have their silence" [263, 1954]) and in the following stanza:

> nothing which we are to perceive in this world equals
> the power of our intense fragility:whose texture
> compels me with the colour of its countries,
> rendering death and forever with each breathing (263, 1954)

But "somewhere i have never travelled" also equates the object of the poet's love as well as the poet himself with a flower—specifically, a rose. Cummings depicts the rose both as it awaits the gentle hands of the spring breeze, in combination with spring rain, to help it unfold its petals and bring it to full blossom, and as this flower closes its petals and folds into itself in preparation for the snow to come:

> your slightest look easily will unclose me
> though i have closed myself as fingers,
> you open always petal by petal myself as Spring opens
> (touching skilfully,mysteriously) her first rose
>
> or if your wish be to close me,i and
> my life will shut very beautifully,suddenly,
> as when the heart of this flower imagines
> the snow carefully everywhere descending;
> .   .   .
> (i do not know what it is about you that closes
> and opens;only something in me understands
> the voice of your eyes is deeper than all roses)
> nobody,not even the rain,has such small hands (263, 1954)

Thus does "somewhere i have never travelled" join the imagery of the flower to the idea of love-and-death, even as *The Glass Menagerie* does the same. Clearly Williams had the tender, frail Laura Wingfield in mind when he chose the epigraph to his play from this poem, for, like the flower in Cummings' work, "Blue Roses" opens her petals when the Gentleman Caller touches her on a warm spring evening after the cessation of "a steady murmur of rain" (85), only to close those petals and "die" once Jim betrays her hopes. Just as clearly,

Williams identified his own self as a flower, at one with Laura: like the "i" or voice of Cummings' poem in communion with his rose, and like his alter ego Tom Wingfield of *The Glass Menagerie*. This narrator cannot leave the memory of his beloved sister behind despite his literally leaving her behind in St. Louis, and one can infer that, as a result, his own loving petals slowly closed themselves off from the world even as he himself may have blossomed as a poet.

Put another way, Tom became a singular or isolated phenomenon, someone who, like Laura, is "one times one" in Jim's words (105) and in the words of E. E. Cummings himself, which Williams almost certainly borrowed from the poet's collection of verse titled *1 x 1* (published in the same year as *The Glass Menagerie*, 1944, but a number of whose poems, if not all of them, had previously appeared in magazines or literary journals). To be sure, "one times one" has a double connotation in Cummings' book, for it also suggests the "wonderful one times one" of budding love and romantic union with another person, of "i love you and you love me" (see "LIV," the final poem in *1 x 1*, n.p.), after which Laura yearns. But "one times one" suggests as well the exclusive or distinctive death-in-life of unrequited love—followed by the miraculous or eternal life-in-death of Romantic absorption in Nature—of the kind Laura experiences in her relationship with Jim, as the following lines from poem "XVI" in Cummings' volume make clear:

one's not half two. It's two are halves of one:
which halves reintegrating,shall occur
no death and any quantity; . . .

one is the song which fiends and angels sing:
all murdering lies by mortals told make two.
Let liars wilt,repaying life they're loaned;
we(by a gift called dying born)must grown

deep in dark least ourselves remembering
love only rides his year.
                    All lose, whole find (*1 x 1*, n.p.)

***

As I intimated earlier, the lighting of Laura Wingfield—called for most prominently by Williams in the "Production Notes" to *The Glass Menagerie*—is as poetic or expressive as the play's lyrical quotations, and signifies just how different or special, if not heavenly, she is in comparison with the Betty O'Connors of this world: "The light upon Laura should be distinct from the others, having a peculiar pristine clarity such as light used in early religious portraits of female saints or madonnas" (9-10). Furthermore, Williams sometimes makes Laura the visual focus of our attention "in contradistinction to what is the apparent center. For instance, in the quarrel scene between Tom and Amanda, in which Laura has no active part [Scene 3], the clearest pool of light is on her figure. This is also true of the supper scene [Scenes 6-7, 83-88], when her silent figure on the sofa should remain the visual center" ("Production Notes," 9). Beyond this, Williams suggests that the light surrounding Laura, as well as Tom, Amanda, and the Gentleman Caller, show "a certain correspondence to light in religious paintings, such as El Greco's, where the figures are radiant in atmosphere that is relatively dusky" (10). "Relatively dusky"—that is, "blue," one of whose definitions is "balefully murky," as in the "deep blue dusk" from which there issues a "sorrowful murmur" in Scene 6 (83) as a summer-like storm abruptly approaches and Laura becomes too ill to sit down to dinner with Jim O'Connor, her mother, and her brother.

Williams calls for "dim" or "poetic" atmospheric lighting throughout *The Glass Menagerie* (see "Production Notes," 9, and Scene 1, 21 and 23), however, not just during the scenes that occur at twilight or dusk (Scenes 3, 5, and 6). He writes that such faint illumination is "in keeping with the atmosphere of memory" (9) in this memory play, but it must also be remembered that the time from twilight to dusk—the time of dim or poetic lighting—was the Romantics' favorite because, in its mixture of darkness and light, it is more infinite, more all-embracing, than any other part of the day. In addition, twilight-to-dusk suggested to them a mind that was half awake and half asleep and therefore in sentient retreat from the workaday world, but alive to the dreamlike workings of memory. As is Laura's mind toward the end of Scene 5, in the "early dusk of a spring evening" (56), when—in response to her mother's demand that she "make a wish on the [little silver slipper of a] moon" (67) that has just appeared—Laura "looks faintly puzzled as if called out of sleep" (67). Not by chance, the moon appears again in Scene 7, when "the air outside becomes pale and luminous as the moon breaks through the clouds . . . [and] the [electric] lights in both rooms flicker and go out" (85). For, in its blending of blackness and brightness, moonlight creates the nighttime equivalent of twilight at sunset.

Twilight can thus be seen as the retiring Laura's favorite time of day, despite the fact that Jim calls it—or its artificial equivalent, candlelight—*his* favorite in the following exchange from Scene 7:

| Amanda: | We'll just have to spend the remainder of the evening in the nineteenth century, before Mr. Edison made the Mazda lamp! |
| Jim: | Candlelight is my favorite kind of light. |

Amanda: That shows you're romantic! . . . Very considerate of [the electric company] to let us get through dinner before they plunged us into everlasting darkness, wasn't it, Mr. O'Connor? (87)

Jim appropriately comes to his "date" with Laura in this scene "carrying [a] candelabrum, its candles lighted, in one hand and a glass of wine in the other" (88), together with a pack of Life-Saver mints (107). The virtually sacramental wine, in combination with his warmth and charm, gradually "lights her inwardly with altar candles" (97), which is Williams's way of saying that Jim's apparent love has touched Laura's soul by way of her eyes. This naturally is the manner in which romantic or spiritual love, as opposed to animalistic or carnal lust, works, and has been thought to do so since the early Renaissance when the sight of Dante's Beatrice (whose name means "blessed") created a hunger for empyreal rather than fleshly beauty: by touching the spirit in emulation of God's love for mankind, man's love of God, and Mary and Joseph's immaculate conception of the baby Jesus.

When Laura realizes that she has misperceived Jim's intentions or that he has unintentionally misled her—that he is already in love with another woman—"the holy candles on the altar of [her] face" are accordingly "snuffed out" (108). Indeed, at the end of the play Laura herself blows out the candles that Jim had brought to their encounter, and she does this in recognition not only of her brother Tom's departure from her life, together with that of her father before him, but also of the Gentleman Caller's leave-taking. The implication is that no gentleman caller will ever enter her life again; none will ever be gentle enough among an American people so crassly materialistic to perceive her inner beauty, to appreciate her love for beauty, to understand her unnatural, if not supernatural, place in a world ruled by science and technology (knowledge and power, in the words of Jim [100]) instead of heart and soul—science and technology that, in the contrary opinion of Amanda, only add to the mystery of the universe rather than clearing it up (86). That Laura requires such a man—*a* man, period—to guarantee her happiness, if not her very survival in an unequal contest with the fittest, is a comment less on the man-made oppressiveness of the patriarchal order or the blind selectivity of the biological one, than on her need-cum-desire to anchor the eternal, unearthly feminine in the world of the temporally masculine. Thus would she unite herself with Nature at least as it is personified by a natural man, if not create offspring in her own image. In this man's world, waiting for the second global war of the century after having recently weathered the economic war of the Great Depression, and therefore a world soon to be "lit by lightning" (115) from mass bombardments, Laura is figuratively condemned to live out her earthly existence in an "everlasting darkness" (87) that has already literally begun to descend (with the onset of the

Spanish Civil War, which is mentioned twice by Tom [23, 57] in his narration) on what will become millions of other human beings.

One of them may turn out to be Tom Wingfield himself, for he is a member of the Merchant Marine in the present or framing time of the play (1943-1944), even as his father was a "doughboy" or infantryman in the First World War. This means, of course, that he was a sailor on the ships that carried weapons and supplies to our armed forces overseas—ships that were prime, and easy, targets for enemy submarines and cruisers, especially when the merchant vessels went unescorted. In the past (1937-1938) of *The Glass Menagerie* as remembered by Tom, he twice discusses his imminent joining of the Merchant Marine—once with Amanda, once with Jim—and in each instance the image of a "sailing vessel with Jolly Roger" is projected onto the screen (51, 78). Now such a vessel is normally a pirate ship flying the traditional skull-and-crossbones flag, which obviously symbolizes death. Yet, as a merchant seaman, Tom will be furnishing food, clothing, and arms to other men and ships, not stealing such resources from them, as murderous pirates would do. So the image of a sailing craft with the skull-and-crossbones flag seems intended both to mock Tom's fantasy of high adventure on the oceans of the world and to augur his own demise, or descent into darkness at sea, at the hands of a *modern* pirate ship, the privateer: a privately owned warship commissioned by a government during hostilities to attack or harass enemy shipping.

Tom's death will leave the world in the hands of people like Jim O'Connor, the mock-pirate of the Gilbert-and-Sullivan comic operetta in which he once sang "O blow, ye winds, heigh-ho, / A-roving I will go!" (91). Jim's real-life adventures, however, will be limited, as he himself says, to accumulating—or dreaming of accumulating—knowledge, money, and power in that order (100). This is the triad on which democracy is built as far as he's concerned, but it is the foundation of rampant capitalism for most of the rest of us. The Gentleman Caller's cravenly opportunistic dream of material success, or coldly rationalistic strategy for achieving monetary gain, may point the direction in which the American-led, postwar free world must go, but Laura and Tom Wingfield's heroically Romantic dream of spiritual or artistic fulfillment doubtless embodies what that world will lose—alas, more than sixty years later, has long since lost—by going there.

Works Cited

Appel, Carl, ed.   *Die "Triumphe" Franceco Petrarcas* [*Petrarch's "Triumphs"*]. Halle a. Saale: Max Niemeyer Verlag, 1901.

Bloom, Harold, ed. *Modern Critical Interpretations: Tennessee Williams*. New York: Chelsea House, 1987.

Brustien, Robert. "The Dreams of Ingmar Bergman" (Reviews of productions of *Miss Julie* and *Long Day's Journey into Night* at the Brooklyn Academy of Music, directed by Ingmar Bergman). *The New Republic*, 29 July 1991, pp. 29-31.

Cummings, E. E. *1 x 1*. New York: Henry Holt, 1944.

—. *Complete Poems, 1923-1954*. New York: Harcourt, Brace, 1954.

—. *Complete Poems, 1904-1962*. New York: Liveright, 1991.

Debusscher, Gilbert. "Tennessee Williams's Unicorn Broken Again." Pp. 47-57 of *Modern Critical Interpretations: Tennessee Williams's "The Glass Menagerie"*. Ed. Harold Bloom. New York: Chelsea House, 1988. Originally published in *Revue Belge de Philogie et d'Histoire*, 49 (1971).

Dickinson, Emily. *The Poems of Emily Dickinson*. Ed. Thomas H. Johnson. 3 vols. Cambridge, Mass.: Harvard Univ. Press, 1955.

—. *The Poems of Emily Dickinson*. Ed. Thomas H. Johnson. 3 vols. Cambridge, Mass.: Harvard Univ. Press, 1963.

Mann, Bruce J. "Tennessee Williams and *The Rose-Garden Husband*." *American Drama*, 1 (Fall 1001), pp. 16-26.

Novalis (Friedrich von Hardenberg). *Heinrich von Ofterdingen*. Trans. Palmer Hilty. New York: Frederick Ungar, 1964.

Stein, Roger B. "*The Glass Menagerie* Revisited: Catastrophe without Violence." Pp. 135-143 of *"The Glass Menagerie": A Collection of Critical Essays*. Ed. R. B. Parker. Englewood Cliffs, N. J.: Prentice-Hall, 1983. Originally published in *Western Humanities Review*, 18 (Spring 1964), pp. 141-153.

Villon, François. *Poésies completes*. Ed. Claude Thiry. Paris: Libraire Gébérale Française, 1991.

Widdemer, Margaret, comp. *The Haunted Hour: An Anthology* [*of Ghost Poems*]. New York: Harcourt, Brace and Howe, 1920.

Williams, Tennessee. *The Glass Menagerie*. New York: New Directions, 1966. First published, New York: Random House, 1945.

—. *Tennessee Williams' Letters to Donald Windham, 1940-1965*. Ed. Donald Windham. New York: Holt, Rinehart and Winston, 1977.

—. *Collected Stories*. Intro. Gore Vidal. New York: New Directions, 1985.

CHAPTER SEVEN

DEATH OF A SALESMAN, LIFE OF A JEW: ETHNICITY, BUSINESS, AND THE CHARACTER OF WILLY LOMAN

In an essay about *Death of a Salesman* (1949), the playwright David Mamet wrote that

> the greatest American play, arguably, is the story of a Jew told by a Jew and cast in "universal" terms. Willy Loman is a Jew in a Jewish industry. But he is never identified as such. His story is never avowed as a Jewish story, and so a great contribution to Jewish American history is lost. It's lost to culture as a whole, and, more importantly, it's lost to the Jews, its rightful owners. (Mamet is quoted in *Michigan Quarterly Review*, 37, #4 [Fall 1998], pp. 821-822, in an interview with Arthur Miller titled "Responses to a Question and Answer Session," in which Miller agreed only with Mamet's characterization of Willy as a Jew and of his story as a Jewish one.)

I would like to propose that the divided impulse in Miller—a division immediately noticeable in his choice of first names for his characters—between making his play and his protagonist Jewish, and making them universal or representatively American, was largely responsible for the flaws in this drama that I am now going to detail.

To be sure, *Death of a Salesman* contains the idea for a great play, and I would maintain that its immense international success comes from the force of that idea prevailing over the defects in execution. The force takes hold with the very title, which is highly evocative—both declaring the significance of a (not "the") salesman's death and finding value in his very ordinariness or anonymity—and is amplified by the opening sight of Willy Loman coming in the door. That sight is a superb theater image of our time, as unforgettable an icon as Bertolt Brecht's Mother Courage and her wagon (another traveling salesman!): the salesman home, "tired to the death" (13), lugging his two heavy sample cases, after having been rejected by the big milk-filled bosom of the nation from which he had expected so much nourishment. What does he sell? The commodity is never identified, for Willy is, in a sense, selling himself, and is therefore a survivor of that early tradition of drummers in this country: men who, viewing their personality—not their product—as their chief ware, claimed they could sell anything.

The force of *Salesman*'s idea, moreover, continues fitfully to grasp at us: the idea of a man who has sold things without making them, who has paid for other things without really owning them, who is an insulted extrusion of commercial society battling for some sliver of authenticity before he slips into the dark. And battling without a real villain in sight. Willy's boss, Howard, comes closest to that role when he fires or retires Willy for poor performance, but Howard's failing is not ruthlessness; it is lack of understanding (as exhibited in one of the last things he says to his ex-employee, "Pull yourself together, kid" [84]), a weakness that links him to Willy himself. The American economy in the late 1940s was dominated not by the Howards of the world, but by large corporations whose charismatic founders, the "robber barons," were long dead. Instead of clear-cut enemies, then, there were vast, confusing hierarchies, and, to his credit, Miller was one of the first writers to comprehend this change. For late capitalism is depicted in his play as having become impersonal and bureaucratic; instead of class struggle, there is simple anomie.

Nonetheless, to read or see *Death of a Salesman* again is to perceive how Arthur Miller lacked the control and vision to fulfill his own idea. First, consider the diction of the play, because a play is its language, first and finally. And *Salesman* falters badly in this regard. At its best, its true and telling best, the diction is first-generation Brooklyn Jewish—the kind of English that not only is spoken with a muscular, guttural, sing-songy Brooklyn accent, but that also retains the poetic imagery, forceful expression, and ritualistic repetition of Yiddish (the "jüdisch" German dialect spoken by East-European Jewish immigrants as a form both of self-assertion and self-defense) while discarding German syntax, grammar, and of course words. (Some examples from the play: "Life is a casting off" [15]; "A man is not a bird, to come and go with the springtime" [54]; "Attention, attention must be finally paid to such a person" [56]; "Money is to pass" [64]; "I slept like a dead one" [71]; "He's only a little boat looking for a harbor" [76]; "You can't eat an orange and throw the peel away—a man is not a piece of fruit" [82]; "Spite, spite, is the word of your undoing" [130].)

Often, however, the dialogue slips into a fanciness that is slightly ludicrous. To hear Biff say, "I've been remiss" (60); to hear Linda say, "He was crestfallen" (15) or "You're too accommodating, dear" (14); to listen to Willy declare, "There's such an undercurrent in him" (15), "That's just the spirit I want to imbue them with" (52), or "The woman has waited and the woman has suffered. [That's] the gist of it" (107); to listen to Biff asking Happy, "Are you content?" (23), to Happy arguing that Biff's "just a little overstrung" (115), and

to Charley finally opining that "Nobody dast blame this man" (138)—all of this
is like watching a car run off the road momentarily onto the shoulder.

The same goes for Miller's deployment of the nominative and
accusative cases as well as the subjunctive mood. This is a play in which you
can actually hear the less-than-educated, Brooklynite Lomans incongruously use
the subjunctive "were" correctly (24), and unabashedly utter "I and Biff" (17),
"You and I" (23, 31, 63), and "Biff and I" (135) as if they were reading out of a
grammar book. ("Him and me" is what people like this would normally say, but
you will hear such an expression only once in *Death of a Salesman*, on page
125.) And if the argument is made that the Lomans (like Jews who value
education, even though they may not have it) merely aspire to speak in an
educated manner—pretending, in keeping with their essential character, to be
more book-learned than they are—I would respond that Miller could have
helped his cause by having his characters make the mistakes that almost all such
strivers make, such as using "I" when "me" is the grammatically correct form
(as in the phrase "between you and me").

Then there is the language of Willy's older brother Ben, the apparition
of piratical success. He speaks like nothing but a symbol, and not a symbol
connected with Willy in any perceptible way. (As in these instances: "When I
was seventeen I walked into the jungle, and when I was twenty-one I walked
out. And by God I was rich" [48]; "Never fight fair with a stranger . . . You'll
never get out of the jungle that way" [49]; "With one gadget [Father] made
more in a week than a man like you could make in a lifetime" [49].) Miller *says*
Ben is Willy's brother, that's all. Furthermore, the very use of diamonds as the
source of Ben's wealth has an almost childishly symbolic quality about it.
When Miller's language is close to the stenographic, the ethnically remembered,
it's good; otherwise, and especially in Ben's case, it tends to literary
juvenility—a pretended return from pretended experience.

Thematically, too, *Death of a Salesman* is cloudy. It's hard to believe
that, centrally, Miller had anything more than muzzy anti-business, anti-
technology impulses in his head; and that muzziness may have been caused by
Miller's subliminal knowledge that Jews conquered the world of American
business (as Mamet implies in the quotation from the *Michigan Quarterly
Review*) in almost every conceivable way. Is Willy Loman a man shattered by
business failure, for example, and by disappointment in his sons? Then why,
when he is younger and at least making a living, when he is proud of his sons
and they of him, does he lie about his earnings to Linda and then have to correct
himself? Why, at the peak of what is otherwise a molehill of a life, does he
undercut his own four-flushing to tell his wife that people just pass him by and
take no notice of him?

The figure that comes through this play, in fact, is not of a man brought down by various failures but of a mentally unstable man in whom the fissures have only increased. (It must be said, however, that what in the 1930s and 1940s was deemed "delusional"—namely, Willy's belief in a link between likeability or "personal attractiveness" [16] and success—is now being regularly confirmed in the national popularity contests we Americans call elections.) Willy is thus shown to be at least as much a victim of psychopathy as of the bitch-goddess Success. When was he ever rational or dependable? Is this really a tragedy of belief in the American romance, or is it merely the end of a clinical case?

The evidence in the play for Willy's psychopathy is plentiful, so much so that it has led to his being diagnosed as manic-depressive before the age of anti-depressant drugs (by Ben Brantley of the *New York Times* in the fall of 1998, in a review of the Chicago revival [and Broadway-bound production] of *Death of a Salesman*), as well as to his being diagnosed as "other-directed"—or possessing a value system entirely determined by external norms—from a sociological point of view (by Walter Goodman in a *New York Times* column of April 1999). Consider, for instance, Willy's many contradictions of himself: evidence that goes beyond normal human inconsistency into the realm of severe internal division, which may have been produced by Willy's other-directedness but would surely have produced psychosis in the man himself, had he not committed suicide.

To wit, he yells at Biff, "Not finding yourself at the age of thirty-four is a disgrace!" (16), but later adds, "Greatest thing in the world for him was to bum around" (67). "Biff is a lazy bum!" (16), Willy grumbles; then, almost immediately thereafter, we hear him say, "And such a hard worker. There's one thing about Biff—he's not lazy" (16). Father gives the following advice to his son before the big interview with Bill Oliver: "Walk in very serious. You are not applying for a boy's job. . . . Be quiet, fine, and serious. Everybody likes a kidder, but nobody lends him money" (64). A few lines later we hear Willy command, "Walk in with a big laugh. Don't look worried. Start off with a couple of your good stories to lighten things up. It's not what you say, it's how you say it—because personality always wins the day" (65).

Willy's memories of past conversations produce similar inconsistencies. He excused Biff's stealing a football by arguing, "Sure, he's gotta practice with a regulation ball, doesn't he? Coach'll probably congratulate you on your initiative!"(30). Yet Willy soon forgets this excuse: "He's giving it back, isn't he? Why is he stealing? What did I tell him? I never in my life told him anything but decent things" (41). One minute "Chevrolet . . . is the greatest car ever built" (34); the next, "That goddamn Chevrolet, they ought to prohibit the manufacture of that car" (36). And, in consecutive sentences, Willy can declare the following without blinking: "I'm very well liked in Hartford. You know, the trouble is, people don't seem to take to me" (36).

For someone like Willy, naturally, the past and the present duel with each other as well as with themselves. He remembers saying, for example, that "the man who makes an appearance in the business world, the man who creates personal interest, is the man who gets ahead" (33); yet he perceives no inconsistency between that statement and this one in the present action of the play: "A man who can't handle tools is not a man" (44). He remembers telling Linda that "[People] seem to laugh at me" (36). But he can tell his grown sons, "They laugh at me, huh? Go to Filene's, go to the Hub, go to Slattery's, Boston. Call out the name Willy Loman and see what happens!" (62). And all of this from a man who has the nerve to wonder aloud, "Why am I always being contradicted?" (17).

But, this mountain of Miller-provided evidence aside, let's assume for a moment, for the sake of argument, that Willy is *not* a psychopath, that he was a relatively whole man now crushed by the American juggernaut. To return to *Salesman*'s theme, what then is its attitude toward that capitalistic juggernaut, toward business ideals? I ask such a question because there is no *anagnorisis* for Willy that would suggest the play's attitude, no moment of recognition for him, let alone a great downfall: he dies believing in money. In fact, he kills himself for it, to give his son Biff the insurance benefit as a stake for more business, and because he confuses materialistic success with a worthiness to be loved. (Ironically, this insurance windfall is something Biff may not want, and which he may not even receive on account of his father's death-by-suicide.)

Willy's other son, Happy, is himself wedded to money values and says over his father's coffin that he's going to stick to them for his father's sake. Similarly, Biff was so aggrandized by his father that he became kleptomaniacal as a boy and even now, after his father-as-idol has collapsed, he can't resist stealing a successful businessman's fountain pen as a niggling vindictiveness against that man's success and his own lack of it. The only alternatives to the business ethos ever produced in *Death of a Salesman* are Willy's love of tools and seeds, building and planting, and Biff's love of the outdoor life. As between romances—neither of which, in this case, is so easily separable from the other, the frontier ethic being nearly synonymous in the end with a rapaciously capitalistic one (as David Mamet's own best plays, *American Buffalo* [1975] and *Glengarry Glen Ross* [1984], have shown)—I'll take business, for all Biff's talk at the end of knowing who he is, where he stands, and what he wants (or imagines he can get) apart from the world of hard-driving capitalism.

Miller confuses matters even further by the success not only of Dave Singleman, the gentlemanly eighty-four-year-old salesman who was Willy's inspiration (and who, according to Willy, died the regal "death of a salesman" [81]), but also of young Bernard next door as a lawyer in the Establishment world with a wife and his own two sons. This is a deserved success for which Willy feels envy—as he does for the success of Bernard's father, Charley, who is a good man like his son (lending Willy money which he knows cannot be repaid, even creating a job for Willy that the latter pridefully turns down), as well as a good businessman with his own office and secretary.

Yet Charley himself contributes to the confusion in *Death of a Salesman*. For, during the play's Requiem, he can be heard to endorse Willy's view of himself when he says to Biff,

> You don't understand: Willy was a salesman. And . . . a salesman . . . don't put a bolt to a nut, he don't tell you the law or give you medicine. He's a man way out there in the blue, riding on a smile and a shoeshine. And when they start not smiling back—that's an earthquake. . . . A salesman is got to dream, boy. It comes with the territory. (138)

In Act II, however, in an attempt to puncture Willy's self-image, Charley had said almost the exact opposite to his next-door neighbor after Howard fired him:

> CHARLEY. . . . The only thing you got in this world is what you can sell. And the funny thing is that you're a salesman, and you don't know that.
> WILLY. I've always tried to think otherwise, I guess. I always felt that if a man was impressive, and well liked, that nothing—
> CHARLEY. Why must everybody like you? . . . (97)

What we are left with in this play, then, is neither a critique of the business world nor an adult vision of something different and better, but the story of a man (granting he was sane) who failed, as salesman and father—or who failed to live up to his own unrealistic dreams of what salesmanship and fatherhood constitute—and who made things worse by refusing to the end to admit those failures, which he knew were true. That is one play, and possibly a good one if it had been realized; but it is quite a different one from *Death of a Salesman*, a play that, in its atmosphere and mannerisms, implies radical perception about deep American ills.

The difference is between pedestrian pathos and exalted tragedy, between the destruction of a decent but unknowing man and a great or special one who simultaneously deserves, and does not deserve, his fate. And, ironically, Miller himself understood this distinction, even if, in his famous essay "Tragedy and the Common Man" (published in the *New York Times*, 1949)—a not-so-veiled argument for the tragic status of *Salesman*—he unwittingly described Willy Loman when he wrote,

Where pathos rules, where pathos is finally derived, a character has fought a battle he could not possibly have won. The pathetic is achieved when the protagonist is, by virtue of his witless-ness, his insensitivity, or the very air he gives off, incapable of grappling with a much superior force.

Miller makes clear by the very title of his essay that the common man is as appropriate a subject for tragedy, in its highest sense, as the royal leader. Yet modern writers have found it difficult to create powerful tragedies with workaday salesmen, let alone corporate executives, as protagonists. There are at least two reasons for this, apart from Miller's own seeming reluctance, in *Salesman*, to associate commonness with Jewishness. First, for us to feel the full impact of the fate the tragic hero brings on himself, he must have a nearly complete freedom of action. In other words, the more we feel that the hero has been able to choose his course of action without restriction, the more we sense the tragic irony of his choices. Second, it is vital that the tragic hero's actions have some deep moral, spiritual, political, or philosophical significance for the whole of his society. For this reason, the classic dramatists generally dealt with protagonists whose lives were lived out in a public arena—so much so that their every act or decision would have a *direct* effect on everyone around them, on all whom they led or governed. As aristocratic leaders, moreover, the significance of their deeds and words could be underlined or highlighted for the audience through the response of the chorus, or, in Elizabethan tragedy, by the reaction of a group of retainers and courtiers.

Modern democratic societies, however, no longer accept the kind of absolute kings whose personal choices are matters of basic public import—and acceptance. Of course, our leaders have great political power, but it is worth noting that few contemporary dramatists have sought to make tragic figures of our presidents and legislators—except, as in the case of a Richard Nixon, where the leader arrogates unto himself a greater power than is lawful. Although these personages lead public lives that might be dramatized in the manner of classical tragedy, they rarely are. For our concept of power in a democracy implies that personal impulses cannot be erected into commands without taking account of the many diverse groups whose consent is necessary to the exercise of authority. Therefore we feel our leaders lack that total freedom of action which the tragic protagonist seems to require.

The pathos of the salesman, by contrast, lies in the fact that he has neither sufficient freedom of action nor demonstrable public significance. Indeed, he is one of many just like himself, and, unlike classical or neoclassical tragic protagonists, appears to have been conditioned passively, even gladly, to accept the very conditions of life that will lead to his own annihilation. (I don't say "downfall" because a character like Willy is such a "low-man" that his fall can hardly be said to be dramatic or striking.) This may in the end be sad, but it does not arouse the same kind of feeling as the classic tragedies. And doubly so in Willy Loman's case, for (in this instance through no fault or flaw of his own) he is a man caught between the two worlds of Christianity and Judaism, and one whose very ethnic or religious identity is therefore in question—apart from what his profession may be, what social standing he has, or what political beliefs he holds.

I'd like to make a few additional points about the play, connected more with its verism than with its attempt at tragedy. When I saw the 1952 film of *Death of a Salesman*, which made the play's environment more vivid (unlike Dustin Hoffman's 1985 television film of the theatrical production in which he had starred on Broadway), I couldn't help wondering why Willy had money worries: he had almost paid off the mortgage on his house, which was a piece of real estate in an increasingly valuable and desirable section, to judge by the building going on all around it. I don't think this is a petty literal point in a realistic play whose lexicon is bill-paying. Further, all the dialogue about Willy's father, with his wagon-travels through the West and his flutes, seems falser than ever, Miller's imposition on this Brooklyn Jewish play to give it historical base and continental (if not Christian) sweep. As with the character of Ben, there is a schism in tenor between such material and the rest of the play.

Last, a point that is strangely more apparent now, I'm guessing, than it was when *Salesman* first appeared in 1949 (to judge from all the contemporary commentary): the drama is set in the late 1940s and reaches back some fifteen years to the early 1930s, yet there is scarcely a mention of the Great Depression—or of World War II, for that matter. How did Biff and Happy escape the war, and, if they did so, were they criticized or attacked for not serving in the military? If they didn't escape military service, wouldn't the reunited brothers have had something to say about it—especially, if they were Jewish, about the Holocaust? And wouldn't the postwar economic boom itself have had some effect in the present on Willy's view of a promise-crammed (if maddeningly competitive) America, not to speak of the Depression's effect in the past on Willy's view of that same America and his decreased earning power in it? (Miller may have tried to make up for this omission with his quasi-autobiographical *The American Clock* [1980], in which a narrator reminisces about the plight of his family during the Depression. But the only consistent effect of this otherwise platitudinous play is the instant pathos that attaches to memory, especially when, in production, the rememberer is standing before us, stepping into and out of the past.)

Make no mistake: I am not implying, as some critics have, that by virtue of its flashback structure—between the immediate postwar period and the time of the Great Depression—*Death of a Salesman* would have made a better film (with its dissolves, cross-fading, and minutely detailed realism as opposed to the modified, simplified, or theatricalized kind) than a play. In fact, in the case of Miller's play, the theater has a superior ability to suggest both the childishness of Willy's sons (by having the adult actors of Biff and Happy "unrealistically" play their boyhood selves onstage) and the momentousness of Willy's adultery (by having it occur, not "on location" in Boston, but on the forestage—right in the Lomans' living room, as it were). And some of the play, as play, is touching or poignant still: Willy when he is at his most salesman-like, the Requiem over his coffin, and even the very flashback structure of *Salesman*. For it suggests that, without the flashbacks originating in Willy's mind, the information conveyed by them—about such subjects as adultery, lying, cheating, and failure—would not be revealed in the present in dialogue among the Lomans, who, unlike the Tyrones of Eugene O'Neill's great, and overtly Irish-American Catholic, family drama *Long Day's Journey into Night* (1941), do not communicate so well or so openly.

But the flashback structure of *Death of a Salesman* suggests something ominous as well, something connected with what I earlier called Miller's divided impulse between composing a Jewish domestic drama and writing a representative play on the American experience. That is, Miller seems not only structurally to have split his play between a climactic frame, covering the last hours of Willy's life up to his climactic suicide, and an episodic form that enacts the Loman past in a series of flashback scenes. The dramatist seems also to have created a formal equivalent for his own divided consciousness on the subject of a Jewish protagonist versus a Christian one. For who is to say that Willy's flashbacks are objectively true, as they are always assumed to be? Might they not be the subjective or expressionistic visions, even hallucinations, of a feverish mind on the verge of collapse, instead of a mere device for explicating past events that the Lomans otherwise do not, or do not want to, talk about? (This is a kind of memory play, after all, and memory, even in a mentally healthy person, is notoriously fallible as well as selectively creative— as we know from at least one other famous memory play, Harold Pinter's *Old Times* [1971].)

Further, might Willy's flashbacks therefore not only be his attempt to remember a pivotal year in his and his family's past, 1931 or 1932 (football star Biff's senior year of high school, during which he discovers his father's adulterous relationship with the woman in Boston, and when Willy purportedly turns down a job in Alaska working for his brother Ben); might these flashbacks also be Willy's attempt to fictionalize part of his past as well as to portray some of it truthfully? After all, no character in the play, except Willy, uses Ben's name or refers to the elder brother's South African business ventures, nor does any character besides Willy refer to his wagon-travels West, as a boy, with his flute-carving father. And most of these references, by Willy, occur in his flashbacks themselves, during conversations with Ben.

Could Ben and the wagon-travels, then, be Willy's invention, his attempt, if you will, as a proxy for Miller (a Jew whose three marriages were all to Christian women, and who never took the stance of a public *Jewish* intellectual during his long career), to Christianize or universalize his past? Might this not be suggested somehow in production, visually as well as vocally, through the use of different actors in the flashbacks in the roles of Linda, Biff, and Happy—whose appearance and manner of speaking would make clear that they were Willy's idealized Christian versions of his real wife and sons? Would such an interpretation of the context of *Salesman*'s flashbacks not be truer to the play as it stands, particularly if this re-imagining were an exculpatory move on Willy's part, to blame his failings on anti-Semitism and thereby suggest that his life would have been better—materially, domestically, psychologically—had he only been a Protestant? And wouldn't such an interpretation be true as well to Miller's acknowledgment in the *Michigan Quarterly Review* interview, in response to David Mamet's remarks, that Willy was in fact a Jew and his story a Jewish one?

Be it in flashback or in the present, much of the material in *Salesman* on Miller's favorite theme, the love-hate of father and son, is itself still touching. (However, too much of the paterf[am]ilial plot does hinge on Biff's discovery, in Boston, of Willy's unfaithfulness to Mom—to judge from the evidence, the only such infidelity [with a woman nearly his own age], not one of any number of promiscuous acts on this husband's part—an incident Biff understandably remembers while implausibly forgetting that he failed math [110], failed to graduate from high school, and consequently forfeited the college football scholarship he had been offered.) Indeed, the political issues in the play—its major one naturally being the plight of the exploited common man in capitalist America—now seem infinitely less urgent than its emotional issues, which are rooted in the play's family relationships. Bottom-line employers such as Howard no longer throw away older workers like "a piece of fruit" (82)—union vigilance and statutes against ageism provide some protection against such abuses, though it's also the case that a man in his sixties like Willy would be called middle-aged today. Protection is also provided by such mechanisms as Social Security, employee benefits, annuity plans, Roths and Keoghs, and similar devices designed to help soften the economic problems of used-up or tired-out workers.

What have remained the same, though, are the family conflicts of these people, and to some extent their spiritual emptiness: again, something that might have been alleviated by the Lomans' Jewish identity, at the very least—had Miller allowed them to have one. And all the more so since much of what power *Salesman* still has derives from the sure-fire conventions of Yiddish domestic theater. As if it were in a direct line from such Jewish-immigrant drama through Clifford Odets, Miller's play climaxes with a rebellious son being reconciled with his estranged father. (Compare Al Jolson, in the film *The Jazz Singer* [1927], being forgiven by his stern Orthodox father for having become a *teaterzinger* rather than a cantor. And compare *Salesman* with Miller's own *The Creation of the World and Other Business* [1972], which was meant to be a Jewish domestic comedy on the *first* father-son story, that of God and Adam, but where, ethnically speaking, the playwright fiddled, faltered, and fumbled once again.)

But these are all sound moments in a flabby, occasionally false, even schizoid work whose only major female character (Linda Loman), I might add, is less a character than a saint, on the one hand, or a co-dependent, on the other. Miller had gift enough to get the idea for *Death of a Salesman*, but then—in the face of his divided dramatic impulse—he settled for the dynamics of the idea itself, supported by a vague high-mindedness, to write his play for him. (For some critics a better play than *Death of a Salesman* and therefore Miller's best, *The Crucible* [1953] itself suffers from a similar defect or division: its last act is a moral-metaphysical drama of adultery, while its first three acts compose a political parable in which the Salem witchcraft trials of 1692 are used as a parallel with Joe McCarthyism during the 1950s.) As the world knows, many viewers and readers have taken the intent for the deed. Some have not.

And my guess is that the latter group will ultimately prevail in any assessment of *Death of a Salesman* and of Miller's career generally. We must recall that several American playwrights, such as Elmer Rice, Robert Sherwood, and Maxwell Anderson, had similarly large reputations during their lives, in the United States as well as abroad, and all during their lives there were a few qualified critics who dissented; now those reputations are past the point even of diminishment. Excepting O'Neill and Tennessee Williams, Miller has the largest international reputation of any American dramatist ever; and, now that he has passed away, the small group of dissenters he himself had during his lifetime should begin to grow in number. For them, there have always been two Millers: the great dramatist in general opinion, and the much lesser, mostly middling one in their view. (The charter members of this minority, incidentally, were Eric Bentley, Robert Brustein, Richard Gilman, and Stanley Kauffmann.)

One reason I have always assumed for Miller's success in foreign countries is that his language improves in translation—which, at its best, is a kind of rewriting. One reason I have always assumed for his success everywhere is that he makes people feel they have gone on daring intellectual-spiritual expeditions when they have really stayed cozily at home the whole time. Miller supplies the illusion of depth, that is, without endangering or enlightening anyone, and he gives his audience a painlessly acquired feeling of superiority just by their having been present at his plays. He does so by dealing exclusively with *received* liberal ideas, whereas the best social dramatists, like Henrik Ibsen, have usually dealt with dangerous or revolutionary ideas. (In 1950 Miller adapted [and lessened] Ibsen's *An Enemy of the People* [1883], but he could not, on his own, have tackled its theme: that the majority is always wrong.)

I am not accusing Miller of cunning; he never tried to put anything over on anyone, like such "serious" filmmakers as Steven Spielberg and Woody Allen. Despite the fact that all of his plays, not just *Death of a Salesman*, suffer to one degree or another from fuzzy concepts, transparent mechanics, superficial probes, and pedestrian diction, he certainly always did his sincere best. True, *After the Fall* (1964) is tainted with a wriggly feeling of exculpation for some matters in his private life (connected with his marriage to Marilyn Monroe and his appearance before the House Un-American Activities Committee investigating Communist infiltration of the arts), but usually the falseness that crops up in his work is of another sort—the peculiar falseness of honest writers who are not talented enough to keep free of dubious artistic means.

So much is this the case that, going back to *Salesman*, Miller's most highly regarded work yet a relatively early one in his career, has been for me like going to the funeral of a man you wish you could have liked more. The occasion seals your opinion because you know there is no hope of change or improvement. Perhaps now that he is no longer around to guard his own reputation—to "sell" it, as it were—the "double" Miller will die away and only the mediocrity will remain.

Work Cited

Miller, Arthur. *Death of a Salesman*. New York: Viking/Penguin, 1949.

CHAPTER EIGHT

SAM SHEPARD AND THE "BURIED" DOMESTIC DRAMA OF *BURIED CHILD*

More than any other contemporary American playwright, Sam Shepard has woven into his own dramatic idiom the strands of a youth culture thriving on drugs, rock music, astrology, science fiction, old movies, detective stories, cowboy films, and the racing of cars, horses, and dogs. The most talented of a generation of dramatists that includes John Guare, María Irene Fornés, Megan Terry, Jean-Claude van Itallie, Rochelle Owens, and Lanford Wilson, Shepard relies heavily on "jazzy" or manic, often monologue-driven language to make his drama; he creates arresting, if not surreal, theatrical images; his characters are sometimes split, often fragmented, and always unpredictable; while his subjects tend to be non-urban. Indeed, Shepard constantly shows people living on the edge, an emotional as well as a physical one—the Western edge of the United States. In the nineteenth century (and beyond), the West lured adventurers, speculators, outcasts, and pioneers and thus became the mythic place for America to reinvent itself (at the same time as such a reinvention dispossessed the Indians). In the twentieth century, Shepard has evoked that elusive myth as a way of showing how desperately the people of our country need to find themselves again amid the consumer trash, media technology, and spiritual displacement or dislocation of suburban American society.

Called by one critic the "poet of the postmodern condition" on account of his subject matter as well as his effacement of the distinctions between high art and popular commodities such as books, dime novels, or television dramas, Shepard to date has written well over forty stage plays—short pieces, full-length works, and collaborative efforts in addition to a radio play, a television drama, short stories, poetry, and several film scripts. With the possible exception of David Mamet, no American playwright since Eugene O'Neill has been so prolific. And, like O'Neill, who went through an extended period of experimenting with non-realistic, even expressionist, drama before turning in his last autobiographical plays to a much more representational style, Shepard too has moved from his initial "vibrations"—his term for the early non-realistic monologues (or monological dialogue) in which he attempted to create the theatrical equivalent of improvisational jazz—to a series of semi-autobiographical, full-length works that appear, at least on the surface, to take a naturalistic view of the nuclear American family.

Shepard began writing plays just as a new movement was flourishing, financed by playwrights and actors and usually produced in non-theatrical settings (churches, cafés, even a hardware store): Off-Off Broadway. At the Village Gate he got to know the head waiter, Ralph Cook, just as Cook was planning an Off-Off venture at St. Mark's Episcopal Church (located in New York's Bowery). Prophetically named Theatre Genesis, the new company opened its doors in 1964 with a double bill of Shepard one-acts titled *Cowboys* and *The Rock Garden*. Both plays received negative reviews, but in the following years, 1965 through 1971, Sam Shepard became one of the best-known playwrights of the Off-Off Broadway subculture with such short plays as *Chicago* (1965), *Mad Dog Blues* (1965), and *Forensic and the Navigators* (1967), also produced at Theatre Genesis; *Red Cross* (1966) at Judson Poet's Theatre; *Dog* (1965), *The Rocking Chair* (1965), *The Unseen Hand* (1969), and *Shaved Splits* (1970) at Café La MaMa (later La MaMa ETC); *Icarus's Mother* (1965) at Caffe Cino; and *La Turista* (1967), *Cowboy Mouth* (1971), and *Back Bog Beast Bait* (1971) at the American Place Theatre.

La Turista was Shepard's first full-length play, and it won him the fourth of what would ultimately amount to ten Obie Awards. Punning on the Spanish word for tourist and the diarrhea that attacks American tourists in Mexico, this satire features two virtually identical acts (like Beckett's *Waiting for Godot*, the first play Shepard ever read); a dysfunctional couple named Kent and Salem, after popular cigarettes; and an ending in which Kent escapes by leaping through the rear wall of the stage. Three years after *La Turista*, *Operation Sidewinder* (1970), his longest play to date, became Shepard's first venture not produced Off-Off Broadway; instead it was performed at the Vivian Beaumont Theater at Lincoln Center, where it was a critical disaster. (Another Shepard play was not produced on Broadway until the revival of *Buried Child* [1979] in 1996.) Traditional audiences were baffled by the convoluted plot that deals with what happens when an Air Force computer designed to find UFOs is disguised as a sidewinder rattlesnake and mistaken by local Hopi Indians for a snake god.

The Tooth of Crime (1972) is the most impressive play of Shepard's middle period, the late 1960s and early-to-mid seventies, when he extended his grasp to produce full-length works (sometimes in one longish act) employing the same kind of surreal, almost otherworldly individuality found in the one-act vibrations of his first phase. These middle plays—including *Geography of a Horse Dreamer* (1974), *Angel City* (1976), and *Suicide in B-Flat* (1976)—are fantasies that borrow from westerns and gangster films, science fiction, cartoons, and other such mass entertainment at the same time as they explore the isolation of the artist in a violent postmodern world. *The Tooth of Crime*, for example, recasts the Western shoot-out as a confrontation between the established rock star, Hoss, and the "gypsy" challenger, Crow. Combining the mythology of the West and popular music, the use of a referee and pom-pom-waving cheerleaders, Shepard drew not only on his own intermittent musical career as a drummer, but even more on his fascination with language. The climactic duel between Hoss and Crow stands out, for it involves a variety of linguistic styles (a synthesis, in the end, of the slangs of rock-and-roll, crime, astrology, and sports) that in turn create striking physical gestures.

In 1974, as he was moving out of his middle period, Shepard began a long association with San Francisco's Magic Theater. It was there that *Tongues* (1978) was performed by Joseph Chaikin, the founder of the Open Theater in New York. This piece, like *Savage/Love* (1979)—also performed by Chaikin at the Magic—is, in Shepard's words, "an attempt to find an equal expression between music and the actor." Really librettos conceived with the intent of being set to sound and music, these two monologues comprise snatches of everyday life and express a range of familiar human experience from the pain of childbirth to the fear of death. Thus, the emotional transformations required of the actor in *Tongues* and *Savage/Love* seem both to underline a major theme of Shepard's drama and to continue the work of the Open Theater, which was noted for its acting exercises in which performers transformed themselves from one state—or one being—to another.

At the Magic Theater at least three plays from Shepard's five-play family cycle were first produced—*Buried Child* in 1978, *True West* in 1980, and *Fool for Love* in 1983—works that mark the third, "mature" phase of his dramatic writing career. Though the world of these five plays (the other two are *Curse of the Starving Class* [1976] and *A Lie of the Mind* [1985]), which are about the disintegration or dysfunction of the nuclear family, may seem more representational than the world depicted in his previous drama, certain thematic motifs as well as scenographic images link them to the wildness-and-craziness of the earlier pieces. One thinks of the magic vegetables in *Buried Child* and the absent-but-present father in *Fool for Love*, off to the side in a chair in a separate stage area, but preternaturally able to confer with the son and daughter who have conjured him up. (Such an absent-but-present patriarch, in the form of a corpse, is also to be found in *The Late Henry Moss* [2001], where two sons battle to uncover the facts of their father's death.) One remembers the two brothers in *True West*, who, as Shepard himself has said, are really parts of the same person, each the alter ego of the other (a device or phenomenon the playwright was later to exploit again in *Simpatico* [1994]). And one recalls that the title of *A Lie of the Mind* derives from the protagonist's inability to separate reality from illusion, which may make him a madman but implicates us all in our preference for fantasy and feeling over rationality and realism. (In the later *States of Shock* [1991], which marked something of a return to Shepard's hallucinatory-cum-improvisational style of the 1960s, a black waitress in the end miraculously heals a maimed young war veteran wheeled around by the Colonel– a military man who may or may not be his father.)

In this family cycle, Shepard follows O'Neill in dramatizing a tragic America mired in sin. All five plays are bound, not by a carryover of specific characters, but by the real or implied specter of the generalized "old man" or father figure, whose sins weigh heavily on the heads and hearts of his children (together with a grandson in *Buried Child*). As a result, the offspring of these patriarchs are obsessed with recapturing a vision of America and the family that may or may not have ever existed. Like Aeschylus' *Oresteia*—which O'Neill himself used as a model for the trilogy *Mourning Becomes Electra* (1931)— Shepard's series of domestic dramas thus explores the mythic themes of guilt-cum-expiation, blood pollution, regeneration or resurrection, physical as well as emotional violence, and sexual passion within the context of the family.

In *Curse of the Starving Class*, for example, the father is guilty of betraying his wife and children by attempting to sell their farm to soulless speculators; and the familial curse is spiritual starvation (expressed through alcoholism, avarice, infidelity, and duplicity) in the land of material plenty. In *True West*, the absent father is a drunk over whose terrain—the vast yet empty desert and, by extension, movie Westerns and the "West" of myth or the imagination—the two brothers duel, since there is no true West over which to fight, that landscape having long since gone the way of the American Indians. Like the real West—of today's Western cities and suburbs, of the nineteenth-century frontier?—the brothers' relationship, or each's character, is an almost schizoid disunity, a play of opposites marked by painful discords.

Fool for Love reiterates the theme of the sinning father, as well as the love-hate relationship between siblings, as it takes place at the edge of a Mojave Desert only conjured up in *True West* and concerns the troubled, incestuous relationship between a half-brother and half-sister. During their confrontation in a motel room, they are observed by a mysterious Old Man, who is revealed to be their biological father—the "fool for love" who loved two women and had two families by them. He declares that "It was the same love, just got split in two, that's all." Unable to reconcile their conflicting passions, the couple separates and the Old Man crumples under the weight of his own foolish, uncontainable passions. Like *Fool for Love*, *A Lie of the Mind* also concerns two troubled families and adds patricide to the theme of incest as it explores the fragility of filial and marital bonds. (Indeed, this play investigates the dissociation from self that is everyone's existential condition, even as it looks forward to an

America whose gentle ways will belie its violent past.)

With *Buried Child*, the second and arguably best work of this five-play cycle, Shepard continued his acerbic, revisionist examination-indictment of the American family. Awarded the Pulitzer Prize for drama in 1979, *Buried Child* features an Illinois family that, unlike the one in *Curse of the Starving Class*, has kept its farm but has not tended the land since 1935. Dodge, the patriarch, is a nasty man in his late seventies who suffers from alcoholism and an unnamed ailment. Covered with a grimy blanket, he reclines throughout on a sleazy couch in the living room, watching television. Halie, the matriarch, is in her mid-sixties, lives upstairs in emotional isolation, and appears to conduct an adulterous relationship with the local Protestant minister. Husband and wife talk long-distance across their seedy farmhouse, shouting at each other but never really listening to what the other is saying. One of their sons, Bradley, is an amputee, having chopped his leg off with a chain saw; another, Ansel, was a military veteran who, to his mother's regret, died in a motel room at the hands of his Catholic in-laws; and a third, the middle-aged Tilden, is at best functionally illiterate, at worst brain-damaged. It is Tilden's son, Vince, who incites the action by returning to the family farm (with his girlfriend, Shelly) after an absence of six years.

The play's central action concerns Vince's quest for his roots or search for his family's long-buried, terrible secret and lost, Edenic dream. Before this lone grandson's arrival, the family was bound together in a situation rife with betrayal, incest, murder, sickness, and sin—a situation symbolized by the infirmity and obliviousness as well as immobility of its patriarch. Shepard ceremonially reinforces that Dodge is a mere shadow of his former self early in Act I, when Tilden brings an armful of unshucked corn into the house from the otherwise fallow fields. As this son shucks the corn and, by the end of the first act, has spread its husks over the length of his father's sleeping body, we realize that Dodge is meant to be viewed as a husk of his former self: one divested of his potency and humanity by age, illness, drink, and guilt.

Tilden can see what is not visible to anyone else at this point—the abundance of vegetables in the fields behind the farmhouse—and he can even literally gather up the ears of corn (in Act II, bunches of carrots), because he alone acknowledges the family's terrible history. That history includes, above all else, infanticide, to which Dodge confesses in Act III: the killing of Halie's baby boy, presumably fathered by Tilden, and the burying of it in the backyard. Now unburdened of his guilt, Dodge divides his worldly goods between Vince and Tilden, then quietly dies of natural causes. Meanwhile, Tilden has unearthed the child's corpse and, as *Buried Child* ends, is carrying its "bones wrapped in muddy rotten cloth" up the stairs to Halie's bedroom, where the baby was apparently conceived. Now that the family's guilt has been exorcised, even Halie can see the corn, carrots, potatoes, and peas growing outside—declaring as much in the play's final speech, before she sees the little "gift" Tilden has brought her.

Vince, for his part, accepts his connection to the past at the same time as he looks forward to his future as the new owner of the family farm (so much so that he stares at the ceiling "as though Tilden wasn't there" when his brother carries the disinterred skeleton into the house). "I just inherited a house. I've gotta carry on the line. I've gotta see to it that things keep rolling," Vince declares. Yet he appears to sacrifice his youth (along with his girlfriend Shelly, who has resolutely departed), and maybe even his sanity, by sinking into his grandfather's paralytic pose on the sofa. Similar to Eman, the protagonist of Wole Soyinka's *The Strong Breed* (1964), Vince can be thought of as a "carrier," willing or unwilling, of the burden to expiate his family's sins by offering up himself. The "old king," Dodge, may be dead, but a new leader, Vince, has come to suffer in his place. Moreover, the exhumed child, Vince's uncle-brother, will surely bring to the family the shame and scandal—perhaps even the legal prosecution—it was killed to avoid.

To preserve its sense of itself as a pure entity, then, this American family did the most unfamilial thing possible, murdering a child, and thus destroyed its capacity to be a loving, communicative family unit. On a metaphorical level, numerous examples will come to mind of the American national compulsion to bury our own sins and to rewrite history so that we always wind up as the good guys: slavery, the Indians, Viet Nam. Nonetheless, the difficult, painful, and uncertain path of full disclosure is the way to spiritual rebirth, as the sudden flowering of the farm in *Buried Child* makes clear. Similarly, Shepard seems to be saying, the future of the United States lies in our acknowledgment of the worst, and reintegration with the best, in our country's more than two hundred years of existence.

Eugene O'Neill was surely saying something similar in such plays as *Beyond the Horizon* (1920), *Desire under the Elms* (1924), *A Touch of the Poet* (1942), and *More Stately Mansions* (1953). Indeed, the "dark elm trees" beyond the screened porch in *Buried Child* are a reminder of O'Neill's *Desire under the Elms*, which, like Shepard's play, focuses on a father-son rivalry and one son's desire to claim his inheritance. In O'Neill's drama, the patriarch takes a young wife who falls in love with his youngest son; when the wife and son have a child, the old man is deceived about its paternity. But the lovers experience guilt, and the wife, unable to bear the thought of separation from her husband's son, kills the baby. In Shepard's play, as we have seen, the wife also bears a child that is not her husband's and was probably fathered by her *oldest* surviving son, but she has the husband murder the little boy.

Shepard ties *Buried Child* not only to *Desire under the Elms*, but also to the parable of the Prodigal Son (Luke 15:11-32). In the Bible, the return of the Prodigal Son was meant to be an occasion for rejoicing. When the wayward son kneels before his father and says, "I have sinned against heaven and you; I no longer deserve to be called your son," the father responds by saying, "Quick! Bring out the finest robe and put it on him; put a ring on his finger and shoes on his feet." And when the Prodigal Son's older brother, who had remained faithful, complains about not being rewarded, the father replies, "You are with me always, and everything I have is yours. But we had to celebrate and rejoice. This brother of yours was dead, and has come back to life. He was lost, and is found."

In *Buried Child*, a number of allusions to Luke's parable appear, but they are amplified and distorted. For instance, there are two prodigal sons. The first is Tilden, who has returned to the family after twenty years of doing nothing in New Mexico. He says to his father that he had nowhere else to go except home, but Dodge retorts, "You're a grown man. You shouldn't be needing your parents at your age. It's un-natural. There's nothing we can do for you now anyway. Couldn't you make a living down there? . . . Support yourself? What'd'ya come back here for? . . . I never went back to my parents." Tilden certainly did not come back to see the twenty-two-year-old Vince, the second prodigal son, who was ostensibly raised by Dodge and Halie but has not seen them or his father since he was sixteen. When Vince appears, Tilden merely stares at him, more or less refusing to recognize his son; instead he declares, "I had a son once but we buried him." Earlier Dodge had also refused to acknowledge Vince, going so far as to deny that he was anybody's grandfather: "Stop calling me Grandpa, will ya? It's sickening. 'Grandpa.' I'm nobody's grandpa!"

The fine robe in which the Biblical prodigal is wrapped is transposed by Shepard into a grimy blanket, stained with Dodge's spittle and coughed-up blood. When Dodge dies, in productions of *Buried Child*, Vince either wraps himself in this blanket or dons his grandfather's baseball cap as a symbol that he has taken over his inheritance. Thus he, his father, and his uncle have each in some way diminished the power of the family patriarch: Bradley ruthlessly cuts off all of Dodge's hair when he is asleep; Tilden produces the evidence—the corporeal remains—of the child Dodge murdered; and Vince usurps his grandfather's place in the house as he lies down "on the sofa, arms folded behind his head, staring at the ceiling. His body is in the same relationship to Dodge's."

Buried Child draws not only on the parable of the Prodigal Son, but also on agricultural myth similar to that found in *Oedipus the King* (ca. 430 B.C.), which begins with the announcement of a curse on the land: "A rust consumes the buds and fruits of the earth; / The herds are sick; children die unborn, / And labor is in vain." In *Buried Child*, the crops have failed or not been cultivated and there has been no rain; moreover, like Sophocles' tragedy, Shepard's play includes the theme of incest and infanticide. Shepard himself has cited the myth of Osiris—celebrated in the ancient Egyptian Passion Play at Abydos—as an influence on *Buried Child*. Osiris was slain by a jealous brother who dismembered the body and scattered its remains throughout the arid Nile Valley, which mysteriously became fertile wherever it held pieces of Osiris' corpse. In *Buried Child*, as we have seen, the land that had cradled the corpse of Halie's murdered baby boy mysteriously yields crops that are gathered up by Tilden– much to the dismay of Bradley. And by the end of the play, we can hear Halie's disembodied voice declare, "I've never seen such corn. . . . Carrots, too. Potatoes. Peas. It's like a paradise out there . . . A miracle. . . . Maybe it was the rain."

Sam Shepard revised *Buried Child* for its 1995 presentation by the Steppenwolf Theatre Company of Chicago (a revision published by *American Theatre* in September 1996). The revised text makes three alterations worth noting: it makes absolutely clear early in the play that Tilden is the father of the buried child, something that is only implied in the first version; the second *Buried Child* attempts to shift the play's focus from Dodge to Vince, whose role as a surrogate for the buried child, Shepard felt, hadn't been fully explored; and the revision adds dark humor—according to the dramatist, "based mainly on Dodge's out-of-the-side-of-the-mouth . . . sarcasm, that strange World War II [gallows] humor"—to a play that its author thought was too heavy in its first production.

Ironically, however, the added humor—the result mostly of new lines spoken by Dodge—serves to create a kind of (unintended) power struggle between grandfather and grandson for primacy in the revised *Buried Child*. Vince is now a stronger character and his place in the family has become clearer, but Dodge still seems to hold sway in this household. Moreover, the added humor may be just that, added or gratuitous, for the original *Buried Child* had its own brand of black humor that derived organically from the Gothic or grotesque nature of its characters and their eerily domestic drama. As for Shepard's clarification of the buried child's paternity, such a realistic filling in of characterological detail, or providing of certain answers to salient questions of exposition, is unnecessary in a work that lives, finally, off its mythological or metaphorical resonance.

Nonetheless, *Buried Child* achieves mythic resonance in the end by exploiting the power of realism and naturalism, not by escaping it. This is the reason we can add Shepard's warring family to the houses of Ibsen's Alvings and O'Neill's Cabots, as well as those of Sophocles' Laius, Aeschylus's Atreus, and Shakespeare's Old Hamlet. Strikingly, Shepard capped a long period of stylistic experiment with a return to domestic, representational drama in his five-play family cycle.   But he was only doing what other indigenous playwrights, such as Elmer Rice, Maxwell Anderson, and Eugene O'Neill, had done before him: find his way back to the American drama's natural mode. For the gradual discovery of American dramatists, starting in the 1930s, was precisely that domestic realism or naturalism was their most effective vehicle for treating larger issues—larger issues, that is, as they affect the lives of "smaller" people like the families in *Curse of the Starving Class, Buried Child, True West, Fool for Love,* and *A Lie of the Mind.*

CHAPTER NINE

AMERICAN DRAMA/AMERICAN FILM: THE CASES OF *WAY DOWN EAST, THE LITTLE FOXES,* AND *EDMOND*

I would like to begin by saying something about the adaptation of drama to film, mainly because so little is understood about the process of adaptation by even the educated filmgoer. Many people still cling to the naïve belief that drama and film, for example, are two aspects of the same art, except that drama is "live" while movies are "recorded." Certainly there are undeniable similarities between the two forms. Most obviously, both employ action as a principal means of communication: that is, what people *do* is a major source of meaning. Live theater and movies are also collaborative enterprises, involving the coordination of writers, directors, actors, designers, and technicians. Drama and film are both social arts in that they are exhibited before groups of people and are therefore experienced publicly as well as individually. But films are not mere recordings of plays. The language systems of these two art forms are fundamentally different, and movies have a far broader range of techniques at their disposal.

Actually, as many commentators have noted, film is closer in form to fiction than to theater. Like fiction, film can move easily through time and space, and, like fiction, film employs narration—sometimes in the first person, through subjective camera and voice-over; rarely in the third person, through the anonymous commentaries that accompany certain documentaries; and most often and most naturally in the omniscient mode, which enables a filmmaker to cut from a subjective point-of-view shot to a variety of objective shots, from a single reaction in close-up to the simultaneous reactions of several characters in medium or full shot. (Every picture may tell a story, but every moving picture is "told"—by a narrator called the camera.) Unlike fiction, or I should say in a more powerful way than fiction, film can go inside human beings to explore interiority. It does this through the voice and the voice-over, through the close up, and through the ability to present multiple states of consciousness, as Federico Fellini does in *81/2* (1963): present awareness, memory, dream, and daydream. A novel could do all this, of course, but its words wouldn't have the immediacy and effect of film, the power of the image and its accompanying sound. To be fair to the novel, the Russian filmmaker and theorist Sergei Eisenstein has shown how such cinematic innovations as fades, dissolves, and parallel editing were in fact taken directly from the pages of Charles Dickens. And to praise the novel, it has learned from film, as has poetry: a number of critics have remarked upon the cinematic qualities of much twentieth-century fiction and poetry, including Joyce's *Ulysses* (1922) and Eliot's "Love Song of J. Alfred Prufrock" (1915).

To talk now about the adaptation of drama into film, the surest sign of the clichéd mind in filmmaking is a feeling of obligation to "open up" plays when they become films and a conviction that this process proves superiority, that a play really comes into its own when it is filmed. We can really go to Italy in Franco Zeffirelli's film of *Romeo and Juliet* (1968), so for some people this picture automatically supersedes stage-bound theatrical productions. We can dissolve and cross-fade more easily in the movie of *Death of a Salesman* (1951), therefore the theater proves yet again just a tryout place for later perfect consummation on screen—despite, in this case, the theater's superior ability to suggest the childishness of Willy's sons (by having the adult actors of Biff and Happy play their boyhood selves) and the momentousness of Willy's adultery (by having it occur, not on location in Boston, but on the forestage—right in the Loman's living room, as it were). And we can go outside in Mike Nichols' film of *Who's Afraid of Virginia Woolf?* (1966), so once more the theater is shown up as cribbed or confined, if not superficially realistic, even though the claustrophobic nature of George and Martha's single-set living room on the stage is part of the point of this long night's journey into day.

The trouble here is a confusion in aesthetic logic, an assumption that we are comparing apples and apples when we are really comparing apples and pears. Fundamentally, film takes the audience to the event, shifting the audience continually; theater takes the event to the audience, shifting it never. Just as the beauty of poetry often lies in tensions between the free flight of language and the molding capacity of form, so the beauty of drama often lies in tensions between imagination and theatrical exigency. To assume that the cinema's extension of a play's action is automatically an improvement is to change the subject: from the way theater builds upwards, folding one event upon another in almost perceptible vertical form, to the way film progresses horizontally. Figuratively speaking, theater works predominantly by building higher and higher in one place; film, despite the literally vertical progress of planes in the image, works predominantly in a lateral series of places.

In this way, action in the cinema is more of a journey in the present than a confrontation based on the past (the usual form of tragedy in drama): the one is filled with possibility or promise, the other with suspense or foreboding.

By its very form, it can then be said, film reflects for spectators in the twenty-first century the belief that the world is a place in which a person can leave the past behind and create his or her own future—hence one of the reasons the cinema took such a foothold, so early, in the history of our relatively young nation.

"Opening up" a play can be successful when the filmmaker knows clearly what he is doing and treats his film as a new work from a common source, as Richard Lester does in his admirable film of Ann Jellicoe's *The Knack* (1965). But most adaptors seem to think that any banal set of film gimmicks constitutes a liberation for which the poor cramped play ought to be grateful. One film that respects its dramatic source almost completely and is nevertheless cinematic is William Wyler's *The Little Foxes* (1941). Lillian Hellman's play from 1939 has undergone nearly no adaptation: for instance, there are no exterior scenes of dramatic action in the film—precisely the kind of scene, I have been arguing, that most directors would have deemed necessary in order to introduce a little "cinema" into this intractable theatrical mass.

The majority of the action in Wyler's film takes place on the same, totally neutral set, the ground-floor living room of a huge colonial house. At the back, a staircase leads to the second-floor bedrooms of Regina and Horace Giddens, which adjoin each other. (Regina and Horace are played by Bette Davis and Herbert Marshall, respectively, and I shall use the actors' names in my discussion of the film version.) Nothing picturesque adds to the realism of this somber place, which is as impersonal as the setting of classical tragedy. The characters have a credible, if conventional, reason for confronting one another in the living room, whether they come from the outdoors or from their bedrooms; they can also plausibly linger in the living room. The staircase at the back plays a role similar to the one it would in the theater: it is purely an element of dramatic architecture, which in this case will be used to set off the characters in the vertical space of the frame. Let's look at the central scene of the film, the death of Herbert Marshall, which happens to take place in the living room and on the staircase. An analysis of this scene will reveal that to be cinematic a film adaptation not only doesn't have to go outdoors, it also doesn't have to feature either a mobile camera or lots of cutting.

First let me summarize the action of *The Little Foxes* up to and just beyond this point, which occurs toward the end. We are in the South at the turn of the century, where and when middle-class capitalism-cum-materialism has more than begun to eclipse aristocratic feudalism-cum-agrarianism. Two brothers, Ben and Oscar Hubbard, believe they can make a fortune by establishing the first mill in their town, which is surrounded by cotton plantations. Lacking the $75,000 needed for the venture, they seek the partnership of their sister, Regina Giddens, who, eager to share in the profits, promises to get the money from her wealthy husband, Horace, president of the local bank. Having just been brought home from the hospital in Baltimore by his devoted daughter, Alexandra, Horace has only a short time to live and refuses to become involved. Therefore, to help his father, Oscar's son, Lee, a clerk in Horace's bank, steals $80,000 in bonds from Horace's safe-deposit box, on the assumption that his uncle will not check the box for six months; and Ben and Oscar complete their business deal. Horace discovers the theft but tells Regina that he will not prosecute her brothers. On the contrary, he will call the theft a loan and make a new will in which Regina will receive only $80,000 in bonds, the exact amount of the theft. Thus Regina will share neither in her husband's fortune nor in the fortune the mill will make. While the two quarrel, Horace suffers a heart attack, but Regina refuses to administer a reviving drug and coldbloodedly stands by as he dies. With her knowledge of the theft, she then blackmails her brothers into assigning her a 75% interest in the mill, lest she prosecute them. Our scene is the quarrel between Regina and Horace, or, to switch back to the actor's names, between Bette Davis and Herbert Marshall, who has revealed to her the theft of his bonds.

Bette Davis is sitting in the middle ground facing the viewer, her head at the center of the screen; the lighting enhances the brightness of her heavily made-up face. In the foreground Herbert Marshall sits in three-quarter profile. The ruthless exchanges between husband and wife take place without any cutting from one character to the other, since the very positions of Davis and Marshall emphasize their separation and antagonism. Then comes the husband's heart attack, during which he begs his wife to get him his medicine from upstairs. From this instant all the drama in this scene derives from the immobility of both Bette Davis and the camera. Marshall is forced to stand up and go get the medicine himself, and this effort will kill him as he climbs the first few steps of the staircase.

In the theater, this scene would most likely have been staged in the same manner. A spotlight could have been focused on Bette Davis, and the spectator would have felt the same horror at her criminal inaction, the same anguish at the sight of her staggering victim. Yet, despite appearances, William Wyler's directing makes as extensive use as possible of the means offered him by the camera and the frame. Bette Davis' position at the center of the screen endows her with privilege and power in the geometry of the dramatic space. The whole scene revolves around her, but her frightening immobility takes its full impact only from Marshall's double exit from the frame, first in the foreground on the right, then in the mid-background on the left. Instead of following him in this lateral movement, as any less intelligent director would have done, Wyler's camera remains imperturbably immobile. When Marshall finally enters the frame for a second time and begins to climb the stairs, the cinematographer, Gregg Toland, acting at Wyler's request, is careful not to bring into focus the full depth of the image, so that Marshall's fall on the staircase and his death will not be clearly visible to the viewer. This artificial blurring augments our feeling of anxiety: as if over the shoulder of the dominant Bette Davis, who faces us and has her back toward her husband, we have to discern in the distance the outcome of a drama whose protagonist is nearly escaping us.

This analysis of Marshall's death in *The Little Foxes* clearly reveals how Wyler can make a whole scene revolve around one actor. Bette Davis at the center of the screen is paralyzed, like a hoot owl by a spotlight, and around her the staggering Marshall weaves as a second—this time mobile—pole, whose shift first out of the frame and then into the background, draws with it all the dramatic attention. In addition, this shift creates tremendous suspense because is consists of a double disappearance from the frame, and because the focus on the staircase at the back is imperfect. One can see here how Wyler uses depth of field: as I've indicated, the director elected to have Toland envelop the character of the dying Marshall in a certain haziness, to have his cinematographer, as it were, befog the back of the frame. This was done to create so much anxiety in the viewer that he should almost want to push the immobile Bette Davis aside to have a better look. The dramatic development of this scene does indeed follow that of the dialogue and of the action itself, but the scene's cinematic expression superimposes its own evolution upon the dramatic development: a second action, as it were, that is the very story of the scene from the moment Marshall gets up from his chair to his collapse on the staircase.

We can see here everything that the cinema adds to the means of the theater, and we can also see that, paradoxically, the highest level of cinematic art coincides with the lowest level of *mise-en-scène*. Nothing could better heighten the dramatic power of this scene than the absolute *immobility* of the camera. Its slightest movement, which a less skillful director would have deemed the right "cinematic" element to introduce, would have decreased the dramatic tension. Furthermore, the camera does not follow the path of the average viewer's eyes by cutting from Bette Davis to the frantic Marshall; instead, it obstructs our vision merely by recording, without full depth of field, the same scene in one continuous take. It is the stationary camera itself, in other words, that organizes the action in terms of the frame and the ideal coordinates of its two-dimensional geometric space. By means of the cinema, William Wyler has mined the artistic depths of this scene at the same time that he has respected its theatrical appearances.

To the real looks the actors would direct at one another on stage, one must add here the virtual "look" of the camera with which our own identifies. Wyler excels in making us sensitive to his camera's gaze. In *Jezebel* (1938), for example, there is the low-angle shot that clearly points the lens directly at Bette Davis's eyes looking down at the white cane that Henry Fonda holds in his hand with the intention of using it. We thus follow the dramatic line between the character and the object much better than we would have if, by the rules of conventional cutting, the camera had shown us the cane from the point of view of Bette Davis herself.

A variation on the same principle: in *The Little Foxes*, in order to make us understand the thoughts of the character who notices the small steel box in which the stolen bonds were locked and whose absence from the box is going to indicate theft, Wyler placed it in the foreground with the camera being this time at eye-level and at the same distance from the box as the eyes of the character. Our eyes no longer meet the character's eyes directly through the beheld object, as in the above-mentioned scene from *Jezebel*, but as if through a mirror. The angle of incidence of our own view of the object is, as it were, equal to the angle of reflection of the character's view, which angle takes us to this person's eyes. In any case, Wyler commands our mental vision according to the rigorous laws of an invisible dramatic optics.

Paradoxically, insofar as Wyler has never attempted to hide the novelistic of theatrical nature of most of his scripts, he has made all the more apparent the cinematic phenomenon in its utmost purity. Not once has the *auteur* of *The Best Years of Our Lives* (1946), *Jezebel,* or *The Little Foxes* said to himself *a priori* that he had to have a "cinematic look"; still, nobody can tell a story in cinematic terms better than he. For him, the action is expressed first by the actor. Like a director in the theater, Wyler conceives of his job of enhancing the action as beginning with the actor. The set and the camera are there only to permit the actor to focus upon himself the maximum dramatic intensity; they are not there to create a meaning unto themselves. Even though Wyler's approach is also that of the theater director, the latter has at his disposal only the very limited means of the stage. He can manipulate his means, but no matter what he does, the text and the actor constitute the essence of theatrical production.

Film, then, is not at all magnified theater on screen, the stage viewed constantly through opera glasses. The size of the image or unity of time has nothing to do with the matter. Cinema begins when the frame of the screen and the placement of the camera are used to enhance the action and the actor. In *The Little Foxes*, Wyler has changed almost nothing of the dramatic text or even of the set: one could say that he limited himself to directing the play in the way that a theater director would have directed it; and, furthermore, that he used the frame of the screen to *conceal* certain parts of the set and used the camera to bring the viewer closer to the action. What actor would not dream of being able to play a scene, immobile on a chair, in front of 5,000 viewers who don't miss the slightest movement of an eye? What theater director would not want the spectator in the worst seat at the back of the house to be able to see clearly the movements of his actors, and to read with ease his intentions at any moment in the action? Wyler didn't choose to do anything other than realize on film the essence of a theatrical *mise-en-scène* that would not use the lights and the set merely to ornament the actor and the text. Nevertheless, there is probably not a single shot in *The Little Foxes* that isn't pure cinema. Indeed, there is a hundred times more cinema, and better cinema at that, in one fixed shot of *The Little Foxes* than in all the exterior traveling shots, in all the natural settings, in all the geographical exoticism, in all the shots of the reverse side of the set, by means of which up to now the screen has ingeniously attempted to make us forget the stage.

I'd like now to treat a work whose melodrama is even purer, or more paradigmatic, than the kind to be found in *The Little Foxes*: D. W. Griffith's *Way Down East* (1920). Among D. W. Griffith's films, *The Birth of a Nation* (1915) and *Intolerance* (1916) are the most famous and, justly, the most praised. Lower in this group is the status of *Way Down East*, but for me it is a picture of persistent strength and of exceptional interest in American cultural history. *Way Down East* was made from a highly successful stage play of the same name, written by Lottie Blair Parker, Joseph R. Grismer, and William A. Brady, which had its premiere at Newport, Rhode Island, on September 3, 1897, and was performed around the United States for more than twenty years. The Parker-Grismer-Brady play came at the end of a century in which the form of melodrama had dominated the American theater—so much so that it spawned several types, such as the rural melodrama of *Way Down East*.

What is a melodrama? The term has often been defined—it is one of the easier dramatic terms to define—but for my purposes I will try one more definition. Melodrama is a dramatic form using monochromatic characters and usually involving physical danger to the "good" protagonist, who is engaged in an external conflict with evil of one kind or another. The single essential ingredient in this recipe is earthly justice. A "straight" drama may merely imply justice or may end in irony at the absence of it; in tragedy, justice, if it comes at all, may come in the hereafter (if *it* comes at all). In melodrama, by contrast, justice may be slow but it is sure, and it is always seen to be done.

By implication, then, melodrama is an artistic strategy designed, *and desired*, to reconcile its audience to the way things are. In the nineteenth century its chief aim was to support the economic and moral system—a great deal was made in these plays of the "poor but honest" theme together with its companion, the "rich but exploitative" motif. (Today, melodrama supports different conventional ideas, as in the case of David Mamet's movie *House of Games* [1987] if not the much earlier play-and-film *The Little Foxes*, which takes place at the same time as *Way Down East* but emphasizes almost exclusively the rapaciousness or acquisitiveness of the "haves.")   Many thousands of farmers saw the play *Way Down East* in the years that it toured the country, and they must have known that this idyllic, Currier-and-Ives version of their lives was a long way from brute fact, but the fiction gave them two compensations: escape from the harshness and unpredictability of agricultural reality, and roles in which to imagine themselves outside the theater. As Eric Bentley once put it, "Melodrama is the naturalism of the dream life."

Nowadays it may be necessary to explain the title of this play/film. "Down East" is an old phrase used to describe the farthest reaches of New England, particularly Maine, which at its tip is considerably east of Boston. The picture tells the entire story chronologically of innocent Anna Moore (including the portion that occurs before the play and is revealed there only through exposition), who lives with her mother "way down east" in the New England village of Belden. When they get into financial difficulties, the country girl goes, at her mother's request, to seek help from their rich and fashionable relatives in Boston, the Tremonts. Mrs. Tremont and her snobbish daughters treat her poorly, but Anna attracts the attention of an unscrupulous playboy named Lennox Sanderson. He has his way by tricking her into a false marriage, which he persuades her to keep secret on the ground that the revelation would anger his father (from whom he derives his support). Back home in her Maine village, Anna obeys until she becomes pregnant, at which time she asks to be publicly recognized as Mrs. Sanderson. The womanizer responds by telling her the truth and then leaving her to cope as best she can.

Some time later, Anna's mother dies, and Anna takes refuge in a rooming house in Belden, where her baby dies soon after its birth. Turned out by her censorious landlady, who suspects that she has no husband, Anna pitifully takes to the road with her few possessions to look for work. She finds a position at the Bartlett farm, near Bartlett village, despite the reservations of Squire Bartlett about hiring someone whose past he and his family do not know. Anna proves her virtue through hard work (how else?), and the squire's son, David, falls in love with her. But when he declares himself, she tells him, without disclosing the reason, that nothing will ever be possible between them. As coincidence would have it (*has* to have it), the "reason"—Lennox Sanderson—lives nearby on a country estate. He soon discovers that Anna is on the Bartlett place and urges her to move on; she tries to obey what the society of her time would have perceived as a male superior, but the Bartletts, who know nothing of the Sanderson matter (though they know him), persuade their "hired girl" to remain.

The plot begins building to its crisis when, some months later, Maria Poole, the Belden landlady, visits Bartlett Village, sees Anna, and tells her story to the local gossip, Martha Perkins. After Martha relays the news to the squire, he goes to Belden to confirm it; when he learns that the story is true, he returns home that night and orders Anna out of his house during a blinding snowstorm. She leaves, but not before denouncing Sanderson, who that very evening is an honored guest at the Bartlett house. Sanderson is thereupon attacked by David Bartlett and shown the door; then David goes out into the storm to find Anna. Hysterical and grief-stricken, she has collapsed on a frozen river just as the ice is beginning to break up in the spring thaw. When David finds her, Anna is being carried downstream on an ice cake toward the falls, yet he manages to follow her from floe to floe and complete his rescue right before she reaches the brink. Himself forgiving, the Squire now begs Anna's forgiveness as well, which she graciously grants; Sanderson offers to marry her authentically but is scornfully refused; and the film of *Way Down East* ends happily with the wedding of David and Anna.

Distinguishing between "plot," which conventionally signifies the sequence of actions or events in a play, and "story," which for my purposes shall designate all incidents and activities that occur before, after, *and* during the play—offstage as well as onstage—I should presently like to examine Griffith's adaptation of dramatic techniques to film and to consider his reasons for telling Anna Moore's story chronologically or episodically as opposed to climactically. The screenplay that Griffith used, the majority of which he himself wrote, is a model of the film adaptation of plays, in the sheerly technical sense. Much of the formal beauty of play design, as he surely knew, arises from limitation: the necessity to limit action and to arrange necessary combinations of characters on the stage. The skill with which these matters are handled can be a pleasure in itself, as well as positive enrichment of the drama. But this skill is not essential to the screenplay, which has infinitely greater freedom of physical and temporal movement, can unfold intertwined material into serial form, and can run virtually parallel actions. The contrast can easily be seen if the Parker-Grismer-Brady play script and the movie scenario by Griffith and Anthony Paul Kelly are placed alongside each other.

That movie scenario, it must be remembered, was written during the silent era. That is, even if the director had wanted simply to film the play as it stood, he would have been unable to do so without the heavy use of titles. This is because Anna's past is revealed through dialogue in the play, which has a late point of attack and therefore begins when she arrives at Bartlett Village in Maine looking for work—after her baby has died and she has been evicted from Maria Poole's rooming house. It is Lennox Sanderson's discovery of Anna on Squire Bartlett's farm, then, that provokes the drama of the Parker-Grismer-Brady play. Griffith, however, must tell Anna's story long before this occurrence: through pictures (and the discreet use of titles), and beginning with this country girl's visit to Boston.

Beyond the merely descriptive or illustrative images of his narrative, Griffith uses nature to evoke characters' inner states where a drama would use, for instance, the soliloquy; he also uses nature as a silent but expressive character. An example of the latter "use" occurs when Anna is thrown out by her landlady, after her baby's death: there is a lovely long shot of Anna starting down a country road, her few possessions in a box under her arm, and this shot bitterly contrasts the beauty of the countryside with this young woman's sorry state. Indeed, the environment underlines Anna's desolation by seeming to overwhelm her—a tiny figure by contrast who becomes even smaller as she walks away from the camera. Shots of nature are used differently, to endorse a character's feelings, in at least two instances in *Way Down East*. In one, Anna meets with David Bartlett near a waterfall that pours into a gleaming, tranquil river, which reflects the couple's contentment even as the cascade represents the passion surging inside them. Similarly, during the storm sequence there is a powerful congruence between the raging blizzard and Anna's turbulent feelings as she wanders all alone at night.

There is plenty of suspense by the time we get to the snowstorm, but what about early in the film? The sources of tension in the play *Way Down East* are the gradual revelation of Anna's certain secret and the definition of her relationship with Lennox Sanderson. But these tensions disappear in the movie because we follow Anna from her very first meeting with Sanderson, after she has arrived in Boston from rural Maine to visit her wealthy aunt. (One big advantage of the film's method, though, is that Griffith can give Anna the experience of betrayal and loss of her child "onstage," thus making her a differently seen, more sympathetic character by the time she reaches the point of what was her first entrance in the play.) Perhaps believing that an equivalent of dramatic suspense would be necessary to hold the audience's interest in his chronological tale of Anna's ordeal, Griffith creates tension in the first half of the film, before his heroine leaves Boston, through *visual* means in addition to creating literal visual tension.

The first type is produced when, several times, a scene from life on Squire Bartlett's farm is inserted into or intercut with the action in Boston. Griffith knew he had the problem of establishing the Bartlett home and his male romantic lead before Anna reaches them—about half an hour into the story. (In the play of *Way Down East*, the reverse is true: Anna does not arrive at the Bartlett farm until fairly late in the first act, most of which is spent introducing David Bartlett and his parents as well as some local types.) So he solved the problem with a device deliberately borrowed from the Dickensian novel: he inserts the title "Chapter Two . . . Bartlett Village" and proceeds to give us glimpses of the place and its most prominent family. We do not know that this is where Anna will eventually seek refuge and find salvation through David, but we assume that the director is showing us these scenes for a purpose that will become clear. In fact, the lack of clarity is itself an enticement, and we eagerly anticipate an explanation of the presence of the Bartletts and their farm in the movie.

Literal visual tension is created in the film of *Way Down East* in two ways. Life in the sophisticated city, in Boston, is filled with verticals—tall doorways, spiral staircases, high ceilings—whereas life in simple, bucolic Maine, in the inserted country scenes, is composed mainly of horizontals—the long porch of the Bartlett family house, the flat land, the background action that crosses the screen from right to left (as when the sheriff drives his horse-drawn wagon up to the farm's gated entrance). In addition to this horizontal-vertical juxtaposition, there is the larger, even more striking one of outdoors against indoors. Almost all the shots of the country in the first half of *Way Down East* take place outside, in the fresh air and sunlight. By contrast, all the shots of the city occur indoors, in darkened, smoke-filled rooms. The atmosphere in Boston is frenetic: there seemingly are round-the-clock parties. The inhabitants of Bartlett village, for their part, are so relaxed that some of them even fall asleep during the day. (This may explain the otherwise curious shot of David in bed on a sunny afternoon, starting suddenly from sleep only when Anna, as yet unknown to him, is entering into the bogus marriage with Sanderson miles away.)

With the aid of such visual tension, Griffith could film the whole of Anna's story, as opposed to solely the plot of the play, and doing that gave him one large advantage: he could make it appear less melodramatic, or, better, he could enhance the *realism* of the melodrama, of its settings and actions. Clearly, Anna is enmeshed in Manichean circumstances in the movie, but, just as clearly, she passes through them, and *we see her do so.* Although she is victimized by Sanderson on account of her rustic innocence, Anna struggles to make her own destiny: she endures the disgrace (at the time) of giving birth out of wedlock and the grief of her baby's death, then creates a new life for herself through hard work at Squire Bartlett's farm. Circumstance intervenes again in the persons of her erstwhile seducer and of her former landlady, who, with Martha Perkins' aid, betrays Anna's past to the squire. And again Anna fights against her victimization: she rightly accuses Sanderson of gross deception in front of his neighbors, then defiantly walks out of the farmhouse into the blizzard to end all blizzards.

Because we witnessed Anna's strength and bravery after she was deserted by Sanderson and were not simply told about them, we find those qualities in her here at the end more believable. Because we witnessed Anna's journey from the Maine countryside to Boston, then from there back to Maine and on to Squire Bartlett's farm, we are more willing to view her final foray into the snow as possible escape rather than probable death. In the play of *Way Down East*, we only hear of Anna's incredible rescue; in the film, we see it happen, seemingly without gimmick, and her rescue thus becomes credible. After this, her forgiveness by Squire Bartlett (because she was tricked into immorality) and marriage to David can be only anticlimax, whereas, in the play, they are meant to be epiphany.

I do not mean to imply that Griffith increases the literary value of the Parker-Grismer-Brady script by expanding it in time and space. *Way Down East* is still a melodrama. What he accomplishes, however, in adapting the play to the screen is to point up a significant difference between the two forms. Not the most obvious one—that theater is more verbal and cinema more visual—but the difference in artistic structure and philosophical assumption between drama and film. The paradigm of dramatic structure in the West up to Ibsen in the late nineteenth century, with the exception of Shakespeare and his coevals, had been intensive or Aristotelian—a form in which, philosophically speaking, the protagonist is caught in a highly contracted situation, his end foretold before the plot begins and his range of choice therefore increasingly reduced, for the plot in this case is enmeshed in the toils of a story with a long as well as a weighty past. Film form is by its very nature *extensive*, for the camera can easily extend itself over time and space as it covers the whole of the story, in this way militating against highly compressed circumstances and always leaving possibilities or alternatives open for the characters, insofar as action is concerned. (Shakespeare's plays are often called "cinematic" precisely because their own structure is extensive.)

In adapting *Way Down East* to film, Griffith essentially dropped the intensive structure in which Anna Moore had been trapped (only to be miraculously-cum-melodramatically rescued from it at the last minute by David Bartlett) into an extensive one, with favorable or liberating results for the melodrama as well as for the character of Anna. What Griffith was discovering, along with his audience, was that film not only satisfies a craving for the replication or redemption of physical reality, but also for freedom—from the restrictions of time and place, from the limitations of language, and *from the past*. Action in film is thus more of a journey in the present than a confrontation based on the past—the one filled with possibility or promise, the other with fatalism or foreboding. And if stage melodrama, in which villainy is punished and virtue rewarded, was a last-second escape from the past, melodramatic film is an extended departure from it.

Stage melodrama provided its audiences in the nineteenth century with momentary relief from a world in which man felt himself a prisoner of his past, possibly of his own origins, and where justice was most often *not* done. The myth of such melodrama was that of spiritual redemption by bourgeois standards. Hence Anna is a secular saint, truly good, suffering for the sins and blindness of her fellows, finally undergoing an agony that reveals her purity. She is betrayed in her trust, she goes through travail, she labors in humility, she declines the happiness of David's love because she is unworthy, and she shows that death holds no terror for her. At last she achieves heaven: on earth.

To extend the analogy, the God in the story is the Squire—the owner of the Eden. It is he who at first is about to expel Anna from the Garden, who finds the largesse in his heart to let her remain on trust, and who at last provides the crucial forgiveness—because when she sinned, she did not know it; she was tricked into immorality, though she thought she was behaving rightly. Not only is Anna forgiven, but when she marries David she wears white, her virginity restored by dispensation of the Squire. Here then, in capsule, is sainthood founded on respectability, which was possibly the chief criterion for social survival in the nineteenth century.

But not in the twentieth, and certainly not the twenty-first century. Yet Griffith had a sense of the continuing function of melodrama in a bourgeois, mock-egalitarian society. He also must have had some sense of the pluralistic nature of the public at any given time, the perception that new, even avant-garde, interests can coexist with old, traditional ones. (For instance, I don't think he would have been surprised that during the 1969–1970 movie season, to take only one, *Easy Rider* and *Airport* were successes simultaneously.) So in 1920, the same year that O'Neill wrote *Beyond the Horizon,* in which Stravinsky and Satie were already known composers, when Picasso and Matisse themselves were known painters, and two years after the end of a world war that had altered certain traditions and beliefs forever, Griffith paid around $175,000—much more than the entire cost of his *Birth of a Nation*—for the screen rights to a twenty-three-year-old rural melodrama.

Griffith himself had plenty of experience in the theater, a theater that was full of plays like this: he had begun acting in 1897 (the same year, to repeat, in which *Way Down East* was first produced on stage), at the age of twenty-two, with a stock company in his native Kentucky; had struggled in a number of other stock and road companies; then had written a melodrama that had been produced, unsuccessfully, in Washington, D.C., in 1907. Out of this experience, evidently, came the conviction that he knew how to make *Way Down East* "work" and that the postwar public had not shed all its old affinities. And, very clearly, he also understood how film was taking over the form and function of melodrama from the theater, expanding it in the directions toward which it had been moving.

One of those directions included the theater's wishful embrace of cinematic form, not only because of that form's photographic realism, but also because, by its very (expansive) nature, film reflected for melodramatically conditioned spectators in the early twentieth century the belief that the world was a place in which man could leave the past behind and create his own future, where earthly justice for past wrongs would become a moot point—to be left in the past. *Way Down East*, then, represents a landmark in the transition between two worlds: of an intensive play structure and an extensive cinematic one, of Aristotelian drama and Eisensteinian film, of nineteenth-century theater culture and twentieth-century movie magic. It is as if, in filming *Way Down East* after the seminally cinematic *Birth of a Nation* and *Intolerance* and late in the historical process that saw film make over theatrical melodrama, Griffith were going back to mark simultaneously his own beginnings on the nineteenth-century stage and his movement into film in 1908, when, out of theater work, he took a job with the Biograph Company of New York. The rest, to alter the phrase only slightly, is film history.

Lastly, I want to consider David Mamet's *Edmond* (2006), whose episodic form, unlike that of the film version of *Way Down East*, mirrors its source's own extensive structure, and whose (mostly) nighttime settings mirror its central character's long night of the soul. Originally produced as a long one-act play in 1982, *Edmond* is an underrated piece, having been written between Mamet's stellar (and original) screenplay for *The Verdict* (1982) and his best drama, *Glengarry Glen Ross* (1984)—itself filmed in 1992—and consequently having suffered in comparison with those two highly publicized works. But *Edmond* stands on its own two feet, in part because it points up—as none of Mamet's other plays do—an aspect of his writing style that, like this particular drama itself, has been neglected. I mean the fact that Mamet's staccato or minimalist dialogue, with its occasional explosions, is essentially expressionistic, even when the plays themselves are not thoroughgoing expressionist works.

Mamet's language thus underscores the paradox of verism-cum-abstraction that inheres in all his work (but is even more apparent in his films, where verism is expected to a far greater degree than it is in the drama). The general linguistic texture is naturalistic, nearly stenographic—the broken sentences, the repetitions, the litanies of the everyday; then, suddenly, with a telegraphic word or phrase, and especially with an entire quizzical or contorted sentence, the vernacular lifts into an arch. As in, "The path of some crazed lunatic sees you as an invasion of his personal domain" (*American Buffalo* [1975]). Or, "People used to say that there are numbers of such magnitude that multiplying them by two made no difference" (*Glengarry Glen Ross*). And, from *Edmond*: "[God] may love the weak, but he protects the strong." With a lesser writer, such lines might seem to be fissures in verism; but Mamet otherwise so thoroughly certifies the accuracy of his ear that in these instances we feel we are flying past the character's actual powers of expression into the thoughts in him that he isn't always able to express. In this way the real is lifted into the abstract—or what I am calling the expressionistic.

That *Edmond* appears more expressionistic than Mamet's other plays stems less from its disgorged or deracinated language, however, than from its episodic form. It's what the Germans call both a "station" drama and a *Wandlungsdrama,* a drama of transformation-cum-regeneration that is composed of a series of stations, or stages (twenty-three in *Edmond*'s case), through which a character progresses as he takes the moral, spiritual, and emotional journey of his life. (A product of European religious drama of the Middle Ages, the original station play consisted of stations that were sometimes literally stations of the cross.) Several commentators have compared *Edmond* to Georg Büchner's proto-expressionistic play *Woyzeck* (1836), but Mamet's drama has more in common with Georg Kaiser's lesser-known expressionistic work *From Morn to Midnight* (1912).

In this play, a bank cashier, whose humanity has been crushed beneath the social conventions, economic system, and political structure of Wilhelminian Germany, succumbs to sexual temptation and both robs his bank and leaves his wife—to embark on a pilgrimage (to a bordello for some sensual fulfillment, to a sports stadium for some passionate gambling, to the Salvation Army for some soulful religion) in search of something beyond the material, the profane, the mechanized, the quotidian. When he doesn't find what he's looking for, he kills himself rather than be imprisoned for his crime. David Mamet's own play covers more than the twelve or so hours of *From Morn to Midnight,* but it, too, is about a character in desperate search of some new intensity, truth, or meaning in his life.

Edmund Burke is a forty-seven-year-old New York stockbroker on his way home early from work after a meeting has been re-scheduled. Low on spiritual fuel, he stops to see a clairvoyant. (Clairvoyants recur in Mamet's plays, one of them being *The Shawl* [1985].) She reads tarot cards and fatefully tells him, "You are not where you belong." (Imagined tarot cards fleck his mind thereafter, until, near the end of the play and the film, Edmond utters a line that is nearly an exact quotation from *Hamlet:* "There is a destiny that shapes our ends . . . rough-hew them how we may.") The result of the clairvoyant's counsel comes that evening at home when, after some clipped dialogue about a broken lamp, Edmond gets up and bluntly tells his wife he is leaving:

WIFE: Will you bring me back some cigarettes? . . .
EDMOND: I'm not coming back.

This simple statement fractures the somnolence of his life. A quick quarrel then discloses that Edmond hasn't loved his wife for years and doesn't think she's attractive: she simply no longer interests him sexually *or* spiritually.

(Mamet, who wrote this film adaptation, puts the wife in bra and panties on screen, as he did not on stage, in order to emphasize Edmond's lack of interest.) For her part, the wife (who is unnamed: more on this later) seems angered less by the bad news than by her husband's detached manner in delivering it. Edmond doesn't care: he just turns his back and walks out on her—and on his mechanical, workaday existence. *Edmond* thus takes place, as it were, after the romance of the archetypal romantic comedy is over—when, in the absence of idealized, romantic love, a desire for a different kind of union or devotion takes over.

In Edmond's case, at least initially, that desire is for sheer sex, primarily of the oral (if not oracular) kind. His first stop after leaving his wife is a bar, where he meets a gabby, suave basketball fan (this "fan" nonetheless makes racist cracks about the black men who play the game) who infers that Edmond feels as if his "balls were cut off." The fan then casually offers some possible solutions to this problem: "money," "adventure," "pussy," "self-destruction." "Pussy" it is, so the man-in-the-bar gives Edmond a tip about a strip club where he can slake his sexual needs. When a pretty, amiable B-girl there tells him her fee for oral sex and also asks him to buy an exorbitantly priced drink, he becomes incensed. Soon Edmond's gotten himself tossed out—the start of a long round of explosive confrontations with hookers, grifters, and pimps in which he keeps heatedly complaining about the cost ("It's too much!"), naïvely trying to apply bourgeois standards to an inherently corrupt underworld into which he nevertheless keeps sinking deeper and deeper.

His odyssey through New York's seedy underbelly takes Edmond to a peep show next and then to a massage parlor, before he decides to try to get his satisfaction out of a hand of three-card monte. (*Edmond* is set for the most part on Manhattan's Eighth Avenue, though the sleaze there has largely been cleaned up since 1982. But this movie could actually take place at any time over the last several decades, and in any American city's tenderloin district—indeed, it happens to have been filmed wholly in Los Angeles.) When, however, he accuses the dealer of running a crooked game (surprise, surprise), the dealer and his shills pull him into an alley, beat him up, and steal his money. So Edmond goes to a pawnshop to trade his wedding ring for some cash—and with no such prior plan, comes out with a knife (unlike Woyzeck, who goes to a pawnshop expressly to buy a knife with which to kill his common-law wife). Thus armed, he first threatens a woman on a subway platform, then uses the knife (and the racial epithets "jungle bunny," "nigger," and "coon," as well) on a leering, gold-toothed pimp who promises to take him to a prostitute but tries to hold him up instead—and in return gets a "knife-whipping" from Edmond that leaves this black man half dead.

Invigorated by this act of violence and experiencing the delirious liberation of living in the moment for the first time in his life, Edmond goes on a manic jag during which he is unable to keep his mouth shut as he babbles first to this stranger, then to that. One of those strangers turns out to be Glenna, a twenty-three-year-old waitress in a coffeehouse, whom he successfully propositions and whom he tells (after bedding her at her place), in a highly racialized speech, how alive beating the pimp has made him feel. An aspiring actress, Glenna—the only named character besides Edmond because, apart from him and in contrast to the generic secondary characters of expressionistic drama in general, she is the most humanized—compares his feeling of almost Dionysian ecstasy to the one she gets when she is acting. She thus fits into, shares, or even becomes a projection of, Edmond's narcissistic framework, but only for a time, since Glenna proves to have a slightly different frame of reference from his. To wit: she refuses to join him in "leaving normal" and renouncing the past.

This provokes Edmond's rage and he kills her with his knife, as the fever of his quest for a higher reality, which has been burning through everything he has been doing, propels him past the rational into the hierophantic, the exalted, the truthful. The truth, that is, according to Edmond Burke, but a grotesque compound of his lifelong frustrations by any other name. (Does Mamet call him by this name in order to connect his reactionary thought with that of his real-life namesake, Edmund Burke [1729-1797], often regarded as the father of Anglo-American conservatism?) After he leaves Glenna's apartment, Edmond goes (like the Cashier in *From Morn to Midnight* after his bordello-visit) to a religious mission (a black Baptist one, no less) to hear a minister preach another kind of truth: that every soul can be redeemed through faith. But before he gets a chance to make his testament in front of all those assembled, Edmond is identified by the woman he accosted in the subway and arrested—at this point, presumably only for the assault of this woman and for the attempted murder of the black pimp. (The woman's coincidental appearance here jars as it would not, or would to a much lesser degree, in the less veristic or make-believe world of the theater.) And after a short reunion with his wife, who serves him with divorce papers, he ends up in a prison cell.

A big black man is assigned to his cell, and Edmond expresses conciliatory feelings toward this African-American as well as blacks in general, musing that "when we fear something, I think we wish for it." (This line echoes, or rather literalizes, the sly observation made by the female psychiatrist to the con artist in Mamet's film *House of Games*: that she wants someone, namely the con man, to take her "into a new thing.") Uninterested, his cellmate beats Edmond into granting him sexual favors. In the last scene, the two men are simply living together (perhaps for life), affectionately; and the film ends as

Edmond says "good night," kisses the other man, then turns over and goes to sleep. He thus ends in an unforeseen domesticity, enforced but safe, yet a domesticity, paradoxically, through which he reaches his apotheosis—and finds the gateway to spiritual freedom, inner peace, and personal transcendence.

All of this as the prison sex slave of his hulking black cellmate, mind you, the emphasis here being not on crushing others in an outside world where every interaction, or transaction, is a struggle for power (the typical Mamet meme), but on the tender mercy of surrender in an inside or inner world of one's own willing. If Edmond's eventual contentment in captivity suggests a Jean Genêt allegory, however, Mamet's hard, syncopated dialogue couldn't be less similar to Genêt's flowery porno-poetry. Mamet never surrenders—or never lets his characters surrender—the armor of expressionist direct-diction, which is to say the prison-house of a kind of language that so strenuously asserts the diminished self as to seal it off insuperably in its own subjective consciousness.

Mamet's theme, then, is not that we all share Edmond Burke's particular frustrations and hungers, but that we all have them in one form or another and can be interested in a man who not only discovers his own, but does so in such a way as to set himself *apart* from us—by feeling nothing beyond his own suffering. In this he again resembles Kaiser's Cashier, who never wastes a thought on the feelings or troubles of the wife and family he abandons, the waiter he cheats, the whores he abuses, the stadium spectator whose death he engineers. Ironically, the Cashier indirectly compares himself to Christ with his last words, "Ecce homo" (the same as those uttered by Pilate, in John 19:5, immediately before Jesus's crucifixion), though *Ecce homo* was also the title of the 1888 book in which Nietzsche unfavorably contrasted Christian ideals with his own superior ideal of the *Übermensch*, or superman. A cashier, of course, is no superman, but he isn't (or hasn't behaved like) a Christian, either—which is precisely Kaiser's point in having him utter words that simultaneously call to mind the Bible and Friedrich Nietzsche.

The same goes for Edmond Burke: he's a slave by the end of *Edmond*, not a superman and not even a Christian slave, and he finds himself in a hell of his own, self-satisfied creation. (Late in his existential descent, after his visit to the Baptist mission, he can be heard openly to ask, "You think there's a hell? You think we're there?") If Edmond is a martyr of a kind, moreover, he is a martyr, not for mankind, like Christ, but for men—specifically for American men of the 1980s, when the straight white male was reeling from his loss of potency at the hands of women, gays, and especially blacks in a climate of rigid political correctness as well as institutionalized affirmative action. So, after sacrificing a female waitress and an African-American pimp, Edmond sacrifices himself: to the woman who identified him as her (and the pimp's) assailant, to the wife who divorces him, and finally to the black who sodomizes him.

Mamet himself, however, has not sacrificed any of Edmond's dialogue (or any other character's, for that matter) from the play to the more visual medium of film. But he does do something that, for all the film's incisiveness, takes away from the form-conscious, almost abstract or removed, effect of the original drama. In the play of *Edmond,* that is, the twenty-three brief scenes follow one another like consecutive yet separate glimpses of a journey, a sort of mobile slide show that gives an ironclad logic to Edmond's fate, paradoxically, because of the very absence of such logic, reason, or causality from the drama's words and actions themselves. In the film, by contrast, Mamet uses connective "tissue" between the scenes or stages of Edmond's "progress," and this connectiveness takes away from the fragmented or desultory (yet nonetheless fated) quality of the play's episodes—a quality that could only be enhanced by shifting sets and characters who enter and exit from the wings, and one that is meant to mirror the fragmented or irrational perception of the protagonist himself as he manically searches out his destiny.

For example, when Edmond arrives in prison, he is dragged nude and shackled down a corridor of cells while other convicts jeer and yell at him: so we are visually told (and Edmond is bluntly informed, before the fact as it were) that this once prim Manhattan businessman has shed his pinstripe respectability, not so much for the prison stripes of an inmate as for the naked vulnerability of a jailhouse punk. In the *play,* Edmond's wife ends her visit to him in prison, the scene ends, and we then immediately find him in his cell with the black man: no transitional journey through a hostile cellblock here.

The play is thus like a medieval morality, modernized: profane, stark, abbreviated, final. The film of *Edmond* is more of a narrative stream: equally profane but less abbreviated (even at eighty minutes or so), more explanatory if not exculpatory, and consequently both less stark and less final. After all, the camera-eye, if not the eye of God, is watching Edmond and telling his tale. The play of *Edmond,* in contradistinction, presents his drama without benefit of a guide or narrator; David Mamet may have written the words, but his presence is otherwise undetectable. Indeed, in medieval terms, he is a *deus absconditus.* And Edmond himself is what Mamet impishly-cum-impiously has left behind: naked, unacccommodated, alienated man.

Edmond was directed by Stuart Gordon, who once ran Chicago's Organic Theater Company and produced as well as directed the original 1974 production of Mamet's *Sexual Perversity in Chicago.* He has since made a name for himself in the horror-film genre by adapting several H. P. Lovecraft stories to the screen, among them *Re-Animator* (1985), *From Beyond* (1986), *Castle Freak* (1995), and *Dagon* (2001). Only one touch here, a spray of blood, belongs in a horror movie; otherwise, Gordon deals fittingly with a script that has its own horror—and, unlike most horror movies, its own alchemical reality (as opposed to science fiction)—about it.

He serves *Edmond* raw, if you will, without padding (except for the aforementioned "connective tissue," which I attribute to Mamet the scenarist) and without any attempt to open the film up any more than, as a drama, it already was "open," or set in a number of different locations. This "open" or episodic aspect of *Edmond* naturally helps it to escape the "filmed play" feeling—a feeling that, unfortunately, the movie versions of Mamet's single-set plays *Oleanna* (1992; filmed 1994) and *Lakeboat* (1970; filmed 2000) could not escape. Something else helps *Edmond* to escape the theatrical trap as well: Gordon's playing of Mamet's stylized dialogue against the ultra-realism of the film's horror-suspense-thriller context, as opposed to overplaying the linguistic stylization for its own incantatory sake (as Mamet-the-writer/director himself seemed to do in *House of Games*) and thereby drying up or (to switch metaphors) flattening out the picture.

Edmond is additionally aided, in its transition from the theater to the cinema, not only by the continuity provided courtesy of Bobby Johnston's breathy, jazz-funk trumpet on the soundtrack, but also by Denis Maloney's cinematography. I'm referring both to the film's "horror look"—its hard-edged lighting by night (making the dark "colorful") and shadow-filled imagery by day (making daylight nearly black-and-white)—and to *Edmond*'s subjective or dream-like quality, as if the whole picture, the whole world, were being seen only though Edmond's feverish eyes. This expressionistic quality in the script can be realized onstage, it's true, but only with difficulty or obtrusiveness, and only intermittently, through the use of a spotlight that "sees out" exclusively from Edmond's perspective. But the point-of-view, or first-person, shot is easy to achieve in so narrative a medium as film, and we see plenty of such camera placements in *Edmond*: most of the time we are right there with the protagonist, in the middle of things, without the "relief" of any sweeping boom shots. The editing (by Andy Horwitz) also emphasizes *Edmond*'s dreamlike or subjectively expressionist aspect: one second, for example, Edmond is looking at a tarot card, and the next he's looking down at a dinner plate—the very kind of abrupt transition that is utterly natural to the dreaming, fantasizing, or "projective" mind.

Edmond's transition from stage to screen is not aided, alas, by the performance of Mamet regular William H. Macy in the leading role. The big-eared, wattle-faced Macy is not a *bad* actor; he's a *supporting* or character actor who does his best work out of the spotlight, or in the shadow of stars. (Witness his supporting performances in such films as *Boogie Nights* [1997], *Wag the Dog* [1997], *Fargo* [1996], and *House of Games*.) Macy's own supporting cast is fine, from Joe Mantegna—another Mamet regular—as the chummily racist basketball fan and Mena Suvari as a brass-tacks prostitute, to Lionel Mark Smith as the raffish pimp turned icy mugger and Julia Stiles as the waitress-cum-actress acting out the (last) scene of her life—all of these performers, with the possible exception of Stiles, seeming to be in a kind of competition to see who can play the sleaziest character. But Macy himself, as the central character, is out of his depth, or, rather, we never sense any real depth of character in his Edmond. (He was better by default as the academic in Mamet's film of *Oleanna,* where he was at least playing someone without a whole lot of depth.)

To be sure, Macy is as authentic as he can be in all the shades of the role; he never sets a foot wrong, but he never sets an especially right one, either. Thus we rarely sense the Edmond Burke in whom all these feelings—about his wife, about sex and sexuality, about race, religion, politics, and vocation—have been repressed for decades and who is now both maniacally gleeful and pitifully frightened by the bursting of his personal dam. The result is that Macy's Edmond at times appears to be an almost comic character. What the role calls for, and what Macy cannot quite provide, is the sense not of a simple robot unleashed but of a complex man who has been imprisoned for years by rote; and whose potency is only now breaking out in the only way it could at this late juncture, through physical force rather than force of character. What the role of Edmond calls for, in sum, is a virtuoso actor like Jack Nicholson—especially as we saw him, playing a similar character, in *About Schmidt* (2002).

Macy notwithstanding, *Edmond* is now available on film, in a lucid version, and I am glad for it. Whatever this version's flaws, Mamet's incantation works again. And *Edmond,* like *American Buffalo,* to name only Mamet's second-best drama (later filmed as well), is above all a species of incantation: profane, yes, but so desperate in its profanity as to take on spiritual overtones. Edmond may not be as vacuous as Don and Teach in *American Buffalo,* but, even as they do, he tries to create through language some sense of autonomous being. The difference is that the middle-class Edmond is reaching for a higher or more authentic being—hence the more singular and expressionistic his search as well as his speech; whereas Don and Teach (and to a lesser extent young Bobby, the third character in *American Buffalo*) are trying to create through their dialogue only some sense of their lowly—and shared—being, a verbal environment in which that being can at least subsist.

There is nothing romantic about *American Buffalo,* then; it is solely (if superbly) an instance of dramatic naturalism. *Edmond* begins in domestic naturalism but quickly extends beyond it, into a kind of super- or supra-naturalism that I am calling expressionism. In the process Mamet's film invokes the spirit (if not religion itself), or the spiritual search for order, meaning, and harmony, in part through its very form, that of a morality or mystery play. Thus, once again, we are indirectly reminded that the cinema began as a profane event and eventually came to include the sacred, by which it is edifyingly represented at least in part in these two films; while its predecessor, the theater (ironically, where *Edmond* originated), began as a sacred event and eventually came to include the profane—by which it is now shamelessly, nay benightedly, dominated on all the world's stages.

CHAPTER TEN

DAVID MAMET, *GLENGARRY GLEN ROSS*, AND SELLING IN AMERICAN DRAMA

David Mamet's rise to the forefront of American drama has been seen as the triumph of a minimalist, the most obvious component of whose signature style is his dialogue. (Only Sam Shepard has a comparably emphatic signature style, but his depends less on the shape and sound of words than on an offbeat, sometimes surreal use of scenic elements.) A reification of the Chicago idiom, that dialogue is carefully heightened—its degree of ebullience or rhythmic confidence being almost always in proportion, paradoxically, to the extent to which the speaker has been denatured by his social role (a denaturing apparent in the sheer number of obscenities employed). As for the other salient feature of Mamet's work, his minimalism, it is evident in the compactness of his dialogue, the relative "plotlessness" of his plays, and their dearth of stage directions as well as descriptions. Such minimalism has strong European parallels, and the downbeat tone of Mamet's drama— its articulation of a poetics of loss without any patent compensatory dimension—together with the palpable stasis of many of his endings, does seem to derive from the theater of Pinter, Beckett, and the Absurdists. But, unlike them, Mamet is more a realist-cum-naturalist and therefore a moralist, who is filled with dismay at the obsolescence and covert predatoriness of certain American myths, particularly the frontier myth as domesticated in the boys' fiction of Horatio Alger.

American Buffalo (1975) was the work that established Mamet as a major voice in the contemporary American theater and framed the distinctive qualities of his drama—qualities that would later be quintessentially reprised in the even more powerful *Glengarry Glen Ross* (1983). These are a nearly exclusionary focus on the sleazy world of masculine power, bonding, and betrayal; a meticulous deployment of his characters' urban vernacular such that, through their fractured utterances and pauses, Mamet is able to chart their inner conflicts and psychological shifts; an examination of the influence of the myths and archetypes of popular culture upon America's citizens; and a recurring concern with the world of American business in its tawdrier incarnations (where even morality is bartered as a commodity).

Set in a rundown, claustrophobic junk shop in Chicago, *American Buffalo* delineates the symbiotic relationships among three men who plan the robbery of a valuable buffalo nickel, only to have their plot go awry. Inhabiting an inner city of resident hotels, cheap diners, and pawn shops, Don, Teach, and Bobby are petty crooks without the intelligence or forethought necessary actually to carry out the robbery they propose. Indeed, their strategies for the break-in, which swing between the starkly vicious and the hilariously incompetent, ensure that their venture never gets off the ground. But the projected heist does serve to illuminate the values of these characters and to focus attention on the nature of their friendship. For these three low-lives are willing to betray each other on behalf of "business" principles that are, in fact, nothing more than selfish moves to achieve material advantage. In the process, they evoke the same hypocritical pieties and maxims as might any big-time businessman in a corporate boardroom.

Thus does Mamet imply that an entire society—of high-life, low-life, and the middle class in between—is engaged in the pursuit of monetary gain to such an extent that it has supplanted or perverted all other forms of behavior. Even in the midst of their ethical confusion and essential isolation, however, Don, Teach, and Bobby long for the compassionate interaction that their own actions constantly subvert, for the humane connection that they have sacrificed for mere survival in the competitive rat-race known as rampant capitalism. This is *American Buffalo*'s pathos, and what makes its otherwise brilliant rendering of callousness and greed, of failed communication, clumsy manipulation, and casual venality, so compelling.

Other plays by Mamet deal more positively with the possibilities of genuine communion in love or friendship. *A Life in the Theatre* (1977) and *Lakeboat* (1970; revised, 1980) are male rite-of-passage dramas and studies of mentor-protégé relationships in which the protégé moves beyond the mentor or removes himself from the mentor's sphere. *Reunion* (1976) depicts the tender meeting between an estranged father and daughter who have not seen each other for twenty years. *The Shawl* (1985) builds to an unexpected communion between a supposed clairvoyant and the wealthy woman he had earlier planned to cheat out of her fortune. *Edmond* (1982), for its part, presents a more complex and even ironic pattern in which "communion" for the protagonist is only reached on the other side of murder, in jail, in a homosexual bond with a black prisoner.

Yet another group of Mamet plays shows nascent love between men and women destroyed by a complicated array of forces not limited to the business "ethic" that dominates *American Buffalo*. In *Sexual Perversity in Chicago* (1974), the romance between an inexperienced pair of lovers is soured not only by the dog-eat-dog atmosphere of the downtown office scene, but also by their own pettiness, hesitancy, and reserve as well as the cynical ministrations of each one's older, same-sex mentor figure. In *The Woods* (1977), Mamet focuses exclusively on two lovers in an isolated cabin, revealing the emotional insecurity together with the metaphysical terror of a male on the verge of deeper commitment. And in *Speed-the-Plow* (1988; followed in 1989 by a sequel titled *Bobby Gould in Hell*), an attraction between a temporary secretary and a jaded film producer is torpedoed by his "buddy," a self-seeking Hollywood agent who decides that the woman's feelings are motivated only by her ego in the promotion of a script, or artistic "property."

The cutthroat world of Hollywood executives is not so different from the equally ruthless milieu of real-estate salesmen in *Glengarry Glen Ross,* who also peddle properties if they do not engage (onstage at least) in the exploitation, objectification, or manipulation of women. But in the process of peddling those useless properties (several of which are referred to in the play's snappy but empty title), the salesmen exploit, objectify, and manipulate *one another*; like the characters in *American Buffalo*, albeit at a somewhat higher level, they sacrifice friendship for money, fellowship for commerce, getting along for getting ahead. Mamet may express his moral outrage at the various salesmen's tactics and actions, but he also communicates his paradoxical respect for their manic energy, endless resourcefulness, and persistent ability to bounce back. Their struggle for something like existence, for triumph even, within the language they speak creates the real dynamic of this biting, funny, harrowing, finally purgative play. And that grinding, salty, relentless language—stripped of all idealistic pretenses and liberal pieties—is what stays in the audience's mind long after a reading or viewing of *Glengarry Glen Ross*. The play is readily available for viewing, since it was filmed in 1992 (though with changes designed to make the salesmen more sympathetic and their world less dark), as was *American Buffalo* in 1996 and *Oleanna* in 1994.

One of Mamet's most controversial works, *Oleanna* was first performed on stage in 1992 and investigates the issue of sexual harassment—particularly as it gets played out in an American academy undergoing profound and interrelated economic as well as social transformations. Mamet's treatment of women in his earlier plays has sometimes drawn fire, and his depiction of Carol, the student in his drama, continues to garner its share. Even the successful female psychologist of his best original screenplay, *House of Games* (which he also directed, in 1987), came under attack by feminists: for she becomes a compulsive thief after being duped, financially as well as sexually, by a gangster and then murdering him in revenge.

Perhaps the more recent *Boston Marriage* (1999) is Mamet's reaction to such criticism, as it examines a blue-blood Victorian relationship between two women and therefore may signal a new direction for this, the most protean as well as Promethean of contemporary dramatists. Then again, that new direction still includes some of the most ferocious, most unbuttoned, most politically incorrect racial and religious slurs in recent American drama, as evidenced by Mamet's *Romance* (2005), a legal farce in the tradition of the Marx brothers that features Jewish, Gentile, and homosexual characters against the background of a peace conference between the Israelis and the Palestinians. Ironically, or perhaps aptly, *Romance* opened in New York at the same time as the staccato realism of *Glengarry Glen Ross* was being revived on Broadway.

Let us now begin a detailed consideration of *Glengarry Glen Ross* and the subject of salesmen or selling. *Glengarry Glen Ross* has two, very different acts. In its three scenes, the first act offers three variations, each cast in duet-form, on the theme of persuasion. The setting is a Chinese restaurant in Chicago. In scene one, Shelly "the Machine" Levene, once a leading salesman but now fading badly, tries with increasing desperation to get the office manager, John Williamson, to give him the best "leads," or appointments with prospective customers—resorting eventually to (but not succeeding in) bribery. In the second scene, the mutually consoling gestures made by the frustrated no-hoper Moss toward the already defeated Aaronow turn out to be a tactic designed to compromise the latter man—by involving him in a plan to rob the real-estate office and sell the "hot" leads. Scene three, like scene two, also involves deception in tandem with persuasion. Richard Roma, the current star salesman and "ruler" of the office, first hypnotizes a Milque-toast called Lingk with some unbuttoned philosophizing, then pounces on his sales prey. Roma seemed to be relaxing as he talked, but in fact he was artfully doing his job. The top prize of a Cadillac in the office selling-contest is almost his. (The second man wins a set of steak knives, while the bottom two salesmen get fired.)

Act II harnesses and combines the dynamic energy of these three encounters in a more or less conventional plot structure. It is the next morning, the real-estate office or "boiler room" has been ransacked, and the leads have been stolen. Throughout the act the salesmen are called into an adjoining room for questioning by a detective named Baylen. Levene joins Aaronow, Moss, and Roma in the office, where he wants to celebrate and recount his "closing" of a big sale—which is later revealed to be a dud. Then Lingk arrives to cancel Roma's sale to *him*. Roma stalls with Levene's clever help, but when Williamson mentions that this customer's check has already been cashed, Lingk rushes out and the deal is doomed. Williamson is abusively berated for opening his mouth, first by Roma and next by Levene, but when the latter lets slip that he knows Williamson lied about the check, he betrays his own guilt for the robbery. Only the thief could have known that Lingk's check, instead of being deposited at the bank, remained sitting on the office manager's desk. Williamson reports Levene to the police. Levene squeals on Dave Moss. And

Roma resumes his predatory quest for the Cadillac—but not before making sure that he takes financial advantage of the pathetic, defenseless Levene.

Such an account of the plot of *Glengarry Glen Ross* barely hints at the linguistic virtuosity of Mamet's writing. There is a rich orchestration of voices, sounding the whirling idiom of sales-speak—"leads," "sits," "closes," boards," "streaks"—which is rhythmically sustained by a constant stream of highly expressive obscenities. The very opacity of the language—its ellipses, parataxis, and concealment (as opposed to exposition)—makes us aware of speech as *act*, as something that functions rhetorically rather than as a lucid medium of transmission or communication. For the salesman is a rhetorician whose job hinges on the power of speech, the act of utterance, the theater of the word. Whatever the words used, the rhythms, the tones, the pauses, the fragments are designed to bully, to cajole, to advance, to retreat, to seduce, to impress. ("High-speed Pinter," wrote one reviewer, and Harold Pinter happens to be the play's dedicatee.) As Mamet himself has said, "The salesmen [where I worked] were primarily performers. They went into people's living rooms and performed their play about investment properties," just as Roma improvises one fiction after another in order to snare Lingk. Indeed, these men seem never to stop performing, even when they are alone with one another: aggressive selling has become for them not merely a profession but a means of *being*, to the point that they are imprisoned within the sales-talking lingo of their lives.

The fiction that the salesmen play out among themselves concerns the "frontier ethic." This is the idea that success is attained not only through self-reliance and hard work, through the drive and initiative of the rugged individualist, but also through the partnership, dependability, and fellowship of other men. Thus Levene can declare at one point that "You have to believe in your*self*," and at another that "your partner *depends* on you . . . you have to go *with* him and *for* him . . . you can't exist alone." The predatory individualism of these men, however, introduces an inevitable, irremediable contradiction into the frontier ethic, which then becomes a vehicle for the domination of others in relationships founded on professional rivalry. Originally practiced at the expense of the Indians as well as other Americans, the frontier ethic in *Glengarry Glen Ross* is practiced at the expense of bottom-feeders like George Aaronow and their cliental counterparts—like James Lingk. He desperately needs to believe in something or someone and is conned into thinking that, through the existential act of purchase, he is affirming his essential, authentic being. What he buys, ironically, is the very land that was once taken from the Indians and has itself become a waste product of our Manifest Destiny.

Often called a *Death of a Salesman* for the 1980s, *Glengarry Glen Ross* may surpass Arthur Miller's play in its assault on the American way of making a living, for it launches that assault without a single tendentious line, without a trace of sentiment, with no social generalizations. At once savage and compassionate, trenchant and implicit, radical and stoical, sad and comic, Mamet's drama does not feature any deaths at its conclusion. A worse death has already begun for its salesmen, who are metaphorical rather than literal victims of a merciless and venal economic system. *Death of a Salesman* (1949) and Eugene O'Neill's *The Iceman Cometh* (1946) do feature deaths at their conclusions, and these two plays about selling call for some discussion, as does Tennessee Williams' *A Streetcar Named Desire* (1947)—yet another drama that has a salesman as one of its principal figures and that, along with the other two, makes up a triumvirate of the most important plays of the 1940s.

Drawing on the cultural archetype of the salesman at a time when America was proudly emerging as the richest and most powerful country on earth, Miller, O'Neill, and Williams exposed the contradictions underlying our apparent success (even as Mamet chose to do so during the booming eighties, when "greed was good"). In all three of their plays, significantly, it is at most vague as to what the salesmen are actually selling. As is well known, we never find out what Willy Loman is selling at all. Stanley Kowalski travels for an unnamed firm that apparently manufactures and markets some kind of machinery, since we hear that Mitch works "on the precision bench in the spare parts department. At the plant Stanley travels for" (40), which is all we ever hear of it. Hickey is described by O'Neill as a "hardware drummer," but we never hear anything about his hardware, which seems to have to do more with sex or death ("hardware" being a slang term for, among other things, that archetypal phallic symbol, a gun) than with any real product. Willy Loman, Stanley Kowalski, and Hickey, then, are disassociated from the merchandise they sell. And the vagueness of their products underlines the allegorical nature of their selling; each is an American everyman, in an America where what is produced becomes ever less tangible, ever more removed from reality. These three don't sell "stuff," they sell illusion—or themselves in the form of their winning personalities.

Oddly enough, however, these three salesmen don't see themselves in this way. All three consider themselves clear-eyed realists, devoted to a reality that seems as tangible to them as the Brooklyn Bridge. The salesmen of *Glengarry Glen Ross* are realists, too, out for all they can get and having no scruples about how they get it; their amorality, particularly in the case of Roma, is the very source of their charm. But these three salesmen of the 1940s are not amoral; they all have a similar moral code, which consists of a stern belief in the necessity of rejecting illusion and facing up to reality. They not only are realists, they preach realism, too—sell it, if you will. Unfortunately for them and those around them, however, their "reality" is an imaginary one, in the end as treacherous as the illusions the salesmen are out to destroy.

Stanley Kowalski himself seems cruder than the other two salesmen. His animal nature is much remarked upon; he drinks beer, copulates, plays games, smashes light bulbs, paws through Blanche's wardrobe, throws plates on the floor, even commits rape. Yet he doesn't just do these things aimlessly or impulsively. Always his objective is to deflate pretense: "Look at these feathers and furs that she [Blanche] come here to preen herself in!" (35). He is proud of having pulled Stella "down off them columns" of Belle Reve, and wants to pull Blanche down off them, too. He is also proud of being Polish, being American, being a Louisianan under the Napoleonic code. As Stanley bellows to his wife and sister-in-law, "What do you two think you are? A pair of queens? Remember what Huey Long said—'Every Man is a King!'" (107). Even his rape of Blanche seems motivated more by a desire to pierce her illusions than her body. Stanley is a dark version of the salesman, selling the idealistic Blanche a harsh reality on the specious grounds that it is somehow good for her, and willing to use force, if necessary, to make the sale.

Willy Loman is a more sympathetic figure than Stanley Kowalski, but ultimately he is even more destructive. His vision of reality is that simply being "well liked" is the key to all worldly and spiritual success: "It's not what you do, Ben. It's who you know and the smile on your face! It's contacts, Ben, contacts! . . . That's the wonder, the wonder of this country, that a man can end with diamonds here on the basis of being liked!" (86). On the face of it, this is a remarkably cynical philosophy, glorifying personal contacts while scorning traditional values like education and hard work. The odd thing about Willy, however, is that he does not think of these views as cynical, but rather as something fine, "the wonder of this country." In other words, like Stanley and, as we shall see shortly, Hickey, he is another realist, preaching his own ideal.

Another odd thing about Willy is that his views don't seem to convince anybody else in the play, any more than they do the audience. Charley, for example, counters Willy's modern view with a more traditional cynicism: "Why must everybody like you? Who liked J. P. Morgan? Was he impressive? In a Turkish bath he'd look like a butcher. But with his pockets on he was very well liked" (97). Furthermore, Willy's philosophy is proved wrong over and over again in the play, as applied to his sons Biff and Happy, to Bernard the boy next door, and to Willy himself, who ends up feeling lonely and not well liked by anybody. "You are the saddest, self-centeredest soul I ever did see-saw," says the tellingly perceptive Woman in the hotel room, Miller's version of the farmer's daughter, who then quickly follows up with the words "Come on inside, drummer boy" (116). Finally, despite all evidence to the contrary, Willy buys his own warped reality for good, by killing himself, foolishly convinced that Biff will benefit materially as well as spiritually from his death.

Hickey in *The Iceman Cometh* is another realist who preaches his own ideal and therefore has a lot in common with Willy. He, too, believes that the key to success is in being well liked: "I'd met a lot of drummers around the hotel and liked 'em. They were always telling jokes. They were sports. They kept moving. I liked their life. And I knew I could kid people and sell things" (233). And sell he did, by playing on people's pipe-dreams and making them like him. Yet, like Willy, Hickey repeatedly complains of being lonely. Like Willy, he has taken up with a woman, or women, other than his wife, a fact that hovers around the play in the form of the sex joke that is never actually told, but which nonetheless gives *The Iceman Cometh* its title. There are several versions of this joke, one of which goes like this: a man comes home and calls upstairs to his wife, "Honey, did the iceman come yet?" "Not yet," she calls back, "but he's breathing hard." The iceman is a salesman who beds another man's wife, and who sells ice—a symbol of coldness, hardness, and death. He is another "realist," a purveyor of the cold, hard truth. In popular slang, to "ice" someone is to kill him, and ultimately Hickey is an iceman too, icing his wife and icing himself in the end.

Like Willy, then, Hickey is ultimately selling death. And who are the suckers doing the buying? Certainly the *Lumpenproletariat* in the bar form a group of them, and Hickey, like Stanley, is trying to sell them a harsh reality, puncturing their pipe-dreams in the way that Stanley brutally punctured Blanche's illusions. In the end, however, the people in the bar aren't buying Hickey's vision, going back to the pipe-dreams that sustain them. In a sense, they are salesmen, too, trying desperately to sell their dreams to anyone who will listen, as well as to themselves. Their pipe-dreams are not just pleasant reveries to sustain them through life's tribulations; they are ideals that they must repeat, over and over, for each sale quickly wears off and creates the challenge to sell it yet again.

A notable difference between Hickey and Willy, like that between Roma and Levene in *Glengarry Glen Ross*, is that Hickey is a *successful* salesman. That is, he *has* been one, until he takes up trying to sell the reality-ideal. Selling was easy for him, so easy that, unlike Willy, he seems to have unlimited amounts of money, and he certainly has not lost his job. He really was "well liked"; his customers who were so easy to sell did not drop him as he got older—instead, he has dropped them. And, of course, the biggest sucker of all was his wife, who always bought his slick tales, and who always forgave him even when he brought her home a case of venereal disease. In the end, Hickey came to hate all the suckers, including his wife, Evelyn, and he killed her. It is as if the seller threw the sucker off the Brooklyn Bridge after having sold it to him, in contempt for his having been such an easy mark, and then dove in after him, in contempt for himself.

The Iceman Cometh is a greater play than *Death of a Salesman* because O'Neill realized, as he did in *Long Day's Journey into Night* (1941) and as Mamet was later to realize in *Glengarry Glen Ross*, that the tragedy of America is not a tragedy of failure but rather one of success. Willy clings to his foolish ideal until the very end, despite its obviously having failed him; Hickey rejects that very ideal, of fitting in and being liked, because it has succeeded for him too easily and too well. Unfortunately, he substitutes for his ideal another one, all the more insidious because it seems so concrete and obvious. In the end, however, it is just as manipulative and condescending to destroy people's illusions as it is to feed, or feed off, them. A realism that ignores human suffering is no genuine realism at all.

And that kind of selective realism began, perhaps more than ever before, to characterize America in the 1940s, when our country had reached the pinnacle of its success. The wars that had brought disaster to much of the world did relatively little damage to us; in fact, they made us stronger and wealthier than ever. At the same time, there was a growing unease in the country. As in Hickey's case, our success seemed easy, yet finally hollow and frustrating. Why, we plaintively asked, wasn't American success recognized as the solid, realistic achievement it obviously was? Why did alien philosophies like Communism appeal only to those with foolish pipe-dreams? Why did traditional societies not abandon their elaborate social structures, their customs and conventions, their myths and rituals—all foolish pipe-dreams of their own in favor of the new Capitalist order in which everyone was equal in his opportunity to maximize his gain? Americans, the great pragmatists, apparently would have to sell their brand of realism to the rest of the world for its own good.

This realism, called Capitalism or Free Enterprise, certainly looked solid. What could be more "realistic" than appealing to human acquisitiveness? A society that rejected tradition and culture, turning everyone into a seller or a buyer instead, was tough, strong, genuine, even moral in its way. The rest of the world was populated by old-fashioned idealistic suckers who would have to learn that greed was good. We would sell them our view, and destroy their illusions. We weren't suckers, we were do-good traveling salesmen to the whole world. Ultimately, we would try to sell our brand of realism to the Vietnamese, the Nicaraguans, the Salvadoreans, even to the Russians and then the Iraqis, if not the Iranians, never realizing that—like Stanley and Hickey and Willy, Roma, Levene, and Moss—what we are actually selling is death.

Works Cited

O'Neill, Eugene. *The Iceman Cometh*. New York: Random House, 1946.
Mamet, David. *Glengarry Glen Ross*. New York: Grove Press, 1984.

Miller, Arthur. *Death of a Salesman*. New York: Viking/Penguin, 1949.
Williams, Tennessee. *A Streetcar Named Desire*. New York: Signet/New American Library, 1947

REVIEW

THEATER CHRONICLE: THE REAL THING

On Broadway these days, disbelief is not so much suspended as it is propped up—with props. As soon as the curtain rose, it was clear that the main attraction of *La Cage aux Folles* was not going to be Gene Barry and George Hearn, playing Georges and Albin, the homosexual lovers who are, respectively, the proprietor and the drag-queen star of the eponymous cabaret. And after the first few bars of the opening number, it was also apparent that Jerry Herman's music and lyrics and Harvey Fierstein's book (based on Jean Poiret's play and the subsequent movie [1980], a cult favorite) were not responsible for the SRO crowds at the Palace Theater.

No, the real attraction was David Mitchell's set of Chinese boxes-within-boxes: a light-studded proscenium that broke in half, rotated, and turned into the exterior, the interior, and the backstage area of the nightclub, then into George and Albin's house, finally into the St. Tropez waterfront. While the sets were transmogrifying, the characters covered the intervening "distance" by walking in place, much like the "break dancers" who have become such a common and tiresome sight on big-city streets—or so I initially thought. I quickly realized, though, that the cast was not composed of mimes who could seem to stroll without making any progress. Once again, Mitchell deserved credit, this time for crafting what appeared to be strips of flooring that could be moved backward at the same time that pedestrians atop them moved forward.

The collective gasp that greeted each successive special effect rivaled the appreciation of moviegoers at, say, *Star Wars*. No doubt a great deal of the audience's reaction was a form of self-congratulation—an appropriate response, it seems safe to say, on the part of theatergoers who had waited weeks to get tickets that were priced at $45, in order to defray the reported $5 million required to produce the show. Even though *La Cage aux Folles* wasn't any damn good, it was (in the fashionable advertising argot) the "Broadway sensation of the year." So acclaim was not so much earned as bought.

More important, the audience was reacting, though with perhaps less self-awareness, to a new mode of theatricality on Broadway. It could be called Hyper-realism, to distinguish it from its Super and Magic counterparts in contemporary painting and fiction. Better still, Idiot Realism, since its intent is not to represent but to replicate, not to engage the imagination (not even a little) but to coerce the senses. "You want to see a cabaret?" I can hear the producer, Allan Carr, asking. "We won't just make something that *looks* like a cabaret. We'll actually *build* one, right there on stage." Indeed, the sets could not have been more realistic—unless they were covered with dollar bills.

What is so odd is that this Idiot Realism should be in the service of a play that is supposed to be about artifice—about men pretending to be women, about lovers pretending to be just friends, about psychological truth that expresses itself in duplicity. *La Cage aux Folles* should be theatrical in the most flamboyant way, its form matching its content. Instead, it is literal-minded to a terrifying degree—so much so that *nothing* in the play seems like anything except exactly what it is. "Les Cagelles," the drag princesses who accompany Albin, look like linebackers in tights. Hearn looks like nothing more and nothing less than a middle-aged man in mascara. (Compare him to the "heroine" of Fierstein's *Torch Song Trilogy*, whose transformation is so shocking, and convincing, because it comes from within, not simply from a make-up kit.) And Barry just looks middle-aged, a has-been television actor whose soft-shoe routine is even harder for the audience to watch than it must be for him to execute.

Worst of all, the title and lyrics of Herman's big number, which brings down the first-act curtain with a whimper, not a bang, have everything backward (which I should have anticipated in a show whose primary purpose apparently was to make transvestism palatable to the bridge-and-tunnel matinee set). "I am what I am," sings Albin defiantly, instead of proclaiming what you would expect from a self-respecting drag queen, confident of his/her non-identity: "I am what I am *not*." I admit that *I* was not interested enough to stay for the second act. Nor would I have lasted past the intermission of Marsha Norman's *'night, Mother*—except there wasn't one.

The play had only one act, stretched to the almost unbearable length of exactly ninety minutes. That's right: *exactly* ninety minutes. I know; I timed it. So did everyone else at the John Golden Theatre—audience, cast, and crew. There was a big clock hanging conspicuously on the back wall of the single set, a "relatively new house built way out on a country road." In yet another deadening display of Idiot Realism, dramatic time matched real time as the timepiece ticked away till the end of the play—when a bell should have signaled (but didn't) our grateful escape from the theater.

With such a mechanical windup, the climax came as no surprise (nor was it supposed to), either to the audience or to the two characters, Jessie Cates (played by Kathy Bates) and her mother, Thelma Cates (Anne Pitoniak). *'night, Mother* takes the form of a debate between mother and daughter over Jessie's decision to commit suicide, but the outcome is rigged. Jessie is quietly determined, Thelma not so quietly deranged. While daughter is patiently cleaning a gun in preparation for the big-bang finale, mother is prattling on inanely about hot chocolate, knitting, television, and a host of lowbrow concerns with which Norman has burdened her in order to let the audience know that this is a drama about Real People.

In keeping with one of the leading principles of Idiot Realism—that "too much ain't enough" (as the sign reads on the Lone Star café in lower Manhattan)—Thelma is only one of the many crosses her daughter bears. Jessie is overweight and homely. Her father has died. Her son is a petty thief. Her husband has deserted her. And if all that were not enough, she also suffers from epilepsy, though (incredibly) no one ever told her about it while she was growing up. In fact, Jessie's reasons for killing herself are so obvious and numerous that a coroner could cite sheer concatenation as the cause of death. (As if her mother's bad taste alone were not enough!) Such an over-determined life (and death) is not worth examining, much less living—or dramatizing. The grinding inevitability of that onstage clock is thus not so much tragic as pathetic, realism at its most unrealistic.

Somehow, *'night, Mother* won a Pulitzer Prize. I suppose the logic was to honor the playwright, not the play; Norman's previous work, *Getting Out*, was more deserving, though no masterpiece, either. I have even heard *'night, Mother* hailed as a display of her range as a writer. But that strikes me a little like praising a baseball slugger for his ability to hit long foul balls as well as home runs. When the range is from very good to very bad, as in this case, I would like to see a somewhat smaller spread, with a lot more of the "hits" approaching the former than the latter.

A Soldier's Play itself won the Pulitzer Prize a couple of seasons back, and, as produced by the Negro Ensemble Company under the direction of Douglas Turner Ward, Charles Fuller's play deserved the award. But, now that the smoke (see below) has cleared, we can see that it deserves criticism as well as praise, and I'd like belatedly to offer some here.

Set in 1944, *A Soldier's Play* could also have been written then; it is a straightforward piece of psychological (as opposed to Idiot) realism that takes the form of a murder mystery. In the first scene, Vernon C. Waters (performed by Adolph Caesar), a Tech/Sergeant in the 221st Chemical Smoke Generating Company, is killed by two unknown assailants. Waters is black, as are the other noncoms and enlisted men at Fort Neal, Louisiana, in the year before the end of World War II. Suspecting that the killers are white and fearing a racial conflict between the soldiers and the residents of nearby Tynan, the white officers restrict the troops to the base and order an investigation.

A black captain, Richard Davenport (Charles Brown), assigned to the military police, arrives at Fort Neal to conduct the inquiry (and to narrate the play, which consists largely of flashbacks in multiple locations, whose identity therefore—and mercifully—had to be suggested rather than idiotically replicated). Davenport is reluctantly assisted by a white captain, Charles Taylor (Peter Friedman), a West Pointer who makes known his antagonism by aggressively announcing, "I never saw a Negro until I was twelve or thirteen." Still, it is clear to both of them that the investigation is supposed to fail, since everyone assumes that the murderers are white and that consequently it will be impossible to bring them to justice in the South. "Don't take yourself too seriously," Taylor warns Davenport, who sardonically acknowledges that "the matter was given the lowest priority."

Nonetheless, the black captain persists, eventually daring to cast suspicion on two white officers, Lieutenant Byrd (Sam McMurray) and Captain Wilcox (Stephen Zettler). By this time, Taylor has grudgingly come to respect Davenport's efforts; in fact, he is even more eager than his black colleague to bring charges against his fellow whites. But Davenport has begun to believe that the case is more than an incident of racial violence. His questioning of the black soldiers gradually leads him—and us—to the uncomfortable realization that the murder was committed by someone under Waters' command.

As the captain digs deeper, a complex portrait of the dead sergeant emerges from the flashbacks that grow out of the interrogation sessions around which the play is structured. A veteran of World War I, Waters is a career man and a strict disciplinarian who expects his troops to toe the white man's line as squarely as he does. When he busts Corporal James Wilkie (Steven A. Jones) to the rank of private for being drunk on duty, Waters complains, "No wonder they treat us like dogs." His favorite target for abuse is a Southern black, Private C. J. Memphis (David Alan Grier), who represents everything he despises. Pleasant but slow-witted, Memphis is the star of the company baseball team, as well as a mournful blues guitarist and singer. But to Waters, a Northerner, Memphis is nothing but an embarrassing exemplar of a "clown in blackface." "Niggers ain't like that today," the sergeant sneers.

Waters is no simple Uncle Tom, however. "This country's at war," he tells his men, "and you niggers are soldiers." To him, they must be more than good soldiers—they must be the best, for their own sake if not the army's. "Most niggers just don't care," he claims. "But not havin's no excuse for not gettin'. We got to challenge the man in *his* arena." In his twisted way, Waters truly believes that the black race can only advance by following his example— by being better than the white man at his own game. "Do you know the damage one ignorant Negro can do?" he asks Memphis. "The black race can't afford you no more. . . . The day of the geechy is gone, boy."

Davenport soon learns the lengths to which Waters went to "close our ranks to the chittlin's, the collard greens—the corn-bread style." During the year before his death, the company team had been so successful that a game with the Yankees was in the works if the Fort Neal soldiers were to win their conference title. But the better the troops do on the field, the worse they do on the base. "Every time we beat them at baseball," the black soldiers complain about their white opponents, "they get back at us in any way they can"—in work details ranging from KP to painting the officers' club. Waters, of course, believes "these men need all the discipline they can get," since he regards their athletic achievements as frivolous, even dangerous, pursuits, because they reinforce the white man's stereotype of the "strong black buck."

To his horror, Davenport discovers that Waters found a way of eliminating Memphis while simultaneously sabotaging the baseball team. The sergeant framed the hapless private for a mysterious shooting on the base ("one less fool for the race to be ashamed of"), and when Memphis hanged himself in the stockade, the players threw the championship game in protest. But the ultimate cost of Waters' demented discipline was a growing desire for vengeance among his troops. As Davenport finally determines, two of them— Private First Class Melvin Peterson (Denzel Washington) and Private Tony Smalls (Brent Jennings)—took matters into their own hands and killed their tormentor. Yet even at the moment of his death, Waters had the last word, or words—the same ones that opened the play. "You got to be like them!" he cries in torment. "And I was! I was—but the rules are fixed. . . . It doesn't make any difference. They still hate you!"

Whatever else can be said about *A Soldier's Play*, Fuller must be credited for creating a truly tragic character for whom those words are an anguished, self-proclaimed epitaph. It is in Waters, then, that the toll of racism is most apparent. To be sure, all the black characters in the drama are representative of different modes of dealing with white oppression: the cautious rationality of Davenport, the self-abasement of Wilkie (brilliantly brought to life by Jones), the unenlightened self-interest of Smalls. Likewise, Memphis embodies the black past, stolid and humble, just as surely as Peterson represents the future, or at least one possible future: righteous but also arrogant.

Yet Waters is unique among the men by being both the engineer of his own downfall and the victim of circumstances not of his own making; like all genuinely tragic figures, he attains universality because of, rather than despite, the stubborn reality of his particularity. From the smallest of his affectations— the pompous, gravelly voice, the pipe-smoking, the military carriage, the cultivated disdain for his inferiors—to the enormity of his crimes against his own people in their name, the costs of Waters' unnatural, willful assimilation to the white man's ways are painfully apparent. ("Any man ain't sure where he belongs," says Memphis, "must be in a whole lotta pain.") Fuller's resolute writing and Caesar's forceful acting have created a positively unlikeable yet strangely sympathetic character, a manifestly unpleasant man who is nonetheless unexpectedly revealing of what we fear are the worst accommodationist impulses in ourselves—racial or otherwise.

Unfortunately, Fuller does not handle the investigation into Waters' violent death as ably as he does his characterization of the sergeant's life. Somehow the murder mystery comes to dominate the other elements of the play, such as the problems of human behavior in adverse circumstances—race war or world war—which become secondary to the whodunit questions of motive and opportunity. True, the investigation gives the drama a certain forward momentum, but not enough to disguise the fact that almost everything interesting takes place in the past. The most compelling figure is the victim, whose life is revealed entirely in flashback; while the action in the present is, for the most part, structured according to the time-honored strategy of revelations leading to further revelations and ultimately to a rather comfortable resolution.

Not too comfortable, mind you: Peterson and Smalls are apprehended, according to Davenport, but

> In northern New Jersey, through a military foul-up, Sergeant Waters' family was informed that he had been killed in action. The Sergeant was, therefore, thought and unofficially rumored to have been the first colored casualty of the war from the county and under the circumstances was declared a hero. . . . The men of the 221st Chemical Smoke Generating Company? The entire outfit—officers and enlisted men—was wiped out in the Ruhr Valley during a German advance.

Fuller is to be commended, as well, for honestly exposing how racism distorts the soul of not just the oppressor but the victim.

For this genuine revelation (as opposed to the convenient revelations that advance the plot) to matter to us, however, it must matter to the character through whose eyes we perceive it. And it is not unreasonable to expect that Davenport's discoveries will change him—somehow. After all, he began his inquiry more or less convinced that the killers were white, and then had to overcome his own prejudices to uncover the truth. He might also have seen something of himself in Waters. Though younger, the captain (who is also a lawyer) must have had to pay the same dues as the sergeant—perhaps even more, to rise to the higher rank and get the college education.

Yet Davenport maintains an eerie emotional distance throughout the play. (This distance is underscored by Brown's rather affectless performance, during which he is so cool that he practically freezes into rigidity.) Perhaps Fuller thereby meant to comment on the captain's notion of soldierly conduct, which causes him to be almost color-blind. Indeed, early in the play, Davenport rebuffs Wilkie's presumption of racial familiarity ("You all we got down here," the private avers.) But this sort of irony seems absent elsewhere, particularly from the author's decision to set the play so far in the past.

I do not think the drama required the segregated army, which came to an end after the war; in fact, the play might have been more pointed had it been set after integration. (As for the war itself, it could as easily have been Korea or Vietnam—or no war at all, for all the difference it makes to the action.) In setting the play before the period of integration, did Fuller believe that the attitudes represented by, say, Memphis and Waters would seem outdated today? That Davenport, too, would seem anachronistic, or even Peterson insufficiently militant? Or did he think (or does he recognize) that setting *A Soldier's Play* in 1944 somehow lets all of us—playwright, cast, audience—off the hook? Or was it that he wanted all concerned to consider the drama purely as art rather than as "relevant" social comment? It is not that I suspect Fuller's motives—it is just that I don't know what they are.

Hence, impressive drama though it may be, *A Soldier's Play* is not a totally satisfying work of art. I regrettably suspect that it has been indulged far more than it deserves, for the mere fact of its subject matter. To be sure, at a time when the problem of race relations is fading from the public consciousness, it takes some courage to confront it—let alone the subject of racial self-hatred—at all on stage. But though they are worth something, good intentions are not enough—particularly not in the drama, where *action*, not intent, is the *modus operandi*.

Now back to the subject of Idiot Realism: one refreshing alternative to the fifty-seven varieties of such Idiocy now bottled on, as well as off, Broadway is Sam Shepard's version of realism in *Fool for Love*, at the Circle Repertory. For lack of a better term it can be called Magic Realism, in honor not of the genre of writing or painting (though it likewise weds realistic form and surrealistic content) but of Martin Esslin's Magic Theatre in San Francisco, with which Shepard has long been associated and where *Fool for Love* was first produced.

Set in a cheap motel room somewhere in the Mojave desert, the drama proceeds along the familiar lines of recrimination leading to revelation, prompting further recriminations and further revelations. Andy Stacklin's gloriously sleazy furnishings, Ardyss L. Golden's wonderfully grungy costumes, the colloquial language, the kitchen-sink style of acting—all suggest at first that *Fool for Love* is yet another down-home drama about Real People. But in his typical manner, Shepard quickly launches the play into the realm of the fantastic, though all the while grounding it in the poetic imagery, visual and verbal, of the mundane.

May (acted by Kathy Whitton Baker) and Eddie (Ed Harris) are trapped together, perhaps voluntarily, in that remote motel. They are lovers, but also—maybe—siblings. Perhaps May is waiting for another man, Martin (Dennis Ludlow); perhaps Eddie is running from another woman (the unseen Countess). Perhaps not. Maybe the Old Man (Will Marchetti) sitting off to the side of the stage is the father of both of them, maybe not. Sometimes he is an invisible spectator to their interaction, sometimes an active participant in it.

"I want to show you something," the Old Man remarks to Eddie, pointing to an imaginary picture on the opposite wall. "Barbara Mandrell [the country singer]. That's who that is. . . . That's realism. I am actually married to Barbara Mandrell in my mind." Later, May tells Eddie: "I can't even see you now. All I see is a picture of you. You and her [the Countess]. I don't even know if the picture's real anymore. I don't even care. It's a made-up picture." "Why should I believe it [what Eddie has been saying about needing May] this time?" she asks still later. "Because it's true," he replies. "It was supposed to have been true every time before," May complains. "Every other time. Now it's true again."

This is not, however, merely *Rashomon*-like relativity, though Shepard does consistently undercut every expectation that he so carefully establishes, as both the writer and director of *Fool for Love*. As the play progresses, it becomes clear that May and Eddie are participating in a familiar ritual of desire and despair that has enthralled them for a long time. "We'll always be connected," he says. "That was decided a long time ago." "Nothing was decided," she retorts. "You made that all up." But making it up is the essence of their relationship. "Lying's when you believe it's true," Eddie proclaims. "If you already know it's a lie, then it's not lying."

The point is not truth, but drama. Each re-enactment gives the lovers a chance to rekindle the lust that consumes them. First May is contemptuous of Eddie; the next moment she can barely keep her hands off him. Then she kisses him passionately, only to knee him in his groin seconds later. And from desire to revulsion and back again, each re-enactment gives them the opportunity to dramatize themselves, to re-create themselves over and over again. "I thought you were supposed to be a fantasist, right?" the Old man asks Eddie. "Isn't that basically the deal with you? You dream things up. Isn't that true?" Most of all, what Eddie and May dream up is different versions of their past, separate and shared. "How many times have you done this to me?" May asks Eddie. "Suckered me into some dumb little fantasy."

It's both dumb and fantastic: characters who exist because they perform a ritual. For an audience, it should be noted: not us, the ticket-holders in our seats, but the Old Man, off to the side. The stage directions in the published version of *Fool for Love* confirm my supposition (which was not shared, incidentally, by most reviewers) that the Old Man "exists only in the minds of May and Eddie." It is only because they see themselves through his eyes that they can be performing at all, instead of just existing for our sake. And it is because of *their* awareness of being on their own stage, in the mind's eye of the Old Man, that *we* are aware of the theatricality of their lives. We see them "living" on stage not for us, but for themselves, for each other, and for their audience of one—and reminding us, all the while, not only of our own "presentation" of self in everyday life, but also of the ritualistic or repetitive nature of all human existence.

This is the essence of Shepard's Magic Realism: positing the theatricality of the mundane, the familiar. In *Fool for Love*, he reveals the essential, and paradoxical, *artificiality* of realism (or naturalism). It is a mode of drama like any other, something that the practitioners of Idiot Realism forget. And it is by no means a "transparent," slice-of-life mode: it has its own artistic conventions, even though they are not often enough acknowledged as such. Shepard self-consciously uses realism not as a transparent mode of dramatization through characterization (his plays are never really "about" their characters or the problems of those characters), but as a theatrical device, a formal mode manipulated to yield up surprising results, in image as well as action.

A play, Shepard knows, does not become more realistic as its sets and effects become more realistic. Just the opposite, frequently. Unlike movies, which can go a long way toward convincing us of the reality of what they represent (violence, monsters, space ships), plays work best on the mind, not the senses—or on the mind *through* the senses. The more the pains taken and the more money the spent on a production, the more conscious we are that what we are seeing is not the real thing but something that *looks* like it: an artificial product bought with dollars, not a work created by art. This is how Idiot Realism undermines itself. But, as Sam Shepard well understands (and as do Charles Fuller and Harvey Fierstein at their best—the latter in *Torch Song Trilogy*, the former in the sparely designed flashback sequences of *A Soldier's Story*), what is most real on stage is what you cannot see.

Spring 1984

PART II:

THEORY IN PRACTICE,
OR DRAMATURGY AND CRITICISM

CHAPTER ONE

RICHARD GILMAN, AMERICAN THEATER CRITIC: AN APPRECIATION

Along with his contemporaries Eric Bentley, Stanley Kauffmann, and Robert Brustein, Richard Gilman (1923-2006) was a major critical voice—one who, in his two collections of dramatic criticism, *Common and Uncommon Masks* (1971) and *The Drama Is Coming Now* (2005), chronicles a major period in American theater history, the 1960s to the 1980s. These were the decades that witnessed the birth or spread of Off-Broadway, Off-Off Broadway, regional theater, non-profit companies, avant-garde performance (of which Gilman was one of the first acute critics, if not the very first), and interest in plays by women and minorities, as well as in *world* drama as opposed to plays exclusively of the Euro-American kind. During this period Gilman served, at different times, as the drama critic for *Commonweal, Newsweek,* and *The Nation*, three well-known magazines that made his name well known among those interested in theater and in the writing about it. In addition, he contributed numerous essays and articles to such important publications as *The New York Times, The New Republic, Partisan Review, The Village Voice, Tulane Drama Review* (*The Drama Review* or *TDR* today), and *American Theatre*.

The pieces gathered in *Common and Uncommon Masks* and *The Drama Is Coming Now* are not academic criticism of the kind even scholars are reluctant to read; they are criticism in the *belles lettres* tradition—deeply felt, scintillatingly reasoned, and beautifully articulated. Gilman had fastidious taste, but he was no prig; he had wide learning, but he did not use it to condescend either to his subject or his reader. He approached plays with the old-fashioned belief that they should be an imaginative entry into another world than our own, and not grist for the latest theoretical mill. In short, Richard Gilman was the kind of critic who is fast disappearing from our cultural scene: unaligned and unafraid, with an interest as much in the life around him as in the life of the mind and the theatrical forms that nourish it. His writing in these books and elsewhere proves, yet again, that criticism is a talent, not something you are automatically equipped to produce just because you have spent the requisite years in graduate school.

Indeed, euphoria is what I feel when I find a writer and critic like Richard Gilman, who used language as if it had never been debased, as if it came shining and newly minted from the best of all possible dictionaries. When I realize, in Wallace Stevens' words, that I will not have to "uncrumple this much-crumpled thing," that an author has freely given me his meaning with all the generosity of which English is still capable, I feel as Robert Frost did after reading D. H. Lawrence's poems: "I wanted to go to that man," he declared, "and say something to him." In *Common and Uncommon Masks* and *The Drama Is Coming Now*, Richard Gilman says something to *me*. He uses words so exactingly here, with so little spill or waste of significance, that, in reading the latter and re-reading the former, I found myself startled again and again into a smile. To see a thing done so precisely gave me an almost *animal* pleasure. I smiled not just because Gilman had surprised me, but because I felt once again that there is life—robust life—in these odd sounds we emit. Only a moment ago, language seemed so lame, so tired, so thick, and now he makes it perform like a daredevil or a dancer.

But the drama was Gilman's subject, not dance and certainly not daredeviltry. And he was a bold, provocative, impassioned, rigorous critic of that drama, rather like a maverick politician who, knowing he'll never be elected, presents himself as an exhilarating witness to the truth. Like all good teachers—and a critic *is* a teacher, in print if not in the classroom—Richard Gilman had, in Ernest Hemingway's phrase, a built-in, shock-proof crap detector. He was forever asking embarrassing questions. Like all authentic artists—and a critic is, in his way, also an artist—Gilman lampooned all who have recourse to the theater's accepted bag of tricks. His appreciation attached strictly to what he considered both meaningfully innovative and artistically well-wrought; he had little sympathy for earnest but unsuccessful drama. Believing that "the theater is only alive . . . when it is being brash, irreverent (or imaginatively reverent), disturbing, antic, dangerous, and even cruel," Gilman simultaneously believed that "reviewers" kill the theater with their kindness toward what is shoddy, pat, showy, cheap, pretentious, and even false.

I want to make a distinction here between reviewers and critics—one that Richard Gilman himself often makes in *The Drama Is Coming Now*, even as he did in his earlier collection of dramatic criticism, *Common and Uncommon Masks*. This distinction is snobbish, if you will, indecorous, perhaps quixotic. But it seems to me that we are never going to get out of the miasma of deceit, self-pity, and wishful thinking that rises from the theater in this country as it does from no other medium, unless we begin to accept the distinctions that operate in actuality between actors and stars, dramas and hits, art and artisanship—and critics and reviewers.

Perhaps the greatest irony in a situation bursting with ironies is the reiterated idea that the *critics* are killing the theater. Now we all know that when theater people or members of the public refer to the "critics," they almost always mean the New York reviewers. It is certainly true that the critics—those persons whom the dictionary describes as "skilled in judging the qualities or merits of some class of things, especially of literary or artistic work"—have long harbored murderous thoughts about the condition of our drama, but their ineffectuality as public executioners is legendary. The reviewers, by contrast, come close to being the most loyal and effective allies the commercial theater could possibly desire. (They are killing the *non*-commercial theater.) But not close enough, it would seem, for this "marriage" constitutes the case of an absolute desire encountering a relative compliance.

As a corollary of its demand for constructive criticism the theater insists on absolute loyalty, and clearly receives a very high degree of it from reviewers, who are all "theater lovers" to one or another flaming extent. And that brings us to our second irony. For "loyalty in a critic," Bernard Shaw wrote, "is corruption." This richly disturbing remark comes near the heart of so much that is wrong in the relationship between the stage and those who write about it from seats of power or places of romantic yearning. From the true critics the theater generally gets what can only be interpreted as gross infidelity, the reason being—as Shaw and every other major observer of drama makes abundantly clear, and as our own sense of what is civilized should tell us—that the critic cannot give his loyalty to people and institutions, since he owes it to something a great deal more permanent.

He owes it, of course, to truth and dramatic art. Once he sacrifices truth to human beings or art to institutions, he is corrupt, unless, as is so frequently the case, he has never had any capacity for determining truth or any knowledge of dramatic art; for such persons, corruption is clearly too grandiose a condition. But at least some reviewers are people of ordinarily developed taste and some intellectual maturity, and it is among them that corruption—in the sense not of venality or outright malfeasance but of the abandonment of a higher to a lower good—operates continually and in the name of that very loyalty which is worn like a badge of honor.

The point about reviewers is that they exist, consciously or not, to keep Broadway functioning within staked-out grounds. They preserve it as the arena for theatrical enterprises that may neither rise above an upper limit determined by a line stretching between the imaginations of Lillian Hellman, William Inge, and Richard Rodgers, nor sink beneath a lower one marked out by the inventiveness and sense of life of Norman Krasna, Harry Kurnitz, and Garson Kanin. (These are names from Broadway's supposed Golden Age; they have changed, but nothing else has.) Whatever creeps into the spaces north or south of this Central Park of the imagination is adventitious, arbitrary, and hermetic; if it is good, if it is art, if it is *Waiting for Godot,* its presence on the Street may confidently be ascribed to someone's idea of a joke that just might pay off. (Beckett's masterpiece was billed in advertisements as "the laugh riot of two continents.")

Outside the theater's hothouse, not part of its clubbiness, its opening-night ceremonies, or its cabalisms, unconsulted about the honors it awards itself every year, and owing no more devotion to it than the literary critic owes to publishers or the art critic to galleries, the serious critic of drama like Richard Gilman is left free—to do what? *To judge.* "There is one and only one justification for the trade of drama criticism," George Jean Nathan wrote, "and that is to criticize drama and not merely apologize for it." Shaw went further:

> A critic is most certainly not in the position of a co-respondent in a divorce case: he is in no way bound to perjure himself to shield the reputation of the profession he criticizes. Far from being the instigator of its crimes and the partner of its guilty joys, he is the policeman of dramatic art; and it is his express business to denounce its delinquencies.

It is this idea of the critic as policeman that infuriates theater people to the limit of their anarchistic temperaments.

Go through the three volumes of Shaw's criticism, or police blotter, covering as many London seasons, and you will find that not once in any sequence of fifteen to twenty reviews was he anything but indignant at what he was called upon to see. Without pity he excoriated the theater of the 1890s, which sounds so much like our own, with its "dull routine of boom, bankruptcy, and boredom," its performers' "eternal clamor for really artistic work and their ignominious collapse when they are taken at their word by Ibsen or anyone else," its lugubrious spectacle of "the drama losing its hold on life." Only when, once or twice a year, something came along that actually had a hold on life did Shaw's critiques turn enthusiastic and positive. But not "constructive"; you do not patronize or act generously toward artistic achievement—you identify it.

For if the critic is not the maker of dramatic art, he is the person most able to say what it is, and at the same time to establish the conditions under which it may flourish or at least gain a foothold. By being negative or *destructive,* if you will, toward everything else, he can help it outlast the ephemera described as "smash" and "riot" and "socko," as "haunting," "riveting," and "stunning." And he will do his championing nearly always in the teeth of the coiners of these inimitable if vacuous terms. To the handful of great journalist-critics the English-speaking stage has had—Shaw, Max Beerbohm, Nathan, and Stark Young; Eric Bentley, Stanley Kauffmann, Robert Brustein, and ultimately Richard Gilman—we owe most of our knowledge of the permanent drama of our time, and in most cases we owe even the opportunity to read or see it.

When, for instance, the London reviewers were doing their best to drive Ibsen back to the depraved Continent (*Ghosts* was "unutterably offensive," "revoltingly suggestive and blasphemous," "a dirty act done publicly"), it was Shaw, along with William Archer, who fought brilliantly and implacably to keep open the door to a resurrected drama. Later, Nathan helped O'Neill past the roadblock of those newspapermen who characteristically admired his "power" while being terrified of his thematic and technical innovations. And, in the 1950s, the truly heroic work of Eric Bentley—both in introducing us to the most vital contemporary as well nineteenth-century European plays and in promulgating standards for a potentially mature American theater—is a monument to the critical spirit at its untiring best. When, for example, in 1959 Jack Gelber's *The Connection* was savaged by the daily newspapers, it was salvaged through the combined support of Bentley and other magazine critics, just as, three years earlier, these intellectual critics had rehabilitated the American reputation of *Waiting for Godot* after its disastrous reception at the hands of such reviewers as Walter Kerr. (The process used to work the way, too: in 1958, Archibald MacLeish's *J. B.* was more accurately evaluated by the weekly critics after *The New York Times* had called it "one of the most memorable works of the century.")

If the history of the modern theater, then, is one of mutual suspicion between the playwright and his audience—or between the playwright and his audience's stand-in, the reviewer—the history of the postmodern theater here in America is one of quick rewards and instant media replay. In this arena, the serious writer fights not poverty and neglect but the fickleness of a culture that picks him up and discards him before he has had sufficient time to develop properly. Like any jaded culture, ours hungers not for experience but for novelty, while an army of media commentators labors ceaselessly to identify something new. In such an atmosphere, where unorthodoxy becomes a new orthodoxy and fashion the arbiter of taste, the function of the vanguard artist, sacrificing popularity for the sake of penetrating uncharted ground, is radically changed. The emblematic avant-garde figure is no longer the expatriate playwright, exiled from nation, home, and church, but rather Julie Taymor— catapulted from the lofts of the Open Theater and the Chelsea Theater Center (where she began) to the Broadway stage, where, through *The Lion King,* she peddles visual emptiness and dramatic pabulum, in the guise of experimental technique, to fat cats and wide-eyed tourists at $100 at throw.

One of the causes of this condition can be found in the peculiar relationship between the American playgoer and the American theater critic, for never before has a handful of reviewers possessed so much power and lacked so much authority. The mediocrity of newspaper, radio, and television reviewing throughout the country is nothing new—it is the inevitable result, first, of the need for haste, and, second, of choosing reviewers from the ranks of journalism (from the sports page, say, or from what used to be known as the women's department) rather than from literary or professional training grounds. What is new, and most depressing, is the scarcity of decent critics *anywhere.* It is almost as if the theater had been abandoned by men and women of intelligence and taste, only to be delivered over wholesale to the publicists, the proselytizers, and the performing seals.

Among them was Clive Barnes of *The New York Times.* It was always difficult to take seriously the judgments of a man, like Barnes, who could speak in nothing but superlatives—who, in the course of a single year, said that five or six different actors were giving the most brilliant performances of their careers, called eight or nine resident companies one of the finest in the country, announced four or five plays to be the best of this or any other season, compared a young writer who had just completed his first play with the mature Chekhov, and identified Stacy Keach as the finest American Hamlet since Barrymore, though Barnes was too young to have seen Barrymore's performance. Barnes's use of hyperbole, with its promiscuous display of the word *best,* exposed not the splendors of the theater season but rather its bankruptcy, for it suggested that his need to identify works of merit or interest had far outrun the theater's capacity to create them.

Obviously, no theater can benefit in the long run from fake approval, partly because the critic becomes discredited, partly because the spectator grows disenchanted, partly because the theater practitioner begins to lose faith in his craft. The very rare work with serious aspirations thus gets lost in the general atmosphere of praise—either because it is ignored or unappreciated, or more likely because it is acclaimed in the same way as everything else. When the inspired and the routine are treated exactly alike, the act of criticism comes to seem arbitrary and capricious; when the corrective impulse is abandoned the whole construct of standards breaks down. A serious *literary* artist can always hope for an understanding review or two in the midst of the general incomprehension, and anyway, regardless of reviews, his book continues to exist for future generations to discover. But the theater artist writes on air, and preserves his work only in the memories of those who see it. In the present critical atmosphere, even those memories are tainted. The marriage that must exist in any art form between the mind that creates and the mind that judges has for the most part dissolved in the theater, with the result that the art form itself is in danger of losing its purpose and direction.

I'm speaking only about the United States, of course. In Rome, Paris, and Berlin, critics like Richard Gilman are likely to be found writing for leading newspapers, rather then being relegated to the back pages of weekly, monthly, or even quarterly intellectual magazines. And the reasons for this development can be found in the history of American theater criticism, which has outlines that, not surprisingly, correspond to large socio-cultural movements. To wit: as American society became less dependent on the theater for diversion (with the advent of film, radio, and the automobile), as the middle class turned into the pseudo-aristocracy, as new wealth gave more people a leisure that had once been restricted to a few, including the leisure to be elegantly bored, there arose a tribe of critics whose principal qualifications were urbanity, wit, and fundamental non-commitment to the theater. In this country a chief haven for that kind of critic has been *The New Yorker,* which, from its outset as well as from its very insignia, has always had a strong streak of Anglophilia— promulgated over the years by such (unidentical) critics as Alexander Woollcott, Wolcott Gibbs, Brendan Gill, and Robert Benchley.

A quite different kind of reviewing also arose in America, out of the same root social causes. Newspaper and mass-magazine reviewing in the first half of the twentieth century was, understandably, in the hands of representatives of this new middle class, men who represented both the appetite for boredom and an equivalent appetite for cultural acquisition at a level that imposed no strain. Mr. Average Man filled the job to the average man's satisfaction, his virtue being that he knew just as little as the common spectator, and sometimes even less. But where American cultural and intellectual life had been relatively homogeneous in the nineteenth century, it was now dividing into major and minor elements—again, for a complex of social reasons.

One of the minority elements found its critical voice around the turn of the century, approximately, with the "arrival" of James Gibbon Huneker and the now-forgotten Percival Pollard. The theme of this "adversary" criticism was that American culture was provincial, puritanical, and benighted, and that mass-media criticism was banal when not together dumb. Huneker, who criticized several arts, developed these ideas about the theater specifically, and his themes, even when unspoken, persisted through the first five decades of the century— usually in magazines of oppositional stance with theater critics like Joseph Wood Krutch as well as the aforementioned Young, Nathan, and Bentley.

This schizoid situation, between popular reviewing and intellectual criticism, altered after the Second World War, again in response to social change. Higher education became democratized, culture "exploded," and the middle class became aesthetically radicalized—very strictly within the limits of middle-class values (themselves now somewhat circumscribed by television) but still with a lot of innocuous daring. The result is that today we live in a critical situation in which the vocabulary and stance (if not the literary style) of the mass-medium reviewer are very different from his predecessor's and much more like those of the adversary critic. The dividing line is no longer a line; only the ends of the spectrum are clearly defined. But what is forgotten in the new joy about the "improvement" of mass-circulation reviewing is that, fundamentally, the critical spectrum still exists.

Richard Gilman himself abandoned his end of the spectrum, and the theater, in 1967, when he gave up regular reviewing just as Clive Barnes was taking it up. He found himself, he wrote in his introduction to *Common and Uncommon Masks,*

> growing desperate to think of ways of saying new things about unchanging evils or ineptitudes. . . . [T]he surprises, the occasions when something original and exciting came along, usually Off-Broadway, and . . . increasingly Off-Off, were simply not frequent enough to make the rest endurable.

> More than this, I had had a notion . . . of being able somehow to affect the theater. Six years of writing criticism and reviews had instructed me in the naïveté of that ambition. The only effect I could discern, apart from the few minds I might have taught to see drama a bit differently, was that I had gained a reputation for being sour, hypercritical, an outsider ranting against the party to which he hasn't been invited.

But then, in 1981, Gilman returned to reviewing the theater on a regular basis, which accounts for several gaps in the table of contents of *The Drama Is Coming Now:* between, for example, his critique of a production of Brecht's *Life of Galileo* on April 26, 1967, for *Newsweek*, and his critique of presentations of Büchner's *Woyzeck* and *Leonce and Lena* on May 30, 1981, for *The Nation*. His reasons for signing on as *The Nation*'s drama critic were several. Domestic offerings might not sustain him (American drama, at the time, being in one of its perennial imaginative slumps), but one of the notable differences between the theatrical situation in New York when he was reviewing for *Commonweal* and *Newsweek* in the 1960s and the theater scene of the 1980s, was the far greater number of new plays and productions that were finding their way to America from Europe or beyond in the latter decade— sometimes with amazing speed. Also to be considered was the mighty increase in revivals of classics from Gilman's beloved modern repertory. Within a couple of months in the spring of 1981, for instance, Ibsen's *John Gabriel Borkman, The_Wild Duck*, and *Little Eyolf* were produced in New York City while *Hedda Gabler* opened at Yale Repertory Theatre in New Haven, Connecticut. In addition, there was a great deal more than in the past of Chekhov, Pirandello, Brecht, Wedekind, and Strindberg, with the latter's *The Father* about to open at the Circle in the Square just as Gilman was getting back into the critical fray as *The Nation*'s "man on the aisle."

Another element that made drama criticism enticing again was the astonishing proliferation of theaters and theater companies, of spaces where people were doing theatrical work of one or another reasonable or bizarre kind. When Richard Gilman began reviewing in 1961, Off-Broadway had only recently come into existence (he once told me he could remember when the Living Theater and the Circle in the Square were the only two established places that weren't Broadway), and Off-Off Broadway was yet to take shape. By the early 1980s, the "Offs" had multiplied; indeed, the physical scene for theater stretched toward the former World Trade Center and the Cloisters. So much so that, on one weekday in March of 1981, there were seventeen *openings* scheduled all over town, plus *Lolita* on Broadway!

Still, much in the American theater (built as it is almost entirely on an economy of financial success) remained false, inept, or painfully familiar, and Gilman knew it. He shared Shaw's famous lament: "I have lavished ideas on the theater; you would think that in my hour of need the wretched institution would have one to offer me." Why, then, in the final analysis, did Richard Gilman want to resume the writing of theater criticism? Because the long view he had taken in the 1970s—in essays, books, and teaching—had left him with an itch to get back in the middle of things, if only for a time. As he so affectingly wrote at the close of his inaugural column for *The Nation*, on April 11, 1981:

> I retain an affection for the live theater, battered though it is—perhaps because it is. I keep an openness to those occasions of pleasure—a performance, a new voice—that come along rarely but are inimitable, restorative. And I guess I have a desire, too, after so many years away from the action, to take on again that function Shaw described when he said that the critic wasn't "the partner of [the theater's] guilty joys" but its "policeman." Ah, but policemen don't only nab malefactors; they help children across streets, give directions to visitors, break up quarrels, and, occasionally, even preside over happy times for all.

Happy times for Richard Gilman were inevitably those in which the drama becomes something other than a repetitive theatrical game designed to comfort the bourgeoisie, those moments when dramatic art renews itself as serious playwrights in every age reinvent their chosen form. Gilman admired all such writers, who know that art is not a complement to life but an increment; that drama is not psychology, sociology, philosophy, or political theory; and that the only new content is new form. He is thus always attentive, in his articles and reviews, to the manner in which plays are made, but he is never concerned with form as embroidery or decoration. Instead, dramatic forms for him are "imaginative dispositions of existential materials seeking deliverance from actuality." They are forms of new knowledge, a mutual freeing of the self—the audience's as well as the author's—from artistic and cultural conventions that limit our sense of possibility.

Richard Gilman's chief interest was always in discovering how new ways of presenting drama and unfolding consciousness aid in revealing character, transmitting ideas, and in general increasing the potential for capturing a sense of "felt life" on stage. Like Eric Bentley, he wisely saw the playwright as thinker—a shaper of modern consciousness—*and* as showman. The best playwrights, Gilman regularly suggests in Common and *Uncommon Masks* and *The Drama Is Coming Now*, are the ones who can turn ideas and problems, moral conundrums and philosophical complexities, into engaging theater. Yet even these fine dramatists, with the exception of Shakespeare, have never held the kind of central position in educated minds that the authors of fiction and poetry have. This must have something to do with the relative difficulty of seeing good performances of great plays, with the trouble most readers have in imagining how a dramatic text would sound and look on the stage (if not in their mind's eye), with (for English-speaking readers) a mistrust of translations that have often well deserved the mistrust they engender. And, I suppose, there is a larger suspicion that drama is an impure medium: commercially exploitable, subject to the vanity or stupidity of actors, unlikely to come off in the theater at all. One goes to a play expecting disappointment, and one usually finds just that.

Richard Gilman's recurrent disappointment with productions is the reason, I sense, that he never became known as a critic of acting. The surface of a theatrical event thus occupies his attention less, in *The Drama Is Coming Now* as in *Common and Uncommon Masks*, than the core of its meaning. That I tend to agree with many of Gilman's criticisms—with their content as well as their nature—may be attributed to the fact that I myself am more interested in dramatic literature than theatrical enactment, in incisive analysis rather than superficial description. And I firmly believe that Richard Gilman gained his most fervent adherents from the ranks of those who would rather read a play than see it performed. Yet the very real charm of Gilman's critical pieces comes, paradoxically, from their suggestion that the author does not entirely believe his own doomsday judgment on the American theater.

After all, it was Beerbohm, a similarly high-minded critic, who wrote the following words back in 1904—partly in indictment of himself:

A critic who wants the drama to be infinitely better than it is can hardly avoid the pitfall of supposing it to be rather worse than it is. Finding that it rises nowhere near to his standards, he imagines that it must be in a state of motionless prostration in the nethermost depths.

To counteract this tendency in himself, Beerbohm (like Shaw), when faced with an evening of despicable entertainment, went home and devised a substitute entertainment of his own, loosely disguised as a review. See in Beerbohm's *Around Theaters,* for example, the little theatrical event this critic stages as his lead into a review of Victor Hugo's *Ruy Blas* in dismal English translation. Gilman, it is true, lacks such playfulness—some would say triviality—but that may be because the American theater itself is almost wholly one of play, of child's play, even when it is ostensibly trying to be serious. And such a theater requires, I think, the stern but stimulating contempt, the acerbic yet arousing intolerance, of a Richard Gilman.

Initially backing up Gilman in his ire were the seminal essays of Francis Fergusson and Eric Bentley, comprising the academic artillery being fired (chiefly from Columbia) at the philistines in Sardi's and Shubert Alley, the entrenched establishment of Lincoln Center and the Actors' Studio, and at the new breed of barbarians storming south of 14th Street past the Living Theater and toward other assorted dead ends. It is not too far-fetched to suggest that Fergusson and Bentley, to be followed by Robert Brustein and Richard Gilman (themselves having moved, like Bentley, to the academy—in their case Yale— in the 1960s), represented an authentic revolution in the modern theater away from the championing of realism of the poetic as well as prosaic variety, toward an appreciation of a still (at the time) undetermined fusion of the ironic and the absurd. With tragedy in tatters and comedy in confusion, these modern critics turned to irony as the only link between the form or formality of theater and the flux of history. Chekhov, Pirandello, Brecht, and Beckett are neither tragedians nor comedians but ironists, and a genuinely ironic sensibility is something unheard of on Broadway. Hence, even on the infrequent occasions of revivals of Chekhov, Pirandello, Brecht, and Beckett, the ironies of their plays are swallowed up by the slobbering sentimentally of a realistic stage tradition; and it takes an "ironic" critic like Gilman or Brustein to point this out.

In this constantly contentious period of cultural history, Fergusson functioned as a remote Hegelian influence on the revolutionaries, Bentley played Marx as he translated Brecht, Brustein was Lenin arriving at the Finland Station on the New Haven Railroad (which would eventually take him from Yale to Harvard), and Richard Gilman wound up playing Trotsky with a tortured self-consciousness that robbed him of nothing except professional stamina (only six years combined at *Commonweal* and *Newsweek* compared with George Jean Nathan's half a century or more on the critical firing line). On the other side, Walter Kerr turned into the Kerensky of the revolution by betraying his academic origins to consort with the hated bourgeoisie, while the drama critics of *The Village Voice* became the left-wing revisionists of Off-Off Broadway.

Like the revolutionary playwrights he loved, and whose work is well represented in *Common and Uncommon Masks* and *The Drama Is Coming Now*, Gilman wanted to raise the consciousness of his readers. The work such a writer does is enormously important, for, on the most obvious level, it teaches people, as the New Critics taught them before, how to read as well as how to see. In its recurrent search for new forms, furthermore, this critical enterprise replenishes the potential of dramatic art. It insists on naming things properly, and on assigning them to their proper places. The only danger inherent in such obsessions is that Gilman may impose a new tyranny on art through his repeated insistence, in *Common and Uncommon Masks* and *The Drama Is Coming Now* as well as in his seminal study *The Making of Modern Drama*, that it break with the traditional forms he finds exhausted. Make no mistake, however: Richard Gilman did not whore after novelty, the imagination's "exotic bird." He may have been attracted by radical departures from theatrical norms, but he was no cultist, the ephemeral or merely clever having no place in his aesthetic. What has already been used clearly had no place for him, either. In fact, he dearly hated all such "use." And that, I guess, was his point; it should never have been *used* at all.

Gilman is ultimately strongest, then, on the dramatists he loves iconoclastically, like Ibsen, Büchner, Strindberg, Beckett, and Chekhov. He excels at precise, economic description of a drama's central effect, as in his definitive review in *Common and Uncommon Masks* of Harold Pinter's *The Homecoming* (positive) and his equally definitive review of Marsha Norman's *'night, Mother* in *The Drama Is Coming Now* (negative). He dissects the "show biz" of Broadway commercial theater with utter precision at the same time that he retains an abundant affection for one of the last serious playwrights it produced: Tennessee Williams. He places the classics (including but not limited to Shakespeare) in what seems to be sensible perspective for today. And, because Gilman has a keen literary intelligence, he is particularly acute, even tough, on the pretentiously "literary" plays of such dramatists as Eugene O'Neill and Edward Albee.

The Drama Is Coming Now includes, in its penultimate section, a review of Jerzy Grotowski's book *Towards a Poor Theatre*, and its subject reminds me of the first piece I ever read by Richard Gilman, as well as the one that kept me coming back to him: a marvelous, detailed essay from 1970 on Grotowski's Polish Laboratory Theater, which concludes *Common and Uncommon Masks*. As one of those who did not manage to get into a performance during Grotowski's first visit to this country, I read Gilman's thoughtful account for clues as to what this visionary Pole wanted, or at least hoped for, in the theater. I was leery of the general response to Grotowski's visit because it seemed to portend a theater of nonverbal physical sensation, of which we had already had alarmingly enough. Richard Gilman found something more in Grotowski's work, and his essay performed a major task of clarification, of synthesis of the theory and practice of the Theater of the Poor. Justifying Grotowski against the charge that his work was all technique and did not "say" anything, Gilman upheld the power of art to put us "in the presence of a life our own lives are powerless to unearth," not merely to imitate the everyday in a lifelike way or to illustrate socially useful sentiments. Here is perhaps the most striking sentence in this piece: "When Beckett said of Joyce that 'he is not writing about something, he is writing something,' he described what all true artists, among them Jerzy Grotowski, do."

Well, Richard Gilman wrote something, too. Put another way, he exemplifies the maxim that it is the critic who makes the subject, and not the subject that makes the critic. In this he represents, not Yeats's cautionary figure, but rather criticism's exemplary one: the man who, instead of making rhetoric out of his quarrel with others, makes poetry out of his quarrel with himself. For Gilman's sake, I am so pleased at the extent to which the essays, articles, and reviews contained in both *Common and Uncommon Masks* and *The Drama Is Coming Now* reveal or reiterate his sense of cultural mission, his graceful style, his predilection for certain artists and themes, his brash independence of mind, and—perhaps most important—his love of good art in any form, theatrical or otherwise.

CHAPTER TWO

ON CRITICISM: AN EXCHANGE BETWEEN ERIC BENTLEY AND BERT CARDULLO

Eric Bentley (born 1916) is a renowned critic, playwright, editor, and translator. Born in England, he became an American citizen in 1948 and currently lives in New York City. In addition to teaching at Columbia University, which he joined in 1953 and left in 1969 (to concentrate on his writing), Bentley was in the 1950s the theater critic for *The New Republic*, where he was known for his blunt, rhetorical style.

He has written many critical books, among them *The Playwright as Thinker* (1946), *What Is Theatre?* (1956), *The Life of the Drama* (1964), and *Theater of War* (1972). His most-produced play is *Are You Now or Have You Ever Been: The Investigations of Show-Business by the Un-American Activities Committee, 1947-1958* (1956). The following interview took place in October 2003 in Eric Bentley's Manhattan apartment. He discusses below the nature, current state, and possible future of American dramatic criticism.

Bentley: Dramatic criticism, today? The standards of the theatre are so low that the talents of a critic of art are not called for. He's really not put to work. If one's interest were poetry, even though there may be no great poets around on the scale of Dante or Shakespeare, nevertheless, the poetic writing is serious and meets a fairly high spiritual standard. But to be a critic of poetry you have to be highly qualified, intellectually speaking, to even see what the differences are between rather good and a little better than that. These finer distinctions, which are the very essence of intellectual work, are totally uncalled for in the theatre because nearly everything there has, at best, crude qualities. Crudely good, if good, and mostly crudely bad. So the talent of a real critic is not called for, is not needed. He should either go and exercise it somewhere else, as in criticizing poetry, classical dramatic literature, the great works of the past, or, if he continues to write on the theatre, to look at the context of it. This is what I had been attempting to do: look at the sociology of it, the history. I think of myself as a commentator on the whole scene. I'm not saying that all criticism is unimportant, just theatre reviewing. I still think that it's good to have a lot of published discussion of cultural matters generally. Journalism at its highest level has some intellectual importance. So have literary magazines. But theatre, well, it's neither like television, which has immense sociological importance, nor poetry, which has immense spiritual importance. It has *no* importance! Anybody of average intelligence can judge plays as well as the newspaper critics, and perhaps better, because many of them aren't even of average intelligence. You don't need a special man to decide that the Broadway playwrights are of no intellectual interest. It's known. It's obvious. No critic would become a dramatic critic. Not for long, anyway.

BC: It seems to me, though, that a good critic does not depend upon the value of what he sees for the value of what he writes. The ideal critic can write as good, as useful, as productive, as intelligent, as brilliant a review of *Getting Gertie's Garter* as he can of *King Lear.* This is proved by some of the things you yourself have written. If you look back on it, you'll find that this is true of every good critic: that some of his best pieces were about plays that nobody would ever dream of remembering except for the fact that he wrote about them. This is certainly true of Bernard Shaw. The level of work he found in the late 1890s was certainly not notably higher than the work you would find if you came back to weekly criticism, and yet, Shaw, like all his really first-rate successors, happened to write extremely well about extremely bad plays. This, I think, can still be done according to a method that you discovered. I think you made a great contribution in teaching us how to write about bad plays—how to say something useful and intelligent about them, not just how lousy they are—by treating them as symptoms of a larger malaise and using them as occasions to discuss this larger malaise. This has been a tremendously valuable contribution to the history of dramatic criticism in this country, and this approach to criticism is what unites the post-Bentley school. This is what makes Robert Brustein's work so good, for example. If the play is nothing as a play, what is its value, what is its interest as a symptom of one of our national sicknesses? But I think dramatic criticism is still of some use in creating, to take a phrase from you, a climate of opinion. This is not to cause this play to flourish and that play to die, but to suggest the possibilities of feeling and seeing and reacting. In other words, the critic uses the play as an occasion for making some sense about the world outside the theatre. I am sure that you would consider *The Rothschilds* (to take one egregious example from the 1970s) as one of the things you left criticism to avoid seeing. Some people are more sympathetic to Broadway mediocrity than you are, but I still can understand fleeing criticism in order not to have to sit through *The Rothchilds*. But I read a review of *The Rothchilds* in which the critic didn't mention the play until the eighth paragraph, and yet he was talking about matters that the play brought up, and I think he was saying something of some use. This is what a critic can do. Even if the theatre is as unimportant as you think, the critic can make some small, useful pieces of discourse, and if he is very, very good, can make a small piece of his own art from even the worst plays. This is what Shaw and Max Beerbohm achieved. They made small masterpieces for which bad plays were the raw material, and as long as this is a possibility (and it's what every good critic should hope for) then there will be some use in dramatic criticism.

Bentley: When I resigned from *The New Republic,* I felt that the particular group of critics active at the time should resign as well, and that I was prepared to lead the way. I don't think anybody followed the lead; I just felt it would be good to have a clean slate. I think since we don't have purges from "above," it would be good if people purged themselves now and again. It's the same on faculties: they have tenure and stay forever. Shaw worked as a theatre critic for four years, and he found that was quite enough. There are many jobs like that, that shouldn't be done for a lifetime. What do people who continue working do, except become exhausted, or develop a talent for something else? I think if I were editor of a magazine, I would either not have the theatre covered at all, especially if it's a national magazine, because outside of New York there's not much interest in theatre, or if it's a New York magazine with heavy emphasis on city readership here, then I would only hire the drama critic for a couple of years with the understanding that it would be more interesting for him to give his place to somebody else.

BC: You have a good point here in that the best critics, Shaw being the best example, but also Beerbohm and Kenneth Tynan, took the job for a few years and then left it to do something else. In many cases, only the mediocrities went on from decade to decade. I do think, however, that it should be *possible* to retain your ability to perceive, your zest, your freshness, your interest. Also, there's another thing involved here. You clearly left because you hated what you were seeing. And I think it's hard to say where ideology stops and taste begins. They have a lot to do with one another, but in the school that descends from you, the school of Brustein and Richard Gilman, the critical school to which I think I more or less belong, one of the principles of their orthodoxy is that in our sick society the theatre that expresses that society has to be sick, that Broadway is absolutely corrupt. And that makes me feel the need to go ahead with something other than criticism. I've never been a full-time critic, and even at this point, I'm a teacher first and then a critic. Teaching means more to me, and it gives me more of the satisfaction I need. Fortunately, I have always been able to do both. I can see that if you did nothing but go to the theatre three or four times a week and write about it, and that was your whole vocational life, that you would begin to get a little squirrely. To quit doing that seems to me an eminently good idea. I don't think that I would take a critical job that wouldn't allow me to teach. But I don't think it's necessary to make that choice. You and Brustein went on teaching at Columbia (and other places) all through your critical careers. That's one of the advantages of writing for a weekly. I agree that if your whole life was this round of opening nights, cigarettes on sidewalks, and newspaper offices, you would get limited, and if you hated the stuff you saw, you would very likely get bitter. So I think it's extremely useful to have a career outside, and most of the good critics have always done this. It's possible to do them both together—not if you go to the theatre four times a week, but if you go to the theatre twice a week, you can certainly teach.

Bentley: I left because I was tired of seeing the same kind of bad show over and over again. The average member of the theatre-going public (if there is such a person) sees a few plays each season: maybe nine or ten, at most fourteen or fifteen. But the critics, especially if they cover Off-Broadway, see dozens and dozens, if not hundreds. It's too many. Few of them can be of any distinction, and even noting the faults, well, oh dear, the same faults appear in thousands of shows. They're easy enough to see; you don't have to be bright. A person who *is* bright, like, in the older generation, George Jean Nathan, or more recently, John Simon, has nothing to do but perfect his waspishness. Why whet your knife when there's nothing to cut but soft, rancid margarine?

BC: I think you have to review in terms of your own standards, or in terms of something that goes deeper than your standards. But I think that one of the forms in which the devil tempts theatre critics is to tempt them so that they conveniently seem to end up having the opinion that will enable them to be most cleverly nasty. I don't think that insincerity need be involved here. This can happen, and it is one of the insidious problems that while you genuinely believe that you are fighting the good fight, you can actually be irresponsibly vicious. It's a minor pleasure: the sense that you've paid someone back for what he's done to you. It's a temptation, and I really try to fight it. When I've written something that I think is extremely nasty in a clever way, I look it over very carefully and ask myself if the play or the film was really that bad. Is this what I think of it? Even if the comment is literally true, does it, taken with the rest of the review, give a false impression? Bernard Shaw said that people who complained about what he said should only have heard what he didn't say. I have taken out wisecracks I was very fond of because the work was really not quite bad enough to deserve them. Now it may be that I have left in others that I ought to have taken out. It's very hard to know when you've gotten corrupted unconsciously.

Bentley: Nonetheless, the theatre in modern times has not been consistently challenging. It has been consistently unchallenging. But once in a while something happens. A play like *Waiting for Godot* opens and the theatre, for the moment, attains a dignity again. It's exciting to be around when Something Happens. Of course, if you're Walter Kerr, you announce that nothing happened after all. Look back at his review of *Waiting for Godot*. But a lot of people knew he was wrong and that something *had* happened between eighty-thirty and eleven that evening. Some people felt that when Bertolt Brecht's plays were first done, that they were witnesses to a Spiritual Event, as in previous generations when Ibsen's plays came along, or when Shaw's plays were produced. Of course, newspaper critics denied it on *all* those occasions! They have an amazing record, those fellows!

BC: Harold Clurman once said that whether the critic is good or bad doesn't depend on his opinions, but on the reasons he can offer for those opinions. The point is not whether or not Walter Kerr likes Samuel Beckett, but *why* he likes or does not like Beckett. What can he tell you about the theatre, American society, mankind, the universe, art, and God, in the course of explaining why he does or does not like Beckett? Of course, there is also the argument that Walter Kerr's reasons for disliking Beckett are extremely bad ones. I suppose that what I am saying is that there is a good case to be made for and against almost every writer, actor, play, and so on. I'm not the first to point this out, but Walter Kerr for his part communicated a sort of *trahison des clercs*. He wouldn't have bothered people so much if he hadn't been an intellectual. I mean, it is just not worth anybody's while to crusade against a Richard Watts because anybody who doesn't understand that a Richard Watts is just not there as a serious critic will not be convinced, no matter what you say. Because Kerr clearly was an intelligent man, however, because he really knew his theatre art—not only in terms of show business, but in terms of Aeschylus on down to the present— because he used to be a university teacher, there was this feeling that he had betrayed something. Stupid men you don't bother with, but intelligent men, they can be dangerous. Also, Kerr, having been critic of the *New York Times* and the *Herald Tribune*, wielded a considerable amount of power. He led the fight against a fair number of the leading writers of the present day. Beckett is the most notable example. He talked about Beckett and Brecht from a point of view that accepts Broadway postulates that you and Brustein regard, not entirely unjustly, as anathema. But again, it seems to me that there is a case to be made for and against almost everybody. Voltaire used to make a very good case against Shakespeare from Voltaire's own point of view. T. S. Eliot used to say that he had never seen a really cogent refutation of Thomas Rymer's strictures on *Othello*, and Rymer called *Othello* "a bloody farce without salt or savor, the moral of which is that housewives should look to their linen." There really is a case to be made against the absurdists. Depending upon what you want, they either have it, or don't have it. They, like all other writers who have ever been born, have their limits. Like all other writers who have ever been born, there is a possibility that their influence can be a pernicious one. It seems to me that a good case for or against any kind of art or artist is a useful service. And Walter Kerr was the very best possible Walter Kerr. For his position, he made a good case. Like Winthrop Sargeant, when you disagreed with him, he forced you to define your own position in disagreement. Also, Kerr had a kind of practical shrewdness. When something went subtly wrong in the theatrical collaboration, he could sometimes put his finger on it in a way nobody else could. He was, among other things, a Broadway director. His experience was useful experience, and he knew how to use it.

Bentley: When I look back in *The Life of the Drama* and see what I myself did with the drama of social indignation, I realize that I was over-hasty. I was trying to concentrate on other things. That passage about indignation and drama is, to me, one of the least adequate parts of my book. I would like to go back and change it a bit. Both there, and earlier in the fifties, when I wrote about Arthur Miller and Lillian Hellman, I put them down too much. It wasn't that I was working myself up into a frenzy I didn't feel. I was opposed to them, and I overdid it. I wrote a piece called "Lillian Hellman's Indignation." I said that indignation is a weak emotion for drama. Today I would want to elaborate on that. There is an incompatibility between that passage in *The Life of the Drama* and my later discussions in *The Theatre of Commitment* and *Theatre of War.* Critics are so unfair! As I look back (of course, one has this objectivity when it's too late) I see how much more favorably I wrote of Rolf Hochhuth's *The Deputy* than of Hellman and Miller, yet, if you'd asked me, at any date, if I thought him a better playwright than they are, I don't suppose I'd have said yes. His play got a better review from me because of various historical "accidents." I think Hochhuth has grave faults, and somewhat the same faults as Hellman and Miller. Just think: had I encountered him at a different time, I might have given him totally bad reviews! If you go back to some of my early stuff, you'll find such a lot of advocacy! I was always a moralist. Always taking up causes. Culture itself was a big cause with me. Do you understand why that was? Culture was a cause, not because I came from a cultural home, but because that was what I *didn't* come from. I was busy *acquiring* culture. Trying to find out for what it stood, and what "standards" were. Like many people in the modern world, both in America and in Britain, where I grew up, I think now that some of my ideas were inexact or even quite wrong. Undoubtedly, I stressed certain truths at the expense of other factors, perhaps because they were self-evident to me at the time. Later, I wanted to go back and look at the whole scene. That is, look at society and even social change . . . I think you have to go outside the aesthetics to judge the aesthetics.

BC: The problem with being a missionary is that to be a missionary you have to have orthodoxy, and I'm not sure that that's a good idea. It can be a limitation. I don't want it ever to happen to me that I can't see something because I'm blinded by the blinkers of my beliefs (though obviously it does and will happen to me, as it happens to everybody). It seems to me that Walter Kerr, for instance, with the best will in the world, was unable to perceive virtues in certain kinds of experimental theatre because his tastes and beliefs just went the other way. Analogously, but oppositely, the orthodox-highbrow school is sometimes incapable of perceiving excellences in commercial theatre because they believe so rigorously that they are not there. Advocacy of one particular kind of theatre can be a useful service. This is what Shaw was doing in the 1890s, and what Tynan was doing in the late fifties, but that isn't what some critics are temperamentally suited to providing. They think that their function is rather to try to sort out what is healthy from what is sick, what is positive from what is pernicious in every kind of theatre: to begin with the notion that there are different sorts of excellences to be found in different places, and to separate out in every context what is excellent, with the understanding that this is extremely colored by their own set of ideas as a perceiver. They try to stay as loose as they can. Shaw said that when you find that a play is absolutely, totally inadequate as X, then it behooves you, in fact, to ask if the play is not really Y. It seems to these critics dangerous to believe that a play must be this or that or the other thing because it interferes with one's ability to perceive. Listen to the work, they say, when it lays down its own criteria, as works always do. They always imply how they are to be judged. Now these criteria themselves can also be judged, but you have to start, says this kind of critic, by trying to see what kind of a thing it is, and not demanding that it be one particular kind of thing. When you see what kind of thing it is, then quite irrespective of your judgment of how good or bad it is at being the kind of thing it is, you can make a judgment about it as a good kind of thing to be or not. But this type of critic thinks it's dangerous to come in with a rigid set of rules. And one further thing. In addition to what the artist has tried to do, you've often got to ask, what has the writer done that he didn't try to do? What is his unconscious doing behind his back? You have to keep open to the possibility of totally unexpected things happening that turn out well. There are a great many plays that offer themselves as serious works of art that fail dismally, and yet, you can't write them off because they do succeed as mild entertainment. That possibility has to be kept open. Everybody's job is to keep possibilities open.

Bentley: I'm quoting now from my article "Oppenheimer, Mon Amour": "I don't actually regard it as more important to write a good play than to tell the truth about Oppenheimer. The life of Oppenheimer is far more interesting than most good plays, and I, for one, would gratefully accept a bad play or a good non-play (a documentary or even a book) provided it made a fascinating contribution to biography and history." If people become what I call overaesthetic, they somehow are assuming that it's more important to write, to produce good works of art, than it could be to do anything else. The people who defended Ezra Pound were people who believed that art is God. If he's a good writer, that transcends all discussion of treason, etc. I'm a little bit closer to the opposite position, though I don't think I'm directly at the other extreme. When it comes to Oppenheimer, a subject that interests me, I'm not primarily interested in the problem, "Has Heinar Kipphardt written a good play?" I want to know if he's got hold of something that makes me see Oppenheimer in a new way. That would validate my evening in the theatre. No, I'm not losing all interest in artistic merit. If Kipphardt can also write a great play, marvelous! But I will settle for less. I have the impression that those who regard themselves as dramatic critics with high standards will dismiss such a work as Kipphardt's *In the Matter of J. Robert Oppenheimer* as soon as they have established to their own satisfaction that it isn't a very good play. To me, this is a very good play. To me, this is a very significant *man*, Oppenheimer, and it would be quite an achievement if you could say something significant about him even without writing a good play. As I said, I don't regard it as more important to write a good play than to tell the truth about Oppenheimer.

BC: I think there is something narrow about your use of the word "aesthetic" here. The Oppenheimer play is an extremely bad play because it doesn't tell a truth of any particular interest. It tells a truth, but that isn't very hard. Every day the *New York Times* comes out with a large number of truths. A fact is a truth. Aristotle said that poetry is more philosophic than history. I disagree. I think that good history is every bit as philosophic as good poetry, but I think that the problem with the Oppenheimer play is that it's not philosophic in that sense. It only grinds away at small facts and misses the really interesting issues implied in that particular confrontation, and therefore, it is lousy history and a lousy play at the same time. And I think that Hochhuth's plays, whatever they are, they're terrible, because the same thing that makes lousy history makes them lousy plays. A good history play is good in both ways. What makes Hochhuth's work lousy history and lousy drama is simply that the man's mind is heavy, cumbersome, literal, and simple. And therefore, whatever specific truths the man may tell in the course of things, he reduces these pieces of history to far less complex, resonant, and significant matters than they really are. I think that you, feeling that these are important plays, that these are the kind of plays that should be written, overlook whether they are written well or badly. It seems to me that if a history play is to be any good, it has to be good history and a good play at the same time. This doesn't mean that it has to be accurate. Shakespeare's history plays are full of inaccuracies.

Bentley: My article on the New Lafayette Theatre contains a totally negative view of the most successful play that group had on in a long while, *The Black Terror*. I thought it was extremely tiresome, even though I agreed with a lot that the author presumably meant. What is more tiresome than merely being in agreement? I have, in fact, seen lots of plays where I am very sympathetic to what the author thinks, but I was so bored! I don't think agreement helps an awful lot. People who go to church agree and fall asleep at the same time . . . In its time I gave a favorable review to *The Psychic Pretenders* but most of my review is not about the writing. I say that the words are the weakest part of that show. I paid compliments where they were due: to a certain type of showmanship and a certain attitude. It was not a "rave," so I don't know if that management did very well out of me. Other people who have had bad reviews from me who could have expected good ones (on the grounds of ideological sympathy) are Leonard Bernstein for *Mass*, Fernando Arrabal for a play supposedly sympathetic to the Spanish loyalists, and the Oppenheimer play itself. I think I was very harsh on a lot of the younger playwrights at the time, Megan Terry and others. "What does he ever do for us?" they used to ask. "And we are writing the actual radical plays!" And that is because I have never been able to praise plays because of my agreement with them. It seems to me that the radical playwright has to make his radicalism active in art by making it very concrete, by making it very ironic. He has to show the contradictions in any situation. It's to be expected, therefore, as in the cases of Brecht and Shaw, that people will find their art less consistent than their theoretical remarks outside the art. They take a position, outside, which has a certain consistency, but in a work of art you show the difficulties or inconsistencies of people: the pull the other way. The shock even—sympathy with the Inquisitor! Shaw tells you in his Preface to what extent he's for inquisitors. In the play the whole reality is shown. I was against the Living Theatre. I thought that was propaganda in the worst sense. I was friendlier to Joe Chaikin and the Open Theatre, because they were less crudely propagandist; they had dialectical movement, or two sides. I acknowledge that there are aesthetic values, and that critics invoke them by being critics. One piece of writing is better than another, period. But such superiority cannot be seen in purely aesthetic terms. Moral elements enter in. That is why I wonder about Ezra Pound. Of course, he was a very gifted writer, and, of course, he also had moral insight here and there. At the same time, if you think that the wisdom of some of the great poets, such as Shakespeare or Dante or Goethe, has anything to do with their talent, as I do (I don't think it's just something they had as an "extra"), then the absence of such wisdom makes Pound a lesser figure than they are. Descending from the sublime to the everyday realities of newspaper drama criticism—all of it is strongly ideological. The man who dominated the New York theatre from the twenties till the early sixties was Brooks Atkinson. Politics and morality entered into his judgments all the time. He favored liberal and humanitarian causes, and he often overpraised plays (aesthetically speaking) when he was in agreement with them. He boosted certain types of good intuitions that never got beyond intuition.

BC: I think it's a mark of honor to be able to see, acknowledge, and expose the faults and inadequacies of work you agree with. It means that no party has you in its pocket. People who overpraise without meaning to do so can be forgiven; people who do it on purpose are liars. We are all tempted to do this sincerely and I think it's a forgivable excess, but when you say, "This stinks, but I'll say it's good," for whatever reason, that's a sin against the Holy Ghost. That's inadmissible. Let me cite Shaw again here. He said, "If my father was an actor-manager, and his life depended on his getting a good notice, I would orphan myself tomorrow morning if his performance was not adequate." (I'm not quoting accurately here.) Shaw says that that is the critical instinct, and I agree. The critic bears witness. That's what he's there for. If he bears a lying witness— for whatever reason—he's betrayed himself and his calling. He's betrayed everything there is for him to betray. Where I got this, I suppose, is from what Matthew Arnold says about culture. As he sees it, the job of critics is not to tie themselves down to any party to the extent that their ability to perceive is warped—which is what happens when you tie yourself down too hard. One very important function of the critic is to be a shit detector, and since shit is found all over, it is very important that the critic's detector work in all directions. (Matthew Arnold doesn't quite talk about it in those terms, but Ernest Hemingway did.) I do see myself, however, as trying to preserve the theatre or to promote a certain kind of cinema, but not by boosting and propagandizing for it. I don't go along with the school of thought that says we have to pretend that it's better than it is, just to keep it alive, because I think that is lying. I didn't go into any of my present professions in order to be a liar. However, it is our function to help keep this or that art alive by talking about it, by demonstrating our own concern with it, by showing that it is possible for intelligent people to still care about it, and by denouncing evil and praising virtue so as to do what you can to create a theatre or a cinema that deserves to live. But I do think it's possible to imagine a theatre, for one art, that just does not deserve to live.

Bentley: It is not one of the critic's duties to try to preserve the theatre because no institution was ever kept going by verbal support from outside. Institutions survive from their own inner energy as accepted by the non-writing public. The locus of the energy is the theatre itself . . . There is a relationship between stage and public, between stage and auditorium, actor and audience. A little encouragement can be given from outside, as by critics, for instance, or even by newspapers which print a notice saying, "The show will take place on Friday." Otherwise there is no audience. Still, I think the main things take place *after* those preliminaries and *before* the critic writes his articles, with just the audience present. Unless a play, like Henrik Ibsen's *Ghosts*, generates a certain energy, on the evening of performance, in *that* theatre—not just among people who write about it, though including them—there is no life in the drama. That's where the life is. It's not totally independent of critics, but neither is it heavily dependent on them. The problems are not with the medium as such, but with the institution as it now exists. The medium is the same medium Shakespeare contributed to; the institution is not. If the play is on Broadway, or anything approaching Broadway, such as the larger Off-Broadway enterprises, the main criterion applicable would be: has this, whatever the author's intentions, by its first night turned into commercial entertainment? If so, the system wants it; if not, the system doesn't want it. Radical authors have been praised when they have met that test and their stuff has ended up as commercial entertainment, and have been dispraised as high-minded but untalented playwrights otherwise. So that's going to happen one way or the other in despite of all individuals. It's of no concern whether Mr. A or Mr. B is writing the criticism. What is left is the weight of the institution. Even writers like Brecht and Shaw are only of interest to this system insofar as they produce the same old commercial entertainment. The theatre isn't commercial because David Merrick was a very commercially minded individual. It would be exactly the same had he never been born: exactly the same. There would be someone else by the same name, or by a different name. So it's not a question of changing the theatre, but of changing the society if you want the theatre also to change. You may change the society and then wait until there's a new theatre, or, like Brecht, figure that the theatre participates in the changing of society. He didn't have very much success along that line, it has to be said. Jean Genêt thought he had none . . . Institutions, theatrical institutions or any other kind, are part of the society in which they exist. They may be rebellious occasionally, but it's very difficult and problematic for theatres to be in total opposition. How can they support themselves, economically, in that case? Generally, theatres have been part of what we call an Establishment, whatever the Establishment was. For Molière or the Greeks, it was organized by the existing ruling class. That would stand to reason. Who else would even have put up the buildings? Therefore, if you have a highly decadent form of society, as many of us feel we have today, it isn't that the theatre's so much worse but that the theatre is an integral part of the whole. If George W. Bush is not a very great president and if his regime doesn't represent a very high degree of wisdom and progress, then it's clear what theatre in his society will be like.

BC: I believe that the theatre works slowly, subtly, subliminally, but that it does work positively on the people who go to it. Perhaps this is just self-serving, blind faith, but it is what I do believe. I don't think that Brecht's contribution was nil, but I still wouldn't say that the theatre is important in any "dramatic" way. I don't think that people go to the theatre and have sudden conversions like Saint Paul on the road to Damascus; that they go in planning to vote for a Republican and come out planning to vote for a Democrat. I think the effect is slower, subtler, more cumulative. It's like marijuana, which doesn't do much to you puff by puff, but as certain scientists once told us, if you smoke it regularly for twelve years, you will begin to be a different person because of it. And I think the theatrical effect is similarly cumulative. It builds up, polyp by polyp, like a coral island. It's slow. It's immeasurable. And, of course, it depends on what you bring to it. But if you bring something to it, it will bring something to you ultimately, and if this is true, then the critic has something to do with helping that process along. All the same, I'm interested in change very much because the theatre is not in such blooming condition that anybody should fight very hard to keep it as it is. As to how the change should come about . . . The point is not to tell an actor you did this and you should have done that, or to tell a writer you did this and you should have done that, because this reduces all your other readers to eavesdroppers. Essentially, you're talking to the public, and whatever you say is, first of all, intended for them. But how then should a critic bring about change? Slowly. The critic should bring about changes in the theatre the way the theatre brings about changes in the world. Not measurably, and perhaps you have to take it on faith that these changes come about at all. But by offering possibilities to your readers, you have some effect on the climate. Not on this play's fate or that play's fate, but on what kinds of pleasure and enlightenment the theatre can afford, how they can be created, what sort of institutions could create them, what the prevailing corruptions are, and how they can be rooted out. Not in the specifics, but slowly and pervasively you hope to have some effect. No critic penetrates very far into the system. Million-dollar investments do not vanish or flourish at a critic's word.

Bentley: I've been writing more *for* the theatre in the latter part of my career, and this is difficult, but rewarding, spiritually speaking. I don't feel that acts of theatre make a tremendous contribution toward changing the world, but they can perhaps make some small dent. Things in the past, like Clifford Odets's *Waiting for Lefty*, didn't overthrow capitalism or even make a sizeable contribution to that end. Nor, adding all the other works of Odets and all the other works of communist or social(ist) realism in the thirties, did they do much. But then again, it doesn't follow that because their contribution wasn't enormous that it's therefore negligible. Yet what can one do? Let's say we were tremendously interested in religion and promoting the cause of religion. We might have a church. We might not believe, as the extreme evangelists do, that we are somehow preparing for the end of the world, getting ready for it fast, and saving people by the million. Most conscientious priests don't have such delusions of grandeur. They think of what they're doing on a smaller scale. They may not be interested in proselytizing much, but if they're not, they're probably very interested in consolidating the forces that they do have. Which means that they do have a didactic church, without being too grandiose in their claims to speed or scope. So things are in the theatre. If we would relate the effort more realistically to the actual audience, we would not fall into the pitfalls of some of the propagandist theatres of the past. If you call yourself a proletarian playwright, and you have not a single proletarian in your actual audience, well, there's something very foolish about that: a lack of self-understanding, let's call it. Let's take something like my project at Yale in the fall of 1972: to do a play about a piece of recent American history, which had certain lessons in it. One of my friends at the time ran a black theatre on the lower East Side. This particular script would not have done much for his audience. They didn't know the public figures in it, they didn't know their careers; they hadn't passed judgment on them, they didn't have arguments about them. It wasn't the material for that particular audience. Contrariwise, it did make sense to present this material on the Un-American Activities Committee, and its treatment of artists and intellectuals, to an audience of Yale students, Yale faculty, and that part of the New Haven population that was friendly with them and mingled with them socially. Many of these people may have disagreed with the point of view I worked into the show. That's legitimate. I'm only saying that the material interested them and concerned them. Was this proletarian theatre? Anything but. It was a theatre of the middle-class intelligentsia. That was a big class, though, in America, and it still is.

BC: To a certain extent, if people like you are not actively demanding that the theatre become better, the chances that it will become so diminish. But I don't think that you are deserting in any way. You have other things to do. You have other, perhaps more important, ways of trying to serve something that ought to be served. I certainly wouldn't argue that criticism is the only way in which the ends of the life force can be served, or even the best way for those who can or want to do it. For me, personally, criticism is still one of the ways—if I weren't writing criticism, I would probably be doing something even less useful! In that context, let me conclude by telling you a story about Sir Henry Irving, the actor. He once scheduled a rehearsal for Sunday, and one of the members of his company said, "Mr. Irving, I noticed that you called a rehearsal for Sunday. Do you think that that is not an impious thing to do? Is it really right that we should be acting on the Lord's day?" And Irving looked at him with the freezing glare for which he was famous, and said quietly, "I think that my work is a *good work*." And that is essentially how I feel about theatre (and film) criticism. I think it's a matter of faith. If you believe it's a good work, you've at least got a chance of making it such—though nothing is guaranteed, God knows.

Bentley: Amen.

CHAPTER THREE

IMAGES IN A VAST WORLD:
HOMAGE TO STARK YOUNG (1881-1963)

Sixty years ago, on the publication of the final collection of Stark Young's dramatic criticism, *Immortal Shadows* (1948), Eric Bentley feared that Young's work was then already on its way to being forgotten. In the years that have passed since that last collection and Young's death in 1963, Bentley's fears have been born out, and Stark Young's immense contribution to the rise of a serious dramatic criticism in America has been passed by as if it never existed: this fate for the man John Gassner called "pre-eminently the artist-critic of our formative modern theatre in America."

In a real sense, the essays by Stark Young that began appearing regularly in *The New Republic* in 1921 signaled the beginning of a new era for the American theatre and its criticism: here was a critic who thought the art of the theatre worth taking seriously, and who, as luck would have it, appeared on the scene just as the theatre in America became worthy of being taken seriously. The rise of the Provincetown Players in New York after World War I and the theatre experiments they initiated were to set off the first native explosion of a modern theatre in America. It was Young's great gift to appreciate this new movement at the outset for what it was, and to see in it what the American stage might become. In his preface to *Immortal Shadows*, Young observed that "not only was the period remarkable, but those of us in it at the time knew that it was remarkable."

As remarkable as the era was Young himself, then just turned forty and arrived at his position as drama critic of *The New Republic* by the most improbable route imaginable. He had been born into a fine old tradition-minded Mississippi Delta family little more than a decade after the Civil War, and for the first twenty years of his life Young had been exposed to what then passed for the education of a gentleman in the public schools of Como and Oxford, Mississippi, and at the University of Mississippi. In his autobiography, *The Pavilion* (1951), Young acknowledged the intellectual inadequacy of his background while conjuring up its great human richness:

I had in a way a distinct kind of education. It consisted not so much in what is usually called education and informed studies as it did in personalities and the general principles that were accepted by them out of life, as it was, and that were to be lived by. Partly by inheritance and partly by the way we live, our people came into an interest in human beings that was not so much psychological or analytical as it was personal, secret, open, and bright.

The sensibility forged by this experience of a post-Civil War Southern upbringing was never to be attuned to abstract theories of drama, to schools of psychology, nor to what Young called "tags of the scientific that was to come into vogue later on." Instead, Stark Young brought to his criticism an intelligence that was acutely sensual, eyes and ears open in an unprecedented way to the nuance and texture of the theatrical moment, and an ability to record what he saw in a manner at once poetic and concrete.

Young wrote dramatic criticism like no one before or after him, for he had a unique way of seeing and listening that must have derived from his childhood. Southerners then and now have a singular way of communicating with each other that goes far beyond the literal into a kind of poetry that Young himself has described as well as anyone:

Things are said that might seem to be nothing at all very much, but that we know without analyzing are the light or serious outpouring from intense or profound or daily and humble sources—a preference for a flower, say, is not just that but also a comment on some quality in life, some soft sweetness or cold or graceful formality, or some old romantic memory or happy or sad association. It might be some shading in the voice, some color of the tone, or the very order itself of the words or phrases, or even what is left out, not spoken at all, that expresses the thing really being said.

It was New York and its theatre, of course, which provided the arena in which Young's sensibility found its vocation. He first came to the city at the age of twenty in 1901 to take a master's degree in literature at Columbia and, in a sense, he never left it after that. Though he did teach at the Universities of Mississippi and Texas and at Amherst before he returned to New York to take up his post at *The New Republic,* New York from almost the moment he arrived there became as important to Young as his Southern childhood.

Two more different worlds cannot be imagined, yet Young loved both passionately. They were not entirely reconciled, however, nor could they be, and the cost of this was a certain amount of paradox both in Young's life and his criticism. A contributor to the famous Agrarian manifesto *I'll Take My Stand* (1930), Young nevertheless devoted his life to the high culture that flourished only in great cities. To explicate this paradox will doubtless be the task of Stark Young's biographer. Here it is enough to note that, while he himself said repeatedly that his experiences of two such different worlds seemed "to bless and feed each other," he was never able to give himself wholeheartedly to one world or the other. He loved New York as only those who have chosen to live there can, but he also claimed that he would "never find it the whole of life, or that . . . its rumor, agitation, and mass could ever be more than images in the vast world."

Aware, then, of a "vast world" beyond the confines of Times Square, Young was able, uniquely among critics practicing when he began, to bring a double-edged perspective to his scrutiny of the American stage. He saw a theatre event for what it was on its own terms ("The wisest course always for the health of art is to admit each thing for what it is and to work from that"), and he saw beyond the event itself to its place in the continuum of an art whose past he knew well and whose future, especially in America, he envisioned with great hopefulness.

It is difficult to write about Young's sensibility. It was all of a piece, at the center of a man who had only disdain for the "little masters of the high moral categories rather than of deeds or facts." Such a sensibility defies easy abstraction, for much of what Young had to say came out in the way he said it, and in that he was true to his Southern heritage. Alfred Kazin, who considered Stark Young "the most interesting American writer on theatre I had ever read," described Young's *modus operandi* in this way:

> Though he sooner or later wove his way round to characteristic observation, he could be alarmingly faithful to the idiosyncrasy of his own mind, and wrote a "drama piece" as if he needed only to satisfy himself. A review by Stark Young was like a rambling, slightly woozy monologue after dinner, punctuated by hiccups as he sat over his walnuts and wine, in the course of which he said more good things about theatre as stylized human behavior, and more interesting things about the Broadway commodity before him, than you would have expected from that great bald Charlus heavily sitting at table in his Southern mansion.

There were underlying assumptions in Stark Young's writing, however, and one in particular: an idea of theatre. For Young, theatre, though it borrowed its constituent elements from all the other arts, in so doing made each of those elements something quite different from before:

> The art of the theatre is not a mere combination of any particular things, settings, actors, recitation, literature, for example; it is a distinct and separate art. It may be composed of many things, but it is none of them. Nothing that goes to compose this art remains as it was before becoming part of it. But what that separate art of the theatre is, can be more easily illustrated than defined.

This passage might stand as the motto behind all Young's criticism. Its final sentence certainly sums up his method, for his writing celebrates those moments of theatre that he called the "idea created," in which form and content are fused so perfectly that something is expressed that could only be expressed by the medium of theatre.

An instance like this occurred only rarely, as in a now-forgotten vehicle for Pauline Lord:

> . . . the greatest single moment I ever saw was that first scene in *Mariners,* where the wife, in her white dressing gown, comes down the stair. It was a silly Clemence Dane play that went to pot long before the last curtain. What Miss Lord did in that first scene seemed to illustrate all life—by what tension, projection, and what technical and mystical combination of excitement, who shall say?

Such moments could be chronicled but never explained for Young, since he treated them as a mystery, happening "as life happens, some of it alive miraculously and unknowably." His columns in *The New Republic* chronicle the presence, the near-presence, and the absence of that mystery, the latter more often than the former, but always in consummate detail. As a chronicle Young's articles from the early 1920s have no equal for their historical value, for they bring alive the rise of Eugene O'Neill, the Provincetown Players, the Theatre Guild, in a way that no other writing of the period does, and none after could.

To the era itself he was only incidentally a chronicler, however, and Young took his function to be much more than that of advisor to audiences seeking their money's worth in the theatre. His greatest responsibility as he saw it was not to the audiences but to the actors, the playwrights, the designers, and the directors. As often as not his essays in *The New Republic* were not only fine descriptions of new productions, but also exquisitely detailed prescriptions as to how the production might be improved. Commenting upon the Theatre Guild's staging of *Caesar and Cleopatra*, for example, he suggested that "the ugly green curtain can be taken out of the banquet scene, the doors at the back of some of the scenes can have thickness added to their walls." Such advice was not offered facetiously by Young, nor maliciously, but in a purely constructive spirit grown out of a great hopefulness for what the American theatre could become. This hopefulness was too often disappointed, especially after the great promise of the early twenties died down, but Stark Young continued to set down his unique observations for a quarter of a century, leaving *The New Republic* in 1947 only after the magazine had changed hands and editorial policy.

Young's criticism needs to be read first-hand and in full—the detail and specificity of it defy excerpting—and for that one must go to the back files of *The New Republic*, since he selected only a small fraction of them for inclusion in *Immortal Shadows*. One of the greatest rediscoveries in the history of our theatre awaits the reader who has the persistence to thumb through those back issues, with their week-by-week chronicles of a great era in American theatre, as it happened. There are his letters as well, published in 1975 by Louisiana State University Press under the title *A Life in the Arts, 1900-1962*.

Finally, as a close to an appreciation of him, a quote from Stark Young that he lived by and that for him was justification for his vocation and the theatre's:

> We see now and again in the theatre great décor, great acting, great drama, but only two or three times in our lives do we see a quality expressed down to the last element in the theatre, a perfect unity in idea, plot, and every other medium of theatrical expression, the music, the setting, make-up, costumes, voice, gesture, and group movement. Such completeness, such unity in essence and form, is the living principle in every work of art, the supreme soul and test of it, first and last.

As a theatre critic Stark Young saw himself, first and last, in the service of that ideal of unity and completeness, encouraging its genesis at the same time as he celebrated its mystery.

CHAPTER FOUR

THEATER (CRITICISM) IN AMERICA: AN INTERVIEW WITH STANLEY KAUFFMANN

Stanley Kauffmann (born 1916) spent ten years, from 1931 to 1941, as an actor and stage manager with the Washington Square Players and has published a large number of short as well as long plays. Since 1958 Kauffmann has been active in criticism. At that time he became the film critic of *The New Republic*, with which magazine he has been associated ever since, except for an eight-month period in 1966 when he was exclusively the theater critic of *The New York Times*. (He continues to write film criticism, at age ninety-two, for *The New Republic*.) He has taught dramatic literature and criticism as well as theater and film history at the Yale School of Drama, the City University of New York, and Hunter College.

Kauffmann has published six collections of film criticism and two collections of theater criticism, *Persons of the Drama* (1976) and *Theater Criticisms* (1983). In 1974 he was given the George Jean Nathan Award for Dramatic Criticism. The following interview was conducted in July 2001 at Stanley Kauffmann's home in Manhattan. He discusses below his tenure as theater critic of the *New York Times*, as well as the state of the American theater and the relationship of that theater to its dramatic criticism.

BC: Could we begin by discussing your tenure as theater critic of *The New York Times*, from January 1, 1966, to August 31st of the same year?

SK: Fine. I had not sought the post; I had been invited by *Times* executives to meet with them. But let me give you some context first. The American cultural climate is changing—not necessarily improving but unmistakably changing—and in connection with this change I *was* something of a pioneer. The spread of middle-class status over the entire social spectrum, the surge of affluence, and the increase in number of college graduates who, whatever their intellects, are aware of being college graduates, all these have produced the current cultural explosion.

The managers of the *Times* were aware of these changes and had wanted their newspaper to respond to them. In the late fifties or early 1960s, they regrouped their various art departments into a Culture Department to facilitate greater "coverage" of culture. They began (as I subsequently learned) to become dissatisfied with several of their reviewers: dissatisfied with some of the old-line newspaper reviewing, couched in glib journalese and buoyed on hollow, dubiously knowledgeable generalities. *The Times's* dissatisfaction increased through 1965 and in fact when they first approached me, in late August of that year, it was not specifically about the job of drama critic but for general consultative conversations. They said they were considering major changes in their Culture Department and wanted "to pick my brains" (their phrase). They and I knew that this was just a gentleman's agreement to avoid any feeling of job-interview; I was even asked to suggest candidates for the drama job—and recommended two men. But in the course of several conversations with various executives, I was asked my opinion of *Times* criticism, in general, as it then was. I replied that in general it seemed to me a "cultural dump." I vigorously excepted Ada Louise Huxtable, their critic of architecture, and Clive Barnes, who had just joined them as dance critic, and later, when Hilton Kramer became one of their art critics, I most certainly excepted him. Otherwise I assured all the editors who consulted me—of the daily and Sunday editions—that I and, in my experience, the intellectual community held most *Times* criticism in very low esteem. They then engaged me.

I understood before I started that my employment was part of the paper's response to the cultural shifts in American life. But Mr. Barnes and Mr. Kramer worked in fields in which consideration of new works *as art* is accepted as the norm. However tawdry or opportunistic a dance recital or a gallery show, no dance impresario or gallery dealer would object to a review because too high standards had been applied; he might be enraged by what he thought was imperception, never by rigor. This is not because people in the dance and graphic art fields are necessarily a finer breed of beings but because mass audiences are not essential to their success, because investments in most dance offerings and all gallery shows are much smaller than Broadway investments, and because their publics *expect* the subject matter to be treated as art. Therefore, although both Mr. Barnes and Mr. Kramer doubtless were cordially disliked by some readers and professionals, the improvements they wrought aroused no concerted opposition. To my knowledge, no protesting delegations of dance impresarios or art dealers marched on *The Times* office to protest their reviews as, I am told, Broadway producers did in regard to me.

Quite objectively, then, I think my appointment can be seen as a frontier operation: an attempt, because of the social pressure of the cultural explosion, to give power to what previously had been tolerated only when impotent: serious theater criticism. The move was based on an assumption that the theater audience was now ready to have plays judged by standards cognate to those in dance and art criticism. To some extent, I certainly think this was and still is true, that there is a large audience being neglected and alienated both by Broadway and by the kind of reviewing that Broadway likes. But the ratio of that audience to the total audience is not large enough—shall I say not yet large enough?

BC: Was there any public reaction to your being appointed *The Times* drama critic?

SK: When my appointment was announced, a week or so before I started, uproar broke out. I had been the film critic for *The New Republic* and the theater critic for the PBS television station in New York, and moving to *The Times*, I meant simply to continue in critical practice whatever I had been able to do in those places. I wasn't naïve about the new job's increased visibility and influence, but I had no image of setting forth bravely to take lofty critical principles into the vulgar newspaper world. Yet this was the assumption, pro and con, of much that was published about the matter. People telephoned to interview me and asked me to comment on my reputation as being anti-Broadway. When I answered that I wasn't anti anything, I was pro theater, the sniffs and grunts I heard suggested that the other person thought I was being more nimble than forthright. Some, a few, put me in shining armor before I wrote a line for *The Times*. This, meant as a compliment, made me feel awkward.

BC: Why did you take the post at *The Times*? Your preceding eight years at *The New Republic* had been almost unqualifiedly pleasurable, had they not?

SK: That's right. To repeat, I went to *The Times* with (I still think) minimal naïveté. Or, as the phrase goes, I knew what I was getting into, at least ninety percent worth. I knew that I was making a trade: a trade that in no way involved my critical standards but that was a barter of some of whatever stylistic range and subtlety I may possess, which had free play in *The New Republic*, in return for the power, the sheer power, of a huge newspaper. I wanted that power—much less for self-aggrandizement (although I am no violet; genuine violets don't become critics) than to serve the theater according to my lights.

I had been trained for the theater through my four years of college, had spent ten years in a repertory company devoted to classics, had written and published plays, had directed in summer theaters and elsewhere, and for the three previous years had been the drama critic of Channel 13, the educational TV station in New York—all of which had produced and sustained in me a symbiotic love and despair. The more one loved the theater, the more reason one had to despair of the New York theater, particularly on Broadway, and not the least because of the general quality of newspaper drama reviewing. The clear implication on *The Times's* part was that I was expected to improve the latter element. I accepted—not modestly but entirely purposefully—because I thought that in some measure I could do it; and thus possibly help the theater itself.

BC: Why did it need your, or any serious critic's, help?

SK: Some historical perspective is essential to an answer so that we may understand the position and condition of Broadway. I am not about to launch into a diatribe against Broadway as the perennial source of all evil, not only because the subject is wearisome but because the thesis is untrue. To insist on it is to misconstrue the present appalling situation.

From its beginnings until late in the nineteenth century the American theater lived throughout America. There were touring companies, particularly on the frontier, but many towns had stock companies, and every large city had its own substantial theater or theaters—Boston, Philadelphia, Washington, Richmond, and so on. A distinguished nineteenth-century actor like William Warren could spend most of his career at the Boston Museum (as that theater was called) without the remotest thought of inferiority or failure because he was not playing in New York. A playwright might as readily take a new play to the manager of a St. Louis or New Orleans theater as to a New York manager. Toward 1900 this situation changed rapidly—principally for economic reasons. Increasingly, the railroads made it more feasible and profitable to book touring shows—complete with scenery—that originated in New York, and increasingly local theaters became local theater *buildings*, temporary habitations for companies passing through. Thus, for *all* intents and purposes, from about 1900 until after the Second World War the American theater was Broadway.

BC: But *most* of its intents and purposes were highly dubious.

SK: Yes, it's true that on Broadway there has always been a preponderance of junk (amongst which I do not include agreeable entertainment), and that preponderance has always been lamented by some. But if you call the roll of American dramatists of note in this century until about 1960, you see that without exception they have all flowered on Broadway. They *aspired* to

Broadway; and though some of them began elsewhere, like O'Neill at the Provincetown Playhouse, Broadway is where they fulfilled themselves. Their works went out *from Broadway* to the rest of America and to the world. Insofar as our theater has produced dramatists of consequence (and it has done so only in this century), Broadway is where it happened.

BC: Well, there certainly have been changes in this situation *vis-à-vis* dramatists.

SK: Right, but let me finish, for there is another important element that continues to apply to Broadway. It is the best yardstick of production quality that we have. Broadway's best work marks the high points in American acting and production. Despite the atrocious productions that always have been available on Broadway and that have proportionately increased in recent years, it is nonsense, I think, to deny that Broadway at its best is still American production at its best. This situation, too, may be changing. It has not yet changed.

Now unless one faces this cultural-historical fact—of the place of Broadway in the *art* of the American theater—it is impossible to understand the gravity of our condition. It is because Broadway has been much more than a money-machine, because for decades it has been both the fountain and funnel of American theater *art*, that the prospects are appalling. Because it is perfectly apparent that Broadway is deteriorating rapidly. There is no slightest touch of romantic nostalgia in this statement. Even statistics have some relevance—the almost continuously decreasing number of productions year by year—because plays of quality have always been in the minority, and if the proportion had been maintained (which it has not been), the number would still decrease. The reason is obvious. Highly increased costs have greatly reduced adventurousness, have caused Broadway to search more feverishly than ever for formulas and for "pre-tested properties," have made it cater even more exclusively to the latest demanding and largest segment of its audience.

For a time in the postwar years, Off-Broadway helped to offset the Broadway decline, but proportionate cost increases there have had proportionate stifling effects. Then there is Off-Off Broadway. The term is more than a semantic nicety: OOB uses mostly nonprofessional actors in improvised environments. It has at least the considerable merit of vitality. There is a certain promise in Off-Off Broadway so long as it doesn't completely justify its existence by being the residence of promise; and so long as its amateurism in performance, imposed by economics, is not exalted into an aesthetic.

Well, then: little is rationally to be hoped for on Broadway, the former source of our theater art; the two other New York theater activities are in a highly doubtful state.

BC: What sane function is there, then, for a New York newspaper theater critic?

SK: Here are the only present justifications I can see for doing the work. I cannot assert unequivocally that the following is the practice I now would be employing if I were still on *The Times*. But the following general ideas were certainly in my mind while on *The Times*; they influenced my actions, and were certainly the goals toward which I moved.

First, the job should not be construed as a contest between art and commerce. Patent commerce should be allowed to be as commercial as it likes, unmolested. The critic should ignore what does not interest him, as do the theater and film critics of good magazines. The newspaper can satisfy its journalistic obligations by running a notice of the opening written by a reporter, who can synopsize the plot, tell us what glamorous figures attended, how many curtain calls there were, how many laughs, and, with musicals, which numbers got the biggest hands. No productions should be criticized except those that clearly aspire to criticism. If the critic is uncertain about an incoming production, he can attend the last preview—which should, it goes without saying, be his standard practice anyway. If he is uninterested, a reporter can go to the opening. Art critics do not review billboards; music critics do not review dance bands and pop singers. Why should a drama critic review *Cactus Flower*? To be ultraclear, this is not an encyclical against light comedy or revues or musicals: for example, I very much enjoyed Mike Nichols' pastry-chef direction of *Barefoot in the Park* and spoke about it at length on television; I praised *The Mad Show* and *Superman* in *The Times*.

BC: Could we talk about this business of reviewing from previews? I know it caused quite a controversy during your stay at *The Times*.

SK: I had discussed at length with *The Times* before taking the job the matter of the opening-night review. This practice means that a critic for a morning newspaper has about an hour and a half—often considerably less—to get from the theater to his office and finish his review. I said that the practice was inimical to good criticism, and since other non-newspaper critics who were consulted had told them exactly the same, *The Times* agreed to take steps to change. They declined to postpone publication of reviews for twenty-four hours—until the morning after the morning after the opening—because of the competitive journalistic situation. I thought this reason irrelevant for a newspaper of *The Times's* standing, and it has become even less relevant. But the management promised to do everything it could to get me into the final previews of plays and to promote the plan with other newspapers. On this matter it kept its word. Indeed, for the first month or so of my tenure, the managing editor himself, Clifton Daniel, did all the telephoning to other newspapers and all the parleying with producers for my preview tickets.

BC: This reviewing-from-the-preview idea wasn't original on your part, was it?

SK: No, it was extremely unoriginal. Except for Great Britain and the U.S., it is more often the rule than otherwise. Attendance by the press at the *répétition générale* is a European commonplace. In Budapest, if a play is to open on, say, a Wednesday evening, there is a special performance for the press on Tuesday morning, with reviews published no earlier than Thursday. My reasons for wanting more time to think and write are obvious to the unbiased. If a play is worthless, as many are, it is easy to dismiss quickly, but even in that case the next day can give one a clearer view of the reasons for its worthlessness or a better way of stating one's dismissal. If a play has some worth, it seems to me little less than critically criminal to complete a review of it—particularly a review with the power of *The Times* behind it—in a maximum of ninety minutes. This for a work that may have taken years to write and has certainly taken at least a year to produce.

BC: What was the response of the other critics to your proposal?

SK: Before I began work, Mr. Daniel informed every other major newspaper critic in New York of the new plan, to obviate suspicion of "scooping" and to invite them to join in the procedure. None of them joined. Except in one case, where there was some reason to expect an understanding response, this was not surprising. To change would have been to admit that they had been misspending their lives. But the quality of their disagreement was unexpected. In reply to Mr. Daniel's telephoned invitation, one critic said, "Isn't this a confession of Kauffmann's incompetence?"—thus equating critical competence with the ability to meet rush deadlines. In fact, for various reasons, I eventually was forced to write a number of opening-night reviews. I had never doubted my ability to do this; and I grew increasingly adept at it; and hated growing increasingly adept.

Another critic, in print, called me "craven." Another was quoted as saying, "Some of us, despite our shortcomings, can do the job." Another was quoted as saying of the preview plan, "Reviews would probably become more negative because as you move away from the experience inside the theatre you tend to lose the fire." So the invitation was met with a solid front of the other critics' competence, guts—the opposite of cravenness—and a wish to keep reviews positive. These days, as you know, the writing of reviews based on previews has become common.

BC: How did theater people themselves react to your plan at the time?

SK: Their first reactions were either favorable or guardedly interested. One producer, Richard Barr, agreed immediately to the plan and drafted a press release endorsing it. He was prevented from distributing it, I was told, by the owner of the theater in which his forthcoming production was housed, who had some contractual control in the matter. (However, Mr. Barr invited critics to previews of his subsequent productions.) I had private comments from actors, playwrights, and directors approving the idea. Then my reviews began to appear, and the climate quickly changed. Within six weeks the League of New York Theaters (a group of producers), the Dramatists' Guild, Actors' Equity Association, and the Society of Stage Directors and Choreographers all voiced formal disapproval of the plan and urged their members to resist it.

BC: What were the reasons these groups gave?

SK: One of the reasons given was that plays are not really ready until the opening night, even as against the last preview on the previous night, and that, at the opening, the performance is always particularly "high." For years I had believed this to be sentimental nonsense, and I soon learned that I was right. While at *The Times* I attended both the last previews *and* the openings of seven productions. These producers wanted me to have a full day in which to write but also asked me to weigh in the opening-night performance before the review went to the press. In six of these cases, the two performances of each play were virtually indistinguishable. In one case, *The Condemned of Altona* at Lincoln Center, the opening performance was markedly inferior to the last preview. If I had taken it into account in my review, I would have had to downgrade my opinion. I did not because I knew what the cast was capable of.
    Another objection was that a cast "ought not to have to go to bat twice" for reviewers—once for me at the last preview and again for the others at the opening. Yet another statement, by one professional group, rejected "the theory that a unilateral decision by a reviewer who bases his report on a performance different from the one his fellows see is valid." These objections made fools of everyone on the second-night press list, all those critics of smaller

magazines and newspapers who regularly see a different performance from the one seen by the daily reviewers. Many producers claimed the right to determine when their productions should be open to inspection; but this right was respected by my going to see the production at the last preview that the public was invited to see. In fact, New York audiences often paid their way into theaters, at previews, for two or three weeks before an official opening. At one final preview I attended, which had been sold out as a benefit, my tickets had a one-hundred-dollar price printed on each. Lastly, the producers repeated the argument of some reviewers: reviews ought to be written "hot," right after the show. Immediacy was essential, they claimed. Why is it any more essential to a play than to a film and why film distributors often show films to critics months before the reviews appear, was not discussed.

BC: O.K., what was the real reason behind all these objections?

SK: Because of the initial favorable reaction to the plan before my reviews started to appear, because of the patent toshery of all these objections, and also because numerous members of these objecting unions and societies wrote me and *The Times* of their approval, I was forced to one conclusion: the official stand was not against the practice but against the practitioner, myself. Whether or not my criticism was sound—a matter that to me and to them is inarguable— the Broadway Establishment objected to a critic who applied the same standards to drama reviews in a major newspaper that he had used on a local educational TV station or that he had used for films on a weekly intellectual magazine.

All this commotion, which quickly took on the coloration of a band of decent folk standing together to resist corruption, was in reality something else: the elements of show biz uniting against someone who treated the theater as an art and only as an art. The theatrical unions that passed resolutions against my preview practice included many artists, but officially—as unions—they are part of an industry. Partisanship among the nonprofessional—and I was fascinated at how many people outside the theater took passionate sides, including many who rarely go to the theater—was an extension of a schism between business and a view to which business is irrelevant. I do not argue a hierarchy: businessmen have as much right, I suppose, to protect their investments as intellectuals have to protect their principles. I do argue a difference. This squabble was the consequence of giving box-office power to a critic who was unimpressed by this box-office power. I know of few similar instances of critics who came from serious magazines to New York daily theater criticism. One of them was my illustrious predecessor, Stark Young, who left *The New Republic* to become the drama critic of *The New York Times* in 1924—and returned to *The New Republic* in 1925.

BC: Were there any public incidents connected with, or growing out of, your policy of reviewing from previews whenever possible?

SK: One producer who objected to the practice sent me tickets for the last preview of an Irish play he was presenting with a note inviting me to use them at, he said, my peril. I went to the theater that evening and found that the preview had been cancelled. The producer gave the press some transparent jokes as his reason. It was obvious that he wanted to force me to write an opening-night review. Later I learned that he had bought up every available copy of the play, which had been published in London and had been imported, so that I couldn't read it in advance.

A mob milled around the closed theater that evening. Photographers were there. A few people applauded me, which made me wriggle. My wife was distressed by all the commotion, and I took her away as quickly as possible. Much was made of the matter in *The Times* next day, and in other papers. My wife shook her head as she read the accounts. "They're *all* wrong," she said. "Even those who like you."

I saw the Irish play on opening night. I thought it was well acted but rather trite. The producer had been clever to publicize it as he had done.

BC: Could we return to the topic of the function of, or justification for, theater criticism, as it butts heads with the business world?

SK: Yes, of course. The present imperative for the critic to review every Broadway show seems to me a debasement of his function, a confusion of territories, and an invasion of a businessman's business rights. A man who manufactures popcorn has the right to sell it, without interference, to anyone who wants to buy it. But the man who manufactures popcorn theater productions has to suffer the intrusion of a powerful dissuader who does not like popcorn. Obviously there are borderline cases, and of these the critic should be the sole judge; but most instances are *not* borderline cases. Alfred Kazin does not try to dissuade anyone from reading Harold Robbins; why should a serious drama critic intrude on the mercantile projects that turn up on Broadway?

For example, early in my stay on *The Times* I saw a show called *The Wayward Stork*, a farce about artificial insemination in which the doctor injects the wrong woman. I had read about the success of its long out-of-town tour with a TV star in the leading role, and indeed at the performance I saw, the audience rocked and screamed around me while I sat numb with revulsion. My review reflected this revulsion. To the argument, which I subsequently heard, that I ought to have recorded the audience's reaction, my reply was—and still would be—that I had been engaged to record my own reactions, not other people's, and that if I applied the reporting principle here, I also would have to report the occasions, which happen, when I laugh and almost everyone else is silent. This prospect of fair play usually squelched the objection, but I have come more and more to believe that my presence at the show was an intrusion between it and a large public that might possibly have enjoyed it for months. It was only nominally a play; my judgment was no more relevant to what was happening on that stage than it would have been to a pie-eating contest where spectators also rock and scream.

BC: Couldn't a second-stringer have reviewed a production of *The Wayward Stork*?

SK: The use of a second-string reviewer for such shows is unsatisfactory. There ought to be an identification between the newspaper and a critical view in the public's mind. Besides, I know from experience that it is discomfiting to see a review in one's own journal with which one disagrees; several times when circumstances kept me from reviewing a play that someone else had to cover, a later visit made me writhe at the opinion that had been voiced in the paper for which I was supposed to be the critic. The only way the critic can be of service to his readers is by providing his own standards—with his own insights and defects—as a frame of reference. The situation in the music and book and art departments is unavoidable because of the far greater number of discussable offerings in those fields than in the theater.

    Friedrich Luft, the eminent German critic, once told me that he had an assistant who reviewed almost all musicals. This must have saved him a great deal of tedium, but I cannot see it as a happy solution here. For one thing, the musical, as we are constantly told, is the prime American theatrical form, and the critic ought to have the right to comment on examples from it. With musicals as elsewhere, there seems to me no rational solution except a division between critic and nonjudgmental reporter, the former to deal with attempts at any kind of valid theatrical art, the latter to serve as a bland medium between sellers and buyers. Some producers might object at first that the absence of the critic is a qualitative tip-off about their productions; still, they might quickly come to prefer this practice to adverse comment.

BC: You said earlier that, first of all, the job of a metropolitan theater critic should not be construed as a contest between art and commerce. You certainly have made that argument; are there any other ones you wish to make about the profession of drama criticism?

SK: My second point is a large one with several subdivisions of, I think, extensive importance. Today the drama critic of a major newspaper ought to consider himself a *national* critic, not a local one who makes sporadic trips to the hinterlands. I began to put this idea into practice during my eight months on *The Times*. I visited about a quarter of the resident professional theaters in the United States (and Canada), several of them more than once, and would have visited three or four more if there had not been an airlines strike in the summer of 1966. The first motive for this practice is sheerly selfish: there isn't enough to sustain a critic's interest in New York; and, if he also writes the Sunday articles, as I did, there is insufficient material for those articles if one is not content to blow Sunday soap-bubbles.

There is a deeper, less personal reason. Broadway was, as noted, the source of our theatrical art for decades; Broadway is strangulating. If the American theater is to survive—no sure thing, in my opinion, despite the statistics—its other areas must prosper: resident theaters, university theaters, small independent theaters. It must complete the cyclical movement of "redecentralization": a return to professional pluralism, a national community of theatrical peers instead of our present status—a flickering sun and a lot of quasi-dependent planets. These out-of-New York theaters, as I have seen them, do not need to be patronized, they need to be criticized, as much for the critic's benefit as theirs. Where merit in some degree exists, it needs to be noticed so that it can be helped; and for his own competence, the critic needs to know what is happening nationally in order to be authoritative in judgment and comparison. The Broadway yardstick of production quality, as I said, has been our best, but now it needs both testing and application: testing to see if it continues to be our best; application to other theaters with the hope of helping them. The latter needs no explanation; as to the former, I saw productions of *Mother Courage* in Milwaukee and *The Last Analysis* in Philadelphia that were better than the Broadway productions of these plays.

As to the metropolitan reader's interest in theaters he is unlikely to attend, it is at least as high as his interest in reviews of concerts that have passed and books he will not read. Very much more so, I would hazard from experience, if he cares about the theater at all.

BC: Are there any other aspects to this matter of a national view or perspective of the theater?

SK: One aspect is the little-regarded but crucially important matter of ego-satisfaction for the members of these outlying professional theaters. Financial rewards are generally small; rewards, in terms of opportunities for good work, are much greater. But *recognition* of this work is generally insufficient. The "William Warren" condition, referred to earlier, had not yet returned to this country. It is not the New York critic's function to publicize a performance in Walla Walla so that the director or leading actor can get a New York job, but he can supply occasional, sympathetically rigorous criticism.

Most cities are even worse off for criticism than New York. Dozens of resident-theater directors and managers have told me how sick they are of the endless meaningless praise they get from the local press, leavened occasionally by equally meaningless carping just to prove the local reviewer's independence. Even though the New York critic can visit any one theater only occasionally, still (granting his competence) these visits can be of value to a valuable theater. The criticism gives the local company a sense of resonance and appraisal—a need that will obtain until and unless local criticism improves. It helps break down a sense of isolation and possibly to expedite the arrival of a truly decentralized theater situation in which these visits by a metropolitan critic will not be essential.

Further, such criticism, if it can be honestly favorable, helps to certify the theater to its community. This is not only a matter of fundraising but of intrinsic audience sympathy. Some administrators of resident theaters have noted that foundation grants have enabled them to choose plays regardless of the community's wishes and taste. When the subsidy is removed, they find themselves with, say, a four-year-old theater and an insufficient audience. I believe in subsidy; and I do not believe in catering to majority tastes. Since, in most cases, local criticism is inadequate, the prestige of a metropolitan critic can, first, help to keep the subsidy forthcoming; second, help to vitalize and enlarge the most responsive segments of the potential local audience.

The growth of diversity in the American theater could have one more most important result. If resident theaters flourish—in every sense—then dramatists may in time come to want productions *there* as they now, mostly, want productions on Broadway or productions that would ultimately move there: another return to a *status quo ante*. Further, other authors of talent, who have been discouraged from playwriting because they refuse to get mired in the Broadway swamps, may become interested in writing for the theater, and this may raise the generally poor level of new American drama. All this a good critic on a powerful newspaper may help to bring about.

BC: Tell me a bit more about what it was like going from a magazine of relatively modest circulation to a huge powerful newspaper.

SK: My stay on *The New Republic* had been very pleasant. One reason for this was my relation—doubtless partly imaginary but nonetheless effective—with the magazine's readers. I felt that I was speaking every week to a responsive and relatively homogeneous audience. Argument and objection reached me in plenty, but it was always dissent within a framework of mutually understood objectives of art and criticism. I said earlier that I had relatively little naïveté about *The Times* job before I began, but there was one matter I had anticipated insufficiently—the change in reader response. *The Times's* readership is not only very much larger than *The New Republic*'s but much more heterogeneous. They virtually brag at *The Times* that almost half of their readers are not college graduates.

From the start my mail was huge, much larger, I was told, than my predecessor's; and from the start there were many letters of commendation, some of them from very flattering sources inside and outside the theater. But the majority of letters opposed me with a heat, I confess, that was shocking. The criticism I was writing—to me, essentially a continuation of the kind I always had written—absolutely enraged many people in this new context. The "Who-do-you-think-you-are?" or "Don't-you-ever-like-*anything*?" letter was common enough in crude and misspelled form; the surprise was in how often that letter was grammatically written and neatly typed: or handwritten in progressive-girls'-school calligraphy of a generation ago. Polished or grubby, these letters all wanted essentially a reviewer who was a kind of shopping service and not too fussy. The proportion of pro and anti letters shifted considerably as the months went on, but the heat of the anti letters did not diminish. I particularly cherished the communiqués from an anonymous backer of *Sweet Charity*, a musical I had disliked. Every week he sent me a copy of the box-office receipts as reported in *Variety*, accompanied by an obscene scrawl.

BC: Aside from the volume of your mail, were there any other visible or tangible indications of your power?

SK: After the first edition of the newspaper came off the press, I would take a copy home with me. If there were any errors in my piece, I would phone in corrections from home. It was one of the few attributes of power I enjoyed, being able to sit home and make changes in *The Times*.

I never understood why there weren't more errors in the paper. One evening about nine-thirty, after I had finished a review, the head of the so-called Culture Department stopped in the doorway of my cubicle to chat. He was standing on some sheets of the copy paper that coated the floor by that hour, and as we talked, his eye wandered down to a sheet under his shoe. He interrupted himself, picked up the sheet, and muttered, "What the hell is this? This was supposed to be in the first edition."

Another power I liked was telephoning in my reviews from far places. I visited resident theaters in other cities, and in the summer I went to theater festivals, and in both cases I had to dictate my reviews over the phone. I had been given a special number to call at *The Times* office. It was always answered by the most bored voice I have ever heard. Slowly, distinctly, I would dictate what I had just written, at the moment the most important words in the world to me, and the voice would say, "Yeah? That all? More? Yeah?" I enjoyed the counterpoint between him and me.

On one of those trips I got a sharp reminder of my power. In Chicago I had agreed to attend a Wednesday matinee of a new theater group if they would drive me to another place by six o'clock. They agreed, and after the performance I got into a car driven by their publicity person, a young woman fresh out of college in her first job. She was eager to do this chore as professionally as possible, and we started off promptly.

What she and the others in her theater had forgotten was that this was rush hour. The road along the lake was jammed with crawling cars, and we were jammed in the middle, crawling with them. My driver knew about my urgency, knew that it was her mission to get this sovereign figure, myself, to his next appointment on time. She began to shake, to beat on the wheel with her fists, to attempt apologies. I was irritated, but she was so distressed that I began to feel sorry for her.

I tried to put her at ease by asking her questions. She answered in short, nervous, machine-gun bursts. How long had she been in this job? "T—two—only two months." Where did she come from? "F—from Chicago, right—right near here." Did she have family here? "Y—yes, my—my mother and—and my brother." She was not getting less panicky. I continued. And her father? "Well—well," she stammered, "he—he's dead at the moment."

BC: Did she laugh as we're laughing now?

SK: No. And she was so nervous she didn't even hear what she had said after she said it.

BC: Your power aside, what was the day-to-day writing of newspaper reviews like before the advent of the word-processor? You had an office, didn't you?

SK: At *The Times* I had a cubicle against the wall of a huge room filled with desks; I had a secretary just outside; I had a key to the back door of the building on 44th Street so that on opening nights I wouldn't have to take time to go around to the front door on 43rd Street if the back were more convenient; I had a credit card.

I disliked the office. Not the people but the idea of newspapers. Clatter and deadlines and hats on the backs of heads, all the movie mystique about newspapers, never held a jot of romance for me. I was there as a critic, I told myself, who happened to be on a newspaper, not as a newspaperman. I even hated the coarse gray copy paper that we typed on and that by nightfall covered the floor. I suppose that now, in word-processor days, there is no such paper drizzle, but it was everywhere then. It seemed to seep up through the floor, like dankness.

I was a technological pioneer. When I was hired, I had asked for an electric typewriter, the kind that I used at home, so that it would be familiar to me. The machine was purchased promptly, the first electric typewriter in the building outside of the executive offices. My secretary, who had worked for some of the theater critics before me, was impressed by the machine. She wanted to help. Just before she left the office at five o'clock on the day I was to do my first review, she switched on the typewriter to save me time when I got there after the play. When I arrived about nine that evening, the typewriter was hot. But it seemed the warmth of concern, hers, so I enjoyed it.

BC: My father was a printer, so I'd like to hear a little bit about your dealings with that department at *The Times*.

SK: In those days of Linotype machines, I had to type one or at the most two paragraphs on a sheet of that copy paper, complete, without a run-on sentence to the next page. This was to help the Linotype operator and to save time. Sheet after sheet. Outside my cubicle waited a copy boy. He took each sheet upstairs to the composing room while I kept typing. I tried to sound calm and experienced as I called "Copy!" and the boy jumped. It was part of the performance.

When the review was finished, I had a sip of Irish whisky from a bottle in my desk. Then I got into a tiny two-person elevator and went up to the composing room. The first paragraphs had already been set, and the proof strips were hanging on hooks outside the composing room. I read the strips and corrected them. By the time I finished them, the last strips were ready.

BC: So you did this for eight months. Did one particular event lead to your dismissal, aside from the issue of previews, which is obviously connected to the one of critical standards?

SK: Before I accepted *The Times* job, I said to the editor with whom the matter was settled, "You know you will have trouble because of me." He replied, "We don't expect you to change your spots. We want you because of your spots." We agreed on a minimum engagement of a year and a half. "But," he said, "that's merely a standard precaution—for both our sakes. We hope this will be for life." The engagement lasted eight months, as we know, until the *Herald*

Tribune died and their drama critic became available, when my contract was settled. Ten minutes after the details of my termination were settled, someone appeared in my cubicle to take away my key to the back door and my credit card. I felt as if he were stripping off my epaulets and said so. He thought my joke out of place.

BC: When did *The Times* divide or split up the traditional function of its drama critic?

SK: That started in September 1967. My successor, Walter Kerr, began to write only Sunday articles, and Clive Barnes, who had been the dance critic of *The Times*, took over the writing of daily reviews. The change in *Times* policy, reportedly suggested by my successor, was ascribed to the diminished number of newspapers and the consequent increase in *The Times* critic's power, and to a wish to provide more than one opinion. If this was the reason, we can wonder why the film critic's function was not thus divided at the same time—also the functions of the music and art critics. Despite the numbers of the latter, *The Times* publishes only one review of any concert or exhibit. Even the double review of a few books is not *policy*: it is not planned that a particular book be covered by a daily staff reviewer and a Sunday free-lancer. The splitting of the drama critic's function—which continues—was in principle a questionable move, seemingly influenced by a democratic-representation concept, a political idea mistakenly applied to art. But at least it is not a first- and second-string ranking.

BC: Before we move to another subject, could you sum up the state of American drama criticism and of the American theater?

SK: Yes, by all means. The difficulties of serious drama criticism, in a position of power, are not new, and I was not a heroic pioneer at *The New York Times*. The theater, more than any other art, has always strenuously resisted serious criticism and tolerates it only when it is relatively powerless. A chief component of this condition is the attitude of much of its audience, who would probably be happier with a one- to four-star rating service, plus a brief synopsis, and who want just enough adverse reviews to make them relish the positive ones—they want to be *permitted* to go. The theater's view of the matter is supported by most newspaper publishers and editors, whose standard in criticism—as anyone can see in almost any newspaper anywhere—is not quality but readability. The writer who can supply bright readable copy, and supply it quickly, is an acceptable critic. If he is also acidulous and full of waspish wisecracks—occasionally alternated with the syrupy sentimentality that inevitably marks such a writer—then he is additionally valuable as being "outspoken." Indeed, "outspoken" has become the most prized adjective a critic can earn, in a publisher's view. Whether the speaking-out is of any intrinsic merit whatsoever is a quite secondary consideration so long as the writer gets himself read and talked about.

In the past the best American drama criticism has been published in journals of relatively little influence. Certainly I do not contend that it has therefore been useless. I do contend that our theater is in a state of acute crisis; that our culture in general is headed either for growth or for horribly swollen, empty inflation; that a junction of newspaper power and good drama criticism can be simultaneously beneficent to the theater and radically helpful to all American culture,

There are two strong countermotions in the present-day theater. On the one hand, expense increases, thus adventurousness shrinks and the number of productions decreases. On the other hand, the educational level of the audience is rising. To this disparity, this absolute opposition, the critic of influence may bring some relief. He can encourage the commercial theater to take account, in its own interest, of the new audience it is missing—a wan prospect. He can help other theaters in New York and elsewhere—in something like the modes described above—to grow in quality, in community with their audiences, and therefore in stability—a somewhat more sanguine prospect. Either way a great deal depends on him. The power of the newspaper critic used to be the capacity to make or break commercial shows. That power was often disavowed, usually by those who had it, but in any case it is now of quite secondary importance. The function of the powerful critic now is either to assist in the birth of a possible new American theater or to be a leading witness of a lengthening eclipse.

BC: Is there *anything* about the state of theater criticism in America that cheers you up?

SK: The only thing that cheers me up about the state of theater criticism—which is a large part of the American theater's problem—is that it's *never* been any good. We think reverently of the great critics of the past, but if you read their contemporaries . . . In terms of power, there is only one critic in this country, and he works for the *New York Times*. It's the most powerful critic's job in the world in any art form.

And playwrights suffer—I mean suffer terribly—from the mindless overpraise dished out by most reviewers. Tony Kushner may be the latest casualty. One thing happens as a result of this, which did not happen in the Broadway of old. You find a playwright writing his sixth, eighth, even twelfth play for Off-Broadway or Off-Off Broadway, with the same faults—curable faults—that he had in his first play. You find wasted talent because of critical pampering and because of the very reaction against the Broadway regimen. There's hope that this situation may be changing now because the profession of dramaturg—another European institution—is coming into some prominence in the United States.

Now, nothing is a solution, but the idea that there should be someone on the staff of a theater, one of whose chief functions it is to be interested not just in finding good plays, but in fostering the art of playwriting, in finding and developing dramatic talent—this is a great step forward. Yet there's been this conduit atmosphere—mostly Off-Off Broadway—in the last forty years or so that implicitly argues: if it exists on paper and has some promise of talent or poetry, let's put it on. And the twelfth play by that author, which is in the same state, is produced as well. I will name one theater—La Mama, run by Ellen Stewart—which has operated on the assumption that it's better to do something that merely shows talent than not to do it at all. And in the long run—and we're getting to be in the long run now after forty years—we come to a situation where people ask, "Where are the new playwrights?" What has happened as a result of this? Part of what has happened is the disappearance of artistic discipline—lack of discipline proceeding from lack of craft if not dearth of knowledge.

BC: There's another problematic point regarding playwrights. Today we have dramatists who come out of some of the best universities in the country, where they are exposed to great dramatic literature, yet they are for the most part incapable of writing anything more than television-level work. Indeed, some of them would *rather* be writing for television or—even better—the movies.

SK: I understand your point but what you're really doing is criticizing an educational system for not creating talent. And that shortage of talent may come down to the fact that the United States is an inheritor country, a scion country of culture that's made its own distinctive contributions but did not originate much in art.

BC: Except in musical comedy.

SK: I said art. And the specialized fact that I've cited, which is an historical one and not a judgmental one, is part of an attitude toward the theater in American writers that's very different from the one in Europe. Europeans operate out of a more homogeneous culture and see themselves as immersed in the tensions, the polarities, of an organism more than Americans do. Why, for example, were there so many good Southern writers in the twentieth century? Because they were—and may still be—the most homogeneously "culture-conscious" of Americans. The English, for their part, believe—despite all the talk of "diversity" on American university campuses—that they're more diverse than Americans within their own particular organism. And because they are, in a sense, more compact or contained, they're more acutely aware of their differences. The class-conscious early plays of Edward Bond—in my opinion his best—are very keenly aware of what it's like to suffer in the English countryside, à la Thomas Hardy. That's something for which we have no exact equivalent in the contemporary American theater.

American plays are trying to sense or satisfy this—let's call it community hunger—by the transmogrification of pop culture. Sam Shepard has done so, particularly in his rock plays. But it is not quite the same thing. I don't know if there's anything to be done about this except for the country simply to live a little longer. I'm just trying to understand in my own mind why more interesting writing is coming from England, Ireland, and elsewhere than we're getting today in the United States. . . . This is not a general American phenomenon; it's an American *theatrical* phenomenon. There is very fine American poetry being written now. There are some fine American novels being produced. And there are good painters and architects at work. I think the problem of playwriting has deep roots in American attitudes toward the theater. In terms of theater *seriousness*, this is a very young nation.

BC: Couldn't substantial public funding for the arts ultimately solve the problem of deficient native playwriting and an anemic American theater?

SK: There's a paradox in this. Our country is, always has been, a democracy, whereas the idea of subsidy that prevails in Europe and elsewhere was originally an aristocratic notion. It's been taken over by many socialist and many democratic countries that have an aristocratic tradition long behind them. It doesn't shock anyone in Germany that huge subsidies go to theaters and opera houses. This doesn't strike Germans as out of the ordinary, because the grand duke so-and-so was doing it over 300 years ago and now they're proud to have taken over the tradition with republican hands. The once-aristocratic system now belongs to the people.

This country was founded on self-reliance, but as applied to the arts that's a blind principle. It assumes that if you open a grocery store on the corner, work hard and deal fairly, you will succeed. And if you open a theater and behave in the same way, the same thing will happen. In point of fact, however, the better your theater is, the less likely it is to make money. The fact that business and art are not analogous has taken about 275 years in this country—from before America was founded—to sink in. There is a further analogy that is harmful. If you work in television or film, your salary corresponds to the market for television and cinema, but if you work in theater, especially a non-profit theater, your salary has no such huge commercial impetus to reflect. Yet you must buy your food in the same supermarket as the television or movie employee, pay equivalent rent, etc. In the theater, the ballet, all but popular music, the situation is ghastly. And it's the kind of situation that, if allowed to burrow down to the roots of arts institutions, may destroy things past recovery.

BC: We can't have a national theater in a country so vast as the United States, but we can and do have city theaters, even "state" theaters. And yet they cannot be compared to the national theaters of Europe in terms of accomplishment.

SK: Here's my definition of a true national theater, derived from European models: a permanent company playing in a repertory that consists to a considerable degree of the great dramatic literature of *that* country. Now the prime handicap here is that there is only a handful of truly great American plays. So that sooner or later, any American artistic director who runs such a theater—if he deals honestly and doesn't want to blow up out of all relativity items that don't really belong on the scale of European names you and I could cite by the dozen—has to make the bulk of his repertory foreign.

     Even that would be fine and necessary from another point of view. If we're not going to have any theater comparable to, let's say, the Comédie Française, then we ought to have in New York City—in many cities—what one might call a museum theater, a theater that is absolutely essential and sadly lacking anywhere in this country. This would be a theater that does for great dramatic literature what, for example, the Metropolitan Opera tries to do for great operatic literature and what the Philharmonic does for great symphonic literature. In other words, give everyone in his lifetime at least some chance to see and hear the great works. Such a museum theater is generally derided nowadays, particularly by young theater people. Derided, I think, because it's outside their competence rather than because of any conviction on their part. I think that a theater like this is culturally imperative as one part of the theatrical spectrum. The reasons that militate against it are obviously expense and obviously, too, the difficulty of retaining anything like a permanent company.

BC: You've painted a despairing picture of contemporary theater in America. What can we hope for in the coming years?

SK: Trouble. Money trouble. Social trouble, too, which automatically means trouble in the theater. But one good thing that theater education has been doing, the education that you're impatient with for not producing masters, is to produce—let's call it—a certain disgust. At least some of the people who are coming out of good educational programs are disgusted with trick-dog theater that sits up when a bored audience snaps its fingers. These people want to do something more with their lives than serve such a theater. We can't look forward to geniuses—that's like pinning your hopes on miracles. But we can reasonably look forward to honor and commitment in the exercise of talent—in the face, moreover, of a cloudy situation that is getting cloudier. It's even not impossible that audiences throughout the United States will get again that sense of possessiveness toward their theaters that once made the theater truly decentralized in this country

And there's one other thing that's part of all this and, in my mind, not one whit less important. There is good reason to hope for some improvement in the level of theater criticism. I don't mean the production of scholarship by professors, but the exercise of critical talent by writers who understand the art of theater—and understand it because they've mastered the other arts as well.

CHAPTER FIVE

AMERİCAN DRAMATURGY: A RE-APPRAİSAL

Dramaturgy is the discipline of a dramaturg, as directing is that of a director, or acting that of the actor. If there is a paradox in an increasing number of dramaturgs encountering increasing confusion about their role, however, it is symptomatic of a larger problem that cannot be answered by explanations or examples from a dictionary. There are still theatres that can plead poverty or ignorance as obstacles to adopting dramaturgical practices; but when a company is rich enough, sophisticated enough, cognizant enough of its own problems finally to hire one or more dramaturgs, and then proceeds not to employ them properly, the reason usually boils down to one thing: there is no dramaturgy to be practiced. Many of our biggest and best known theatres produce play after play without the benefit of dramaturgy, or—in my definition of the word—without any attempt to make sense of the production, for the theatre itself and its practitioners as well as for the audience. The question is: how and why did this come about?

The reluctance to accept dramaturgy and dramaturg as English words reflects a deeper resistance to thinking about the theatrical process as a whole. As busy practitioners we pretend that we do not have time to question the philosophical basis of what we are doing, or that we can take for granted unspoken agreement on the subject. Even in the atmosphere of university theatres, reputed to provide more time and security for exercising the mind, very little thought goes into choosing a play for reasons other than the number of female parts. It is as if we were afraid to ask "why?" in case the answer might negate the value of asking. This is a strange paradox given the philosophical bent of characters like Hamlet and Prospero, who remain more popular than ever on our stage.

The main job of a dramaturg is precisely to keep asking why. Why are we doing this play? Why this season? Why here? Why does our theatre exist? Why do we exist? Why has theatre thrived elsewhere or in the past? Why do our audiences come? Why does ninety to ninety-five percent of the local population stay away? Why are we, inside the theatre, excited about the plays we are doing, and why are we not spreading our excitement to the community?

A sound etymological and working definition of dramaturgy is thus "making drama work." Everybody in the theatre should be involved in the process of playmaking or making drama work. But given the enormous human and technical complexity of preparing even the most straightforward production so that it can open on a certain date (determined long before any of the difficulties that inevitably arise could have been foreseen), it is hardly surprising that everybody in a theatre company concentrates on the mechanics of how to get the job done, hoping that the why will take care of itself. Yet, as Victor Frankl pointed out long ago in *Man's Search for Meaning* (1959), life works exactly the other way around. He observed that the only survivors of the Nazi concentration camps were those who knew why they wanted to live; those who could not find meaning in their lives died faster than those from whom they stole bread. In order to find the "how," therefore, we must first know the "why."

Meaning is central to human existence and art. And every artist must seek meaning for himself. In the performing arts, the quest is more complicated because some kind of consensus has to be reached first within a group of artists and then within the larger tribe represented by the audience. The drama does not work, and it cannot be made to work, if the artists and audiences that are involved in producing and watching it do not seek the meaning of their own roles, as well as that of the work itself. I am not suggesting that there are always answers when the questions are asked, only that there can be no meaning to playmaking without a conscious quest for that meaning. Every good production is the quest itself.

It would be too simplistic and neat to say that the dramaturg asks the "why," or seeks the meaning, and that the director deals with the "how," or accomplishes the doing. Clearly, the latter must also ask why, and the former has to be aware of the limitations to which every production is heir. But it is important to distinguish in the theatre between the text that represents the thinking of usually one individual mind, who is often rooted in a different time or place, and the performance that is the result of a collective consciousness. The text is inert but lasting, the performance is evanescent yet alive; and the two are fused for a few hours to create a unique meaning. This dramaturgical process is exclusively for those people who choose on a particular occasion to come together on stage and in the auditorium. If there is no meaning there, a great many people will have wasted their time. This central fact about the theatre has not changed one jot for two-and-a-half thousand years; it is probably the reason why the theatre survives as an important institution in the face of overwhelming competition from the commercialized mass media, not to speak of personal computers, cell phone, iPods, and the like. As Martin Esslin once put the matter in "The Role of the Theatre," in his book *Reflections* (1969):

... in a world from which spontaneous human experience is more and more disappearing through the cancerous growth of over-organized, over-mechanized, and ready-made patterns of work, behavior, thought, and even emotion, the genuine need for theatre is growing apace—for a theatre in which human beings can regain their autonomy of feeling, in which the denizens of a thoroughly secularized, demythologized, emotionally dehydrated society can return to the roots of what need not be called religious experience, but which might be called a contact with the ultimate archetypes of the human condition, the awe and mystery, the grandeur of man's lonely confrontation with himself, the universe, and the great nothingness that surrounds it.

The dramaturg, inasmuch as he is concerned with the text—or with "meaning" as Esslin conceives it—must have a more lasting perspective both backwards and forwards in time than the director, who is in charge only of the momentary performance or production. The best directors I have worked with, however, have also been the best dramaturgs: their primary motivation and talent lay in carving, shaping, and creating a meaning out of the text, rather than imposing on it some flashy but nonsensical concept that is sometimes mistaken for meaning.

Having pronounced these rather lofty principles about the nature of theatrical meaning, I must now point up the significant difference between the theatre in Europe, where dramaturgs have existed for over two centuries, and the English-language stage, where concepts of dramaturgy have generally failed to take root or adapt. That difference is the gulf that separates a public institution from a private concern. Despite the revolution brought about by the establishment of many hundreds of non-profit theatres in England, Canada, and the United States since the end of World War II, there has been little thought given to the organization and responsibilities of what are supposed to be, after all, public institutions. Yet theatre is our oldest institution in Western civilization, and there are many well-documented examples of what it has been and why it has existed in many different societies.

An organization, after all, reflects a power structure: who has it, who should have it, and what responsibilities power entails. The smallest public company owned by private shareholders is more regulated and held accountable by the Securities Exchange Commission and other governmental watchdogs than any of our major theatres, which are given millions in public funds or tax-exempt donations each year. For this reason, one can only conclude that the profound differences between private and public theatre are understood very imperfectly in most communities. And we are occasionally made aware of this by controversies that seem to erupt from nowhere.

For example: back in 1980 the Mark Taper Forum was admonished by Dan Sullivan, the theater critic of the *Los Angeles Times,* for producing Neil Simon's *I Ought to Be in Pictures* as an obvious tryout for Broadway. Sullivan argued that the Taper is being funded publicly to take risks on lesser known playwrights and not to underwrite the commercial risks for Broadway producers. Artistic director Gordon Davidson countered that Neil Simon should have the same right of access to the Taper as any other American playwright, and that it is in the public interest for his theatre to make money from commercial productions, so that it can continue to take risks greater than the one involving Neil Simon. Both arguments have merit, but what surprised even the arguers is that a debate could erupt with such bitterness at a time when the regional theatre movement had reached some maturity, and the Mark Taper Forum had proven itself to be one of its paragons.

Money is not the only issue. When the Prospect Theatre in St. Louis was threatened in the early 1980s with loss of public funds for producing Christopher Durang's *Sister Mary Ignatius Explains It All for You,* the problem was not simply an attempt at censorship by a special group (Catholics), or the separation of church and state. Surely the question in all such debates is to what extent a public theatre can go against the wishes of a large part of its public. For another example, the Salt Lake City Acting Company stages a revue every summer called "Saturday's Voyeur," which mercilessly satirizes Mormon religious tenets and every aspect of Mormon life. The show sells out without the benefit of any advertising and subsidizes the company's winter season. The Church of Jesus Christ of Latter Day Saints clearly could exert pressure on the producers to moderate or even close the show. So why is it still running, and in a building that used to be a Mormon church? Because in a highly regulated society, the theatre serves a number of public functions, whether to legitimize some forms of dissent, to demonstrate the tolerance of a ruling ideology, or to provide laughter and release. The tragic poets of ancient Athens, as well as Aristophanes, constantly made fun of the official state religion in the midst of what was after all a religious festival, and very rarely did any one of them get into hot water for impiety.

How does dramaturgy fit in with such issues? Dramaturgy is much more a function of the public than of the private theatre. It is the rebirth of the public theatre that has created, more than any other factor, the profession of dramaturgs and literary managers in English-language countries. The private commercial theatre, it's true, has known the dim shadow of the dramaturg for a long time, but only under the restrictive yet nevertheless revealing name of "play-doctor"—that is, someone who is called in only when the play is in danger of dying. Having attended a number of such deathbed scenes, I am familiar with the smell of fear and panic on such occasions. But, of course, dramaturgy involves a great deal more than surgery or resuscitation after the vital functions cease (if there were any to begin with); it is not even preventive medicine. A preferable medical analogy is that of midwife: the dramaturg routinely assists at the birth of a play or production, without any presumption of complications or miscarriage.

Ideally, there will be a dramaturg present at the birth of theatre itself, or of *a* theatre. G. E. Lessing, for instance—the father of modern dramaturgy—was invited to Hamburg precisely for the purpose of articulating the goals of a new kind of theatre. His *Hamburg Dramaturgy* chronicles one particular attempt to create a national theatre in Germany. Lessing's critical essays on plays and productions, which the theatre itself published and disseminated, served the administration's purpose by involving the public in a debate about what it was doing, and how that fit in with the literary and theatrical trends in other parts of Europe. Similarly, the famous eighteen-hour discussion that led to the founding of the Moscow Art Theatre took place between a director with the immortal name of Stanislavsky and Vladimir Nemirovich-Danchenko, the producer, playwright, and dramaturg better known in English as What's-his-name.

By contrast, it took Great Britain more than a hundred years of debate, during which time she grew less and less great, to establish a National Theatre, something no Balkan country would be caught without. Canada, Australia, and the United States are still far from comprehending even the concept. Paradoxically, it was the very vitality of the English theatre tradition, largely fed by generations of great actors, which blinded many people to a three-hundred-year aberration in its history. To wit: from the Restoration of Charles II in 1660 to the rise of publicly funded, non-profit companies following the Second World War, the theatre of the English-speaking world was largely private. I call this an aberration, because from its primitive and Greek origins Western theatre has been in most countries, and for most of its three thousand years of history, very much a public place, vitally concerned with political, social, and religious issues. So much so that Shakespeare had lost enough meaning in less than two generations for even John Dryden to find his masterpieces rude and unpolished. Samuel Johnson did not understand *King Lear* and William Hazlitt thought it was unproducible. Until very recently, in fact, the classics were rarely done, and done even less in order to make dramatic sense of them. And it still caused something of a sensation in our own age when Peter Brook tried to make sense of Shakespeare with help from a dramaturg like Jan Kott.

What we were seeing in England was the tentative revival of the idea of a public theatre, after the violent caesura of Cromwell's Protectorate and the subsequent degeneration for three hundred years. Although the theatre was restored, it was not the same as before: the silly *beau monde* of Charles II's court, with a theatre-going audience of two to three hundred fops, cannot be compared with the dozen competing public theatres of Elizabethan and Jacobean London, the biggest of which could accommodate up to three thousand people at a performance, or three percent of the total population. Later, the rise of Drury

Lane established a new kind of criterion for theatrical success, which was completely unknown to the Greeks, the medieval guilds, or even the companies dependent on royal and aristocratic favor. It remains predominant today: the box office.

The box office, which is the sole criterion for play selection, casting, and every other decision on the commercial stage, ideally plays no such role in the public theatre. In Athens, poor people were paid to go and see plays as part of their civic duty. Wealthy citizens vied for the honor of producing at the great Greek dramatic festivals; their only return was public approbation and honor. In contrast, total commercialization has led to a narrowing of the dramatic scope. Bernard Shaw had to prove himself at the box office before his ideas would be taken seriously; even then he could express himself better in the prefaces to the published plays. Shaw's plays are produced today in English mainly because they are amusing and theatrical despite their seriousness; but in the public theatres of the world they are heard for the same reason that he wrote them: the ideas that they contain. Here, even among theatre people, he is considered a bit of a bore, while abroad it is accepted that not every drama has to be a hoot. European dramatists whom he championed, like Ibsen and Brieux, never became huge commercial hits, because in their own countries where there was a public theatre, they did not have to make similar artistic compromises. It is for this reason that many of the best foreign playwrights continue to find very slow and limited acceptance in the English-language theatre.

Despite the proliferation of literally hundreds of non-profit theatres in postwar America, then, I think (or I hope) it is still too early to predict whether the idea of a public theatre will take root in a land that did not have it before—in a country, moreover, founded by the same Puritans who were responsible for killing the public theatre in England. This is not the usual doom-saying about the health of the theatre, but simple acknowledgment that in America theatre is part of the entertainment business, where commercial factors can bring about very rapid and cataclysmic changes in a relatively short period of time. For example, I have not seen the following facts on too many trivia quiz shows: in 1900 there were approximately 5,000 so-called legitimate theatres in the United States, which had declined to 200 by 1946 and to 90 by 1949. Fewer than two percent survived a half century during which the American population doubled, with an even greater shift to urbanization. There are no forces in the public sector that can destroy, or create, cultural institutions at even one-tenth of the rate that commerce can. Lincoln Center's failure, though unique in some particulars, is a reminder that shiny buildings named after wealthy benefactors are no guarantee of permanence even in a city so rich in patrons and talent as the nation's theatrical capital. The Kennedy Center in the political capital is an example of what happens to the concept of public theatre in a society that has no understanding of what it is: instead of presenting the best American plays of the classic or current repertoire, it is used as a dumping ground for bad commercial plays that do not even make it to Broadway.

This historical perspective is necessary if we are to understand that the dramaturg in the English-language theatre is evolving from causes and needs that may be deeper than perceived. For I do not believe that dramaturgy is a completely forgotten, eighteenth-century German discovery that took this long to be dusted off. After all, other ideas in the theatre have spread a greater distance and much faster than Artaud's plague. For example, the director as a separate functionary is a little over a hundred years old; his rise to absolute power in the theatre has been parallel rather than coincidental with Prussian absolutism and the general love affair we had with totalitarianism in the twentieth century. Nonetheless, there were many opportunities, notably when Max Reinhardt and Stanislavksy came to be known and admired here, or when scores of Americans visited Moscow in the twenties and thirties, to observe how dramaturgs work and note their impact on productions. But the connection was not made, because English-language visitors (even one as acute as Edward Gordon Craig) never had anything to which to relate the dramaturgical function within the structure of the private theatre that they knew.

It was only with the emergence of public theatres, where the box office is no longer the sole criterion for producing plays, that certain dramaturgical functions are becoming recognized as essential. The change is evident in the shifts of meaning in theatrical terminology. A company no longer means just a haphazard collection of actors hired for particular parts who stay together only for the run of one play and disband when the show closes. Today the word may denote a collective united by similar aspirations and ideology, or theatre artists brought in to work together for a whole season of plays under the aegis of a resident theatre. The word "season" itself until recently referred only to all the plays by different producers that were presented within a year on Broadway or London's West End. Now it is as likely to denote a list of plays produced by *one* theatre company.

It was the need to sell to a stable, definable audience a whole season of plays rather than just one that more than anything else led to the use of dramaturgs and literary managers in the American theatre. Whereas the commercial stage operated for centuries on the assumption that every new play should be as much like the previous success as possible (which is why it is so hard to tell Restoration comedies, Victorian melodramas, or French farces apart), it does not make sense to produce for a subscription audience six or seven plays that are exactly alike or even in the same genre. Whereas a road company that brought to town the latest Broadway hit from New York had no responsibility to a local audience beyond putting on the show for a week or two and spending the rest of the time like tourists, most of the playmakers of the resident, season-producing theatres are members of the community, have their children in local schools, pay taxes, and enjoy civic benefits as well as responsibilities. Hence a bad season or a controversial play will influence subscriptions—and playmakers' livelihood— for several years to come, whereas the road company always moves on whether their show bombs or triumphs in a single town.

The concept that a season should have diversity—a mixture of classics and contemporary works and a smattering of new plays—is now widely accepted. But I do not think that this practice has been examined critically, or lately for that matter. The standard subscription drive, as originally popularized by one Danny Newman, uses familiar merchandising techniques to sell the idea of going to the theatre itself rather than the content of the plays themselves. This assumes that people will want to attend the theatre six or seven times a year regardless of what they see, just as they watch a daily or weekly series on television, or buy the main selections of the book club. Yet, because of the initial success at building audiences from scratch in communities that had been without local theatre for two or three generations, there has been a general blindness to the costs and flaws in the system of establishing and maintaining subscriptions.

I have space here to mention only some of the drawbacks. After a few years when the subscription audience stabilizes at ten or twenty thousand, the success of any play in the season is determined by the average number of non-subscribers who happen to attend during its pre-determined run (which is identical to the runs of the other plays in the season). Non-subscribers are those who by definition do not come regularly to the theatre except when they are interested in seeing a particular production. But as anybody who works in the theatre knows (except perhaps Danny Newman), plays are not like other merchandise: that is why some plays run for five years and others close before they open. Some appeal to more people because of subject matter, the name of the author, or the quality of the writing, acting, directing, and other production values. Therefore the idea that an unsuccessful play—be it classic, contemporary, or new—must run the same length of time as a runaway success is illogical, yet almost every major resident theatre gets locked into this absurdity. Maintaining the same subscription level becomes the main agenda for such theatres: letting it fall or rise too rapidly can affect adversely the scheduling for an entire year. And the way that theatres believe they can best maintain their subscription audience is to provide more of the same, to become as predictable as possible. Plays that do not fit the standard menu (as opposed to those that do but are otherwise unsuccessful) either do not get produced or are shunted to a studio, a second or even third stage. Suddenly there is a new category: not a comedy, tragedy, domestic drama, or farce, but a second-stage play, i.e., one that might rock the boat on the main subscription season. These days, the majority of new plays—and, I would add, the most interesting plays—are done on a second stage, which becomes on a miniscule scale what public television is to the networks.

Yet the subscription levels do not necessarily hold. As with any static population, a substantial number each year do not renew, because people get older, turned off, they move, and they even die. What might appeal to one generation bores another; the differences between movie and television audiences are not simply matters of taste, but also age and geography. Moreover, unlike the mass media, the theatre is a local phenomenon, and the various pressures on a non-profit theatre from a board of directors, national and local funding agencies, educators, and even audiences are more akin to those experienced by a school board than by commercial show business.

The greatest impact on a theatre and its policy is exercised by the Board of Directors, even when it is manifested only in a single function: the power to hire and fire the artistic director and other senior personnel. This happens with sufficient frequency that some boards may be said to be bored of directors. The boards of major cultural institutions tend to be composed of public-minded, wealthy, and influential citizens or their spouses, and they wield ultimate power usually through a small executive committee. The Board of Directors of a typical non-profit institution in America is designed on a corporate model. It is made up of largely the same types you would find on corporate boards: lawyers, accountants, businessmen, and socialites. The rationale for such a board is twofold: fiscal responsibility for public funds should be in the hands of people who understand money; and they can attract corporate and private donors to supplement public funds that are never adequate. However, the public proportion of financing for the arts has steadily grown during the past thirty-five years or so, while the contribution of the private sector has proportionately declined. Yet the composition of boards of directors has not reflected this shift; instead, a narrow elite in each community has extended its considerable private power over the public arts, with consequences that are directly reflected in the art that is produced.

Boards are self-perpetuating, as you might guess: new members are proposed by old members, as in any social club, which is essentially what they are. It is rare to find a union official, a senior citizen, a teacher, let alone an artist sitting on a board. So when a theatre is in trouble (usually measured by falling subscriptions towards the bottom line), the board fires the artistic director and hires a new one, repeating the process until the balance sheet improves. I have yet to hear of a whole board, or its executive committee, resigning, admitting in the process its own mistake for having hired the wrong artistic director and thereby run the theatre into the ground. The board remains intact, ostensibly as a guarantee against undue political influence by governments and their funding organizations.

Yet it should be evident by now that the main problem is not one of too much political control, but too little. In the old court theatres of Europe, there was a direct and uncomplicated relationship between the sovereign as patron and the players. Now that constitutional governments have replaced the kings and princes, a direct line of responsibility is being maintained between the elected minister of culture, the mayor or city council, and the appointed heads of major cultural institutions. Yet there has been no attempt to establish an equivalent model of public accountability for the public arts in America. In effect, we do not have public arts in this country, but rather organizations partially funded by the public purse that remain under private control. Boards of directors are not elected and represent a much smaller constituency than they sometimes claim: the ninety percent of the population that does not attend plays and concerts, subsidizes the ten percent that does. The ninety percent is not just unrepresented on the board: with some notable exceptions, there is no conscious attempt to expand the repertory to attract its members as part of a new audience. As I have argued, once the subscription roster has stabilized, there is very little room for newcomers, except to take the place of someone who cancelled or died.

This goes a long way toward explaining why so few theatres have worked out a philosophy, or public policy, which might guide the selection of plays as well as their interpretation. The political process, which is what makes public theatre important and even essential, has been deliberately removed. The sanitized and private tastes of a well-meaning but unrepresentative social class have thus replaced the public agenda that many of the plays discuss. Shakespeare, Shaw, and Ibsen are played for entertainment, not for what they have to say: that is why most productions of the classics are unintelligible. Foreign and native playwrights who have something important to say (but are not "entertaining") often languish in obscurity because they have been rejected by the commercial theatre. The box office, whether in maintaining subscriptions or developing a property for Broadway, dictates the season—just as it does in the commercial theatre—not the concerns of the community. That is why our theatre, in the British director Michael Kustow's telling phrase, has no audience, only customers.

In sum, there can be no public theatre without dramaturgical functions, whether these are performed by dramaturgs, directors (artistic or otherwise), or, after opening night, by the local critics. Non-profit theatre itself is not necessarily public theatre, especially if its ultimate aspirations are only validated by the box office or Broadway success. I would like to believe that issues of dramaturgy continue to surface now because there is a faint but growing recognition that something is missing from the seasons and productions of non-profit theatres, that the frantic activity of maintaining subscription levels, of selling seven plays for the price of six, of producing always the same few classics, of putting on one play after another for the same length of time—all this is extremely tiring if there is no meaning to the production and no *raison d'être* for the company. There are as many different meanings as there are localities, and each company must find the connections between its activities and the community, between the text and the human condition.

I would suggest that the dramaturg is a trained professional who, ideally and if permitted, can identify such meanings and bring forward public issues both for the company and its audience (including those who do not but might attend)—and, most importantly, who can translate those issues from or into a dramatic text. One of the most obvious ways is by preparing adequate program notes to place the production in a meaningful context. This is performed in almost every European theatre by dramaturgs, but hardly ever in America even by those companies that employ dramaturgs.

Much of the intellectual debate over the last twenty years or so about theatre in the United States has been trying to reconcile the *Hamburg Dramaturgy*—the "program notes" of Europe's, if not the world's, first dramaturg—with what I would call a Hamburger Dramaturgy: a fast-food, mish-mash metaphor for the American quick-fix in the arts. If the rather fragile public theatre is to survive, however, American dramaturgy will evolve in the long term not according to the European or any other model, but for the same reasons as everywhere else. That is, it will be defined not by a list of tasks—whether so much time is taken up by reading scripts and so much by working on productions—but rather by an agenda for making plays within a community that is consistent with the public agenda. However, the real debate, which is still to come, will not be about whether dramaturgs are essential or a luxury, whether they help or complicate the artistic process. The battle still to be fought is between those who have established corporate replicas of the private court theatres and those who are working towards creating a genuinely public theatre; between those who have evolved new forms of non-profit hucksterism, where the public is made to take the risks and the baths instead of private investors and producers, and those theatre artists as well as audiences who desire, nay demand, to see a wider meaning in the art and practice of theatre.

POSTSCRIPT

PERFORMANCE ART VS. PERFORMED DRAMA: EXPERIMENTAL PLAYWRITING AND PRODUCTION IN THE UNITED STATES

In the "happenings" of the painter Allan Kaprow from the late 1950s—the original "performance art" in the sense that visual art was "performed" by objectified human bodies—we begin to see the cultivation of performance as art unto itself, apart from or superior to any *a priori* text. So much so that, first, attempts were made by artists other than Kaprow to move theatre outside the confines of traditional, or text-based, theatres and to put it into more accessible, less formal surroundings. Second, emphasis was shifted in "happenings" from passive observation to active participation—from the artistic product to the viewing process—with each spectator thus becoming partial creator of a piece and deriving whatever meaning he wished from the experience, much to the downplaying of the artist's intention or even existence. Third, simultaneity and multiple focus tended to replace the orderly sequence of conventionally, even unconventionally, scripted drama, there being no pretense that everyone at such a multimedia event could see and hear the same things at the same time or in the same order. Many of these ideas were carried over into "environmental theatre," a term popularized by Richard Schechner for something in between traditional productions and happenings.

In this kind of theatre, among other things, all production elements speak their own language rather than being mere supports for words, and a text is not even necessary and therefore there may be none. In other words, fidelity to text, that sacred tenet that had so long governed performance, has become irrelevant, as postmodernism, both as critical inquiry and as theatre, continues to challenge whether any text is authoritative, whether a dramatic text can be anything more than a performance script—whether, in fact, the play exists at all before it is staged. In *Blooded Thought*, Herbert Blau conceded that "so far as performance goes, the Text remains our best evidence *after* the fact, like the quartos and folios of the Elizabethan stage." But what, he asks, is "the nature of the Text *before* the fact?" "The *idea* of performance", he suggests, "has become the mediating, often subversive third term in the on-again off-again marriage of drama and theatre" (37). And performance *groups* such as Mabou Mines and Grand Union, for their part, have become concerned less with what they are saying, with content, than with form and formal experiment: with the means of communicating, the places where theatrical events take place, the persons employed as performers, and the relationship of performers as well as performance to the audience. (As such, the theatrical avant-garde in America has always been rooted more in performance than in text, in a radical performance technique that dismantles and then either discards or refashions the overwhelmingly "well-made" drama of the American stage, as the work of the Wooster Group, the Living, Open, and Bread-and-Puppet Theatres, Robert Wilson, and Ping Chong also attests.)

Something similar can be said about the formalists who practice—however marginally—"experimental" or "alternative" playwriting in America, and who trace their lineage back to Gertrude Stein. (In rejecting cogency of plot and idea in favor of the sensuality or pure form of gesture and space as well as language, Stein was surely the first thoroughgoing American avant-garde dramatist.) Even in those plays of theirs that seem, on the surface, to obey established or conventional dramatic norms (those of farce, say, in Charles Ludlam's *Reverse Psychology* [1980]), these writers encourage us to step back and linger over the elements of performance longer than we are use to doing, seeing how those elements contain clues to the largest meanings of the drama. The design of space, the passage of time, the rhythms of speech and movement: these "invisibles" of theater, once meant to disappear when stories or characters are compelling enough, instead emerge from the background to tell their own stories.

The very setting of the "other" American drama seems to take on a life of its own. Landscape becomes an extension of its inhabitants, reflecting anxieties or ambitions only partly expressed in words. "The rooms besiege me" says Jean Peters in Adrienne Kennedy's *A Movie Star Has to Star in Black and White* (1976), and as she struggles against them, she reveals a hypersensitivity shared by many other characters in these plays. Jeep fears the walls closing in on him in Shepard's *Action* (1975). Marion's spirit suffocates in her husband's townhouse in María Irene Fornés's *Abingdon Square* (1987). The different kinds of compartments in Jeffery M. Jones's *Night Coil* (two adjacent chambers), Len Jenkin's 1988 work *American Notes* (a motel room and lobby, a forest hideaway), and Suzan-Lori Parks's *Imperceptible Mutabilities in the Third Kingdom* (the hull of a slave ship, measured obsessively throughout the play) all serve as psychological pressure-cookers for their occupants. The more they know about space, the less they feel able to control it.

Outside, the landscape is just as restless, forcing characters to acknowledge emotions they would prefer to avoid. In Lee Breuer's *B. Beaver*

Animation (1974), a flood reduces the stage to a pile of planks, all that remain of B. Beaver's dam. Nature won't stay outdoors in Tina Howe's *One Shoe Off* (1993), where roots break through the floorboards, branches wind themselves around the beams, and ivy crawls up the furniture. And consider how many writers—Ronald Tavel (*Boy on a Straight-Back Chair*, 1969), Murray Mednick (*Switchback*, 1994), David Greenspan (*Son of an Engineer*, 1994), John Steppling (*Standard of the Breed*, 1988)—come immediately to set their plays in vast wastelands. A catastrophe seems imminent, or perhaps has just occurred. Either way, one senses that the space has won only a temporary reprieve from change—whether it comes in the form of urban warfare in Eric Overmyer's *Native Speech* (1985), nuclear holocaust in Constance Congdon's *No Mercy* (1986), or the death of a moon in Mac Wellman's *The Hyacinth Macaw* (1994). In each of these plays, an enormous sky stretches above measureless darkness. Characters use up all their emotional resources just keeping their small pools of light from dwindling away. All of them could be asking the question Rhoda asks in Richard Foreman's *Rhoda in Potatoland* (1975): "How can I relate to this place?"

As we map this new theatrical territory, we will also have to acknowledge the effect of time, another element of performance we can no longer take for granted. When narrative is observed, its passage can be excruciating: in *Action*, one intensely felt minute gives way to another, just as unremitting, as if the present tense dilated to ensure that the subtlest gradations of experience are dramatized. Equally disorienting are those plays where the past won't remain in the background and the future won't wait its turn. The former aren't mere memory plays: OyamO (in 1981's *The Resurrection of Lady Lester*), Congdon, and Kennedy each create a remembered world that is capable of sucking characters irretrievably into its vortex. And the latter aren't standard-issue fantasias: for John Guare (*Muzeeka*, 1968), Arnold Weinstein (*Red Eye of Love*, 1961), Naomi Iizuka (*Tattoo Girl*, 1994), and Richard Caliban (*Rodents and Radios*, 1990), the speculative selves available in dream or fantasy slip the leash for the characters who summoned them, wreaking havoc on the best-laid plans for narrative. In fact, it is the rare character in these plays who doesn't exist in all three tenses at once. Time becomes an almost tangible element of the environment—groped through, wallowed in, pushed back—capable, like a tornado, of dispersing a character among numerous contexts; ready, like a flood, to overwhelm him all at once with worlds ordinarily visited one at a time. This ordeal is rarely as moving as in Suzan-Lori Parks's theater, where time *is* space for different versions of the same character (African, and later American) on opposite sides of a single ocean.

Self-division is epidemic in all this theater: it is as if stage-time acts as an acid on its inhabitants, breaking apart images valid only for the moment they are perceived, revealing the composition of personalities beneath the surface of ordinary behavior, and sometimes allowing us to see a self and its ramifications (the kind of person a character denies, fears, or hopes to become) at the same time. The spectacle is unsettling: the person on stage, fickle about his form, can't be trusted, nor can he trust himself. Shepard's Shooter identifies a condition known to many characters when he describes seeing a collection of limbs that, despite his best efforts, he can't claim: "When I look at my hand, I get terrified. The sight of my feet in the bathtub. The skin covering me. That's all that's covering me." He is "afraid to sleep for fear his body might do something without him knowing."

Standard psychological language is useless when it comes to describing such characters. They're not just "alienated," for instance, when the floor barely supports them, the walls close in, and their entire world sheds a skin just when it starts to seem familiar. ("I got no references for this," says Jeep, "Suddenly it's shifted.") "Ambivalence" doesn't begin to suggest their radical fracturing of will. (Kennedy's Clara sits in the margins watching movie stars "star in her life" and speak her thoughts.) "Nostalgic" or "idealistic" temperaments aren't to be found here; only characters so unmoored to a context that, like Fornés's Marion, they feel as if they're "drowning in vagueness" and "have no character." Nor are they simply "insecure" or "confused," but rather suffer such an extreme form of self-consciousness that the self dissolves under the laser-like scrutiny of consciousness. (Foreman's Rhoda can't reconcile her body with her "body of knowledge.") Indeed, when we look at that place onstage where a character is supposed to be—a figure bearing the burden of biography on the road to realized choices—instead we see phantoms and mannequins, and the debris of their struggle to become complete. There are figures like Dinah in *One Shoe Off*—donning and doffing costumes from famous plays, unable to find one that suits her self-image—and the heroine of Craig Lucas's *Reckless* (1983), frequently changing her name and so, she hopes, her destiny. There are the malcontents in *Muzeeka*, *Red Eye of Love*, Jack Richardson's *Gallows Humor* (1961), and *Rodents and Radios*, casting aside jobs and family roles in their quest for their essential identities. There are the characters in Ed Bullins's theater—say, *The Man Who Dug Fish* (1967)—refusing to accept racial roles without irony. And finally there are the collages and force fields that stand in for character in the works of Kennedy, Breuer, and Foreman—everything that the critic Elinor Fuchs has called (in the major study of this development, *The Death of Character*) "ephemeral constellations of thought, vision, and action."

One senses that these playwrights are never sure of their characters, who seem in the shifting landscape of a play to be more than merely the sum of their actions and utterances. Yet for all their determination to penetrate their mysterious surroundings and redeem the promise of the promised land, these characters never feel they arrive. Up to the last moment, their skepticism battles their faith: Individuals who began by scorning received definitions of their lives are careful not to settle for their own. They think there is always another corner of the setting to discover, another variation of their identity to try. Potential lives and future destinations remain more seductive than current experiences. Are such characters destined for days of self-contradiction—needing clarity and self-integration, on the one hand; on the other, drawn to a life of continuous reinvention? Which state will make them feel more alive, not merely present? Which offers the most security, the most freedom?

The questions are left hanging, and the statements of these characters point to something—a place, a quality, an image of oneself—that has yet to be experienced, something that remains invulnerable to cheapening and misunderstanding. Entire plays are summarized in these abbreviated lines: "I just wanted to be . . .," says Philip in *Gallows Humor*, and as his voice trails off, the play opens up to reveal a picture of the need and sadness (and also the hope) behind the workings of the imagination. "I want to become—touch some part of—," says Jack Argue in *Muzeeka*, and here again speech arches forward, trying to reach the perfect expression and the perfect attitude, to present the most convincing incarnation of the self. By the time we get to *Action*, the state of expectation is familiar, but there are still no words for what's expected: "I'm looking forward to my life. I'm looking forward to uh—me . . . My true position . . . up for grabs." Another failed declaration? Or rather, a deliberate evasion of identity, for fear of its being interpreted too narrowly? So many characters are poised on similar precipices—wondering if the next sensation will be the one to illuminate the meaning of their lives, but also dreading its consequences. Revelation rarely comes, and perhaps that's why they sound ecstatic: the thrill is in the search, and in speaking of the search. "I roam," says one character. "I keep looking for the action!" says a second. From still another: "Let's keep pushing!"

The texture of much of this writing suggests that a passionate encounter is going on just beneath its surface, in which a playwright pursues rather than merely dramatizes lives and events. Each scene is another stab at knowledge, written less to prove a point or demonstrate a theme than to gather evidence. Some pages even read as if the playwrights are quarreling with their own styles, trying to elude habitual turns-of-phrase and signature rhythms. At such moments, one imagines the writers urging themselves to stick with difficult subjects or characters until they bend, past the point where they seem merely understood. Perhaps then something unexpected—and truly revelatory—will emerge. For a writer of such an analytic temperament, characters are propositions, meant to be tested against the writer's sense of the full force of thought and action. Staging becomes a form of inquiry; language and movement, the instruments of that inquiry. And writing, for the most anxious of these writers, thus becomes *writing-towards* in which dramatic form is always in question.

Enter "performance art," privileging the indeterminacy and unpredictability of the event over the finish and fatedness of the text. And it is performance art of a kind so loosely defined in the Unites States that all the following qualify as, or have called themselves, "performance artists": Madonna, Karen Finley, Anna Deavere Smith, Amy Taubin, Eric Bogosian, Ann Magnuson, Martha Clarke, Stuart Sherman, Chris Burden, Linda Montano, Laurie Anderson, Jack Smith, Holly Hughes, Vito Acconci, Winston Tong, Meredith Monk, Spalding Gray, Rachel Rosenthal, Tim Miller, John Fleck, John Leguizamo, John Kelly, Joan Jonas, Gilbert and George, Deborah Hay, Bill Irwin, Bob Berky, David Shiner, the Kipper Kids, Michael Moschen, Avner ("the Eccentric") Eisenberg, and the Flying Karamazov Brothers. Anything can be called "art," in other words, as long as it is consecrated in performance— often only of the narcissistic self.

Works Cited

Blau, Herbert. *Blooded Thought: Occasions of Theatre.* New York: Performing Arts Journal Publications, 1982.
Fuchs, Elinor. *The Death of Character.* Bloomington: Indiana University Press, 1996.

BIBLIOGRAPHY

This is a general bibliography of critical works on American drama and theater. It does not contain books on single playwrights, but it does include volumes that treat ethnic or racial groups—both as creators of American drama and as they have been depicted on the American stage overall.

Abbotson, Susan C. W. *Thematic Guide to Modern Drama.* Westport, Conn.: Greenwood, 2003.

Abramson, Doris E. *Negro Playwrights in the American Theatre, 1925-1959.* New York: Columbia University Press, 1969.

Adler, Thomas P. *American Drama, 1940-1960: A Critical History.* New York: Twayne, 1994.

Adler, Thomas P. *Mirror on the Stage: The Pulitzer Plays as an Approach to American Drama.* West Lafayette, Ind.: Purdue University Press, 1987.

Allen, Carol D. *Peculiar Passages: Black Women Playwrights, 1875 to 2000.* New York: Peter Lang, 2005.

Anderson, John. *The American Theatre.* New York: Dial, 1938.

Anderson, Lisa M. *Mammies No More: The Changing Image of Black Women on Stage and Screen.* Lanham, Md.: Rowman & Littlefield, 1997.

Andreach, Robert J. *Creating the Self in the Contemporary American Theatre.* Carbondale: Southern Illinois University Press, 1998.

Arata, Esther Spring, and Nicholas John Rotoli. *Black American Playwrights, 1800 to the Present: A Bibliography.* Metuchen, New Jersey: Scarecrow Press, 1976, 1978.

Aronson, Arnold. *American Avant-Garde Theatre: A History.* New York: Routledge, 2000.

Auerbach, Doris. *Sam Shepard, Arthur Kopit, and the Off-Broadway Theater.* Boston: Twayne, 1982.

Auslander, Philip. *The New York School Poets as Playwrights: O'Hara, Ashbery, Koch, Schuyler, and the Visual Arts.* New York: Peter Lang, 1989.

—. *Presence and Resistance: Postmodernism and Cultural Politics on Contemporary American Performance.* Ann Arbor: University of Michigan Press, 1992.

Bean, Annemarie, ed. *A Sourcebook of African-American Performance: Plays, People, Movements.* London: Routledge, 1999.

Bentley, Eric. *The Dramatic Event: An American Chronicle.* Boston: Beacon Press, 1954.

Berkowitz, Gerald M. *New Broadways: Theatre Across America.* New York: Applause, 1997.

—. *American Drama of the Twentieth Century.* New York: Longman, 1992.

Berney, K. A. *Contemporary American Dramatists.* Detroit: St. James Press, 1994.

Bernstein, Samuel J. *The Strands Entwined: A New Direction in American Drama.* Boston: Northeastern University Press, 1980.

Bial, Henry. *Acting Jewish: Negotiating Ethnicity on the American Stage and Screen.* Ann Arbor: University of Michigan Press, 2005.

Bigsby, C. W. E. *Confrontation and Commitment: A Study of Contemporary American Drama 1959-1966.* Columbia: University of Missouri Press, 1968.

—. *Contemporary American Playwrights.* New York: Cambridge University Press, 1999.

—. *A Critical Introduction to Twentieth-Century American Drama.* Volume 1: 1920-1940. New York: Cambridge University Press, 1982.

—. *A Critical Introduction to Twentieth-Century American Drama.* Volume 2: Williams, Miller, Albee. New York: Cambridge University Press, 1985.

—. *A Critical Introduction to Twentieth-Century American Drama.* Volume 3: Beyond Broadway. New York: Cambridge University Press, 1985.

—. *Modern American Drama, 1945-1990.* New York: Cambridge University Press, 1992.

Black, Cheryl. *The Women of Provincetown, 1915-1922.* Tuscaloosa: University of Alabama Press, 2002.

Blatanis, Konstantinos. *Popular Culture Icons in Contemporary American Drama.* Madison, New Jersey: Fairleigh Dickinson University Press, 2003.

Bloom, Clive, ed. *American Drama.* New York: St. Martin's Press, 1995.

Bonin, Jane F. *Prize-Winning American Drama: A Bibliographical and Descriptive Guide.* Metuchen, New Jersey: Scarecrow Press, 1973.

Bordman, Gerald. *The Oxford Companion to the American Theatre.* New York: Oxford University Press, 1992.

—. *American Theatre: A Chronicle of Comedy and Drama,* 1869-1914. New York: Oxford University Press, 1994.

—. *American Theatre: A Chronicle of Comedy and Drama, 1930-1969.* New York: Oxford University Press, 1996.

Bottoms, Stephen J. *Playing Underground: A Critical History of the 1960s Off-Off-Broadway Movement.* Ann Arbor: University of Michigan Press, 2004.

Brater, Enoch, ed. *Feminine Focus: The New Women Playwrights*. New York: Oxford University Press, 1989.

Brewer, Mary F. *Staging Whiteness*. Middletown, Conn.: Wesleyan University Press, 2005.

Brietzke, Zander. *American Drama in the Age of Film*. Tuscaloosa: University of Alabama Press, 2007.

Bronner, Edwin. *Encyclopedia of the American Theatre, 1900-1975*. San Diego, Calif.: A. S. Barnes, 1980.

Broussard, Louis. *American Drama: Contemporary Allegory from Eugene O'Neill to Tennessee Williams*. Norman: University of Oklahoma Press, 1962.

Brown, Janet. *Taking Center Stage : Feminism in Contemporary U.S. Drama*. Metuchen, New Jersey: Scarecrow Press, 1991.

Brown, John Mason. *Upstage: The American Theatre in Performance*. New York: W. W. Norton, 1930.

Brown-Guillory, Elizabeth. *Their Place on the Stage: Black Women Playwrights in America*. New York: Praeger, 1990.

Brustein, Robert. *Dumbocracy in America: Studies in the Theatre of Guilt, 1987-1994*. Chicago: Ivan Dee, 1994.

—. *Reimagining American Theatre*. New York: Hill and Wang, 1991.

Bryer, Jackson R, ed. *The Facts on File Companion to American Drama*. New York: Facts on File, 2004.

Burke, Sally. *American Feminist Playwrights: A Critical History*. New York: Twayne, 1996.

Burton, Richard. *The New American Drama*. New York: Thomas Y. Crowell, 1913.

Bzowski, Frances D. *American Women Playwrights, 1900-1930: A Checklist*. New York: Greenwood Press, 1992.

Carpenter, Charles A. *Dramatists and the Bomb: American and British Playwrights Confront the Nuclear Age, 1945-1964*. Westport, Conn.: Greenwood Press, 1999.

Cerf, Bennett. *S. R. O.: The Most Successful Plays in the History of the American Stage*. New York: Garden City Publishing, 1946.

Chinoy, Helen Krich, and Linda Walsh Jenkins, ed. *Women in American Theatre*. 3rd ed, revised and expanded. New York: Theatre Communications Group, 2006.

Clurman, Harold. *The Fervent Years: The Group Theatre and the Thirties*. New York: Harcourt, Brace, Jovanovich, 1975.

Coad, Oral Sumner, and Edwin Mims, Jr. *The American Stage*. New Haven, Conn.: Yale University Press, 1929.

Cohn, Ruby. *Anglo-American Interplay in Recent Drama*. New York: Cambridge University Press, 1995.

—. *Dialogue in American Drama*. Bloomington: Indiana University Press, 1971.

—. *New American Dramatists, 1960-1990*. New York: St. Martin's Press, 1991.

Colakis, Marianthe. *Classics in the American Theater of the 1960s and Early 1970s*. Lanham, Md.: University Press of America, 1993.

Connolly, Thomas F. *George Jean Nathan and the Making of American Dramatic Criticism*. Madison, New Jersey: Fairleigh Dickinson University Press, 1999.

Cotsell, Michael. *Theater of Trauma: American Modernist Drama and the Psychological Struggle for the American Mind, 1900-1930*. New York: Peter Lang, 2005.

Couch, William, Jr. *New Black Playwrights*. Baton Rouge: Louisiana State University Press, 1968.

Counts, Michael L. *Coming Home: The Soldier's Return in Twentieth-Century American Drama*. New York: Peter Lang, 1988.

Coven, Brenda. *American Women Dramatists of the Twentieth Century: A Bibliography*. Metuchen, New Jersey: Scarecrow Press, 1982.

Craig, Carolyn C. *Women Pulitzer Playwrights: Biographical Profiles and Analyses of the Plays*. Jefferson, North Carolina: McFarland, 2004.

Craig, E. Quita. *Black Drama of the Federal Theatre Era: Beyond the Formal Horizons*. Amherst: University of Massachusetts Press, 1980.

Crespy, David A. *Off-Off-Broadway Explosion: How Provocative Playwrights of the 1960s Ignited a New American Theater*. New York: Back Stage Books, 2003.

Davis, Walter A. *Get the Guests: Psychoanalysis, Modern American Drama, and the Audience*. Madison: University of Wisconsin Press, 1994.

Debusscher, Gilbert, and Henry I. Schvey, ed. *New Essays on American Drama*. Amsterdam: Rodopi, 1989.

Demastes, William W, ed. *American Playwrights, 1880-1945: A Research and Production Sourcebook*. Westport, Conn.: Greenwood Press, 1995.

Demastes, William W. *Beyond Naturalism: A New Realism in American Theatre*. New York: Greenwood Press, 1988.

Demastes, William, and Iris Smith Fischer, ed. *Interrogating America Through Theatre and Performance*. New York: Palgrave Macmillan, 2007.

Demastes, William W, ed. *Realism and the American Dramatic Tradition*. Tuscaloosa: University of Alabama Press, 1996.

Dickinson, Thomas H. *The Case of American Drama*. New York: Houghton Mifflin, 1915.

—. *Playwrights of the New American Theater*. New York: Macmillan, 1925.

Donoghue, Denis. *Third Voice: Modern British and American Verse Drama.* Princeton, New Jersey: Princeton University Press, 1959.

Downer, Alan S. *American Drama.* New York: Thomas Y. Crowell, 1960.

—, ed. *American Drama and Its Critics: A Collection of Critical Essays.* Chicago: University of Chicago Press, 1965.

—, ed. *American Theater Today.* New York, Basic Books, 1967.

—. *Fifty Years of American Drama, 1900-1950.* Chicago: Regnery, 1951.

—. *Recent American Drama.* Minneapolis: University of Minnesota Press, 1961.

Duffy, Susan. *The Political Left in the American Theatre of the 1930s: A Bibliographic Sourcebook.* Metuchen, New Jersey: Scarecrow Press, 1992.

—. *American Labor on Stage: Dramatic Interpretations of the Steel and Textile Industries in the 1930s.* Westport, Conn.: Greenwood Press, 1996.

Dukore, Bernard F. *American Dramatists, 1918-1945.* New York: Grove Press, 1984.

Dunlap, William. *A History of American Theatre.* New York: J. & J. Harper, 1832.

Durham, Weldon B, ed. *American Theatre Companies, 1888-1930 and 1931-1986.* 2 vols. Westport, Conn.: Greenwood Press, 1987, 1989.

Eddleman, Floyd E, and Daniel Lanelle, ed. *American Drama Criticism: Interpretations, 1890-1977.* Hamden, Conn.: Shoe String Press, 1979, 1989, 1992, 1996.

Elam, Harry J, and David Krasner, ed. *African American Performance and Theater History: A Critical Reader.* New York: Oxford University Press, 2001.

Erdman, Harley. *Staging the Jew: The Performance of an American Ethnicity, 1860-1920.* New Brunswick, New Jersey: Rutgers University Press, 1997.

Fearnow, Mark. *The American Stage and the Great Depression : A Cultural History of the Grotesque.* New York: Cambridge University Press, 1997.

Feingold, Michael. *Grove New American Theater.* New York: Grove Press, 1993.

Fenn, Jeffery W. *Levitating the Pentagon: Evolutions in the American Theatre of the Vietnam War Era.* Newark : University of Delaware Press, 1992.

Fisher, Judith L, and Stephen Watt, ed. *When They Weren't Doing Shakespeare: Essays on Nineteenth-Century British and American Theatre.* Athens: University of Georgia Press, 1989.

Fleche, Anne. *Mimetic Disillusion: Eugene O'Neill, Tennessee Williams, and U.S. Dramatic Realism.* Tuscaloosa: University of Alabama Press, 1997.

Flexner, Eleanor. *American Playwrights, 1918-1938: The Theatre Retreats from Reality.* New York: Simon and Schuster, 1938.

Frazer, Winifred L. *The Theme of Loneliness in Modern American Drama.* Gainesville: University of Florida Press, 1960.

Freedman, Morris. *American Drama in Social Context.* Carbondale: Southern Illinois University Press, 1971.

Furtado, Ken, and Nancy Hellner. *Gay and Lesbian American Plays: An Annotated Bibliography.* Metuchen, New Jersey: Scarecrow Press, 1993.

Gagey, Edmond M. *Revolution in American Drama.* New York: Columbia University Press, 1947.

Gardner, Bonnie M. *The Emergence of the Playwright-Director in American Theatre, 1960-1983.* Lewiston, New York: Edwin Mellen Press, 2001.

Gavin, Christy. *American Women Playwrights, 1964-1989: A Research Guide and Annotated Bibliography.* New York: Garland, 1993.

Geis, Deborah R. *Postmodern Theatric(k)s: Monologue in Contemporary American Drama.* Ann Arbor: University of Michigan Press, 1993.

Gerould, Daniel C. ed. *American Melodrama.* New York: Performing Arts Journal Publications, 1983.

Gewirtz, Arthur, and James J. Kolb, ed. *Art, Glitter, and Glitz: Mainstream Playwrights and Popular Theatre in 1920s America.* Westport, Conn.: Praeger, 2003.

Gewirtz, Arthur, and James J. Kolb, ed. *Experimenters, Rebels, and Disparate Voices: The Theatre of the 1920s Celebrates American Diversity.* Westport, Conn.: Praeger, 2003.

Glassberg, David. *American Historical Pageantry: The Uses of Tradition in the Early Twentieth Century.* Chapel Hill: University of North Carolina Press, 1990.

Goldberg, RuthLee. *Performance Art: From Futurism to the Present.* Rev. ed. New York: Abrams, 1988.

Golden, Joseph. *The Death of Tinker Bell: The American Theatre in the Twentieth Century.* Syracuse, New York: Syracuse University Press, 1967.

Goldstein, Malcolm. *The Political Stage: American Drama and Theater of the Great Depression.* New York: Oxford University Press, 1971.

Gottfried, Martin. *A Theatre Divided: The Postwar American Stage.* Boston: Little, Brown, 1967.

Gould, Jean. *Modern American Playwrights.* New York: Dodd, Mead, 1966.

Greenberger, Howard. *The Off-Broadway Experience.* Englewood Cliffs, New Jersey: Prentice-Hall, 1971.

Greenfield, Thomas A. *Work and the Work Ethic in American Drama, 1920-1970.* Columbia: University of Missouri Press, 1982.

Guha Majumdar, Rupendra. *Central Man: The Paradox of Heroism in Modern American Drama.* New York: Peter Lang, 2003.

Harriott, Esther. *American Voices: Five Contemporary Playwrights in Essays and Interviews*. Jefferson, North Carolina: McFarland, 1988.

Harris, Andrew B. *Broadway Theatre*. New York: Routledge, 1994.

Harris, Richard H. *Modern Drama in America and England, 1950-1970: A Guide to Information Sources*. Detroit: Gale Research, 1982.

Hart, Lynda, ed. *Making a Spectacle: Feminist Essays on Contemporary Women's Theatre*. Ann Arbor: University of Michigan Press, 1989.

Hatch, James V. *Black Image on the American Stage*. New York: DBS Publications, 1970.

Hatch, James V, and Abdullah Omanii. *Black Playwrights, 1823-1877: An Annotated Bibliography of Plays*. New York: Bowker, 1977.

Hay, Samuel Arthur. *African American Theatre: An Historical and Critical Analysis*. New York: Cambridge University Press, 1994.

Herman, William. *Understanding Contemporary American Drama*. Columbia: University of South Carolina Press, 1987.

Herron, Ima H. *The Small Town in American Drama*. Dallas, Texas : Southern Methodist University Press, 1969.

Hewitt, Barnard. *Theatre U.S.A, 1668-1937*. New York: McGraw-Hill, 1959.

Hill, Errol G, and James V. Hatch. *A History of African-American Theatre*. New York: Cambridge University Press, 2003.

Himelstein, Morgan Y. *Drama Was a Weapon: The Left-Wing Theatre in New York, 1929-1941*. New Brunswick, New Jersey: Rutgers University Press, 1963.

Houchin, John. *Censorship of the American Theatre in the Twentieth Century*. New York: Cambridge University Press, 2003.

Hughes, Catharine. *American Playwrights, 1945-75*. London: Pitman, 1976.

Hughes, Glenn. *A History of the American Theatre, 1700-1950*. New York: Samuel French, 1951.

Isaacs, Edith J. R. *The Negro in the American Theatre*. New York: Theatre Arts, 1947.

Jerz, Dennis G. *Technology in American Drama, 1920-1950: Soul and Society in the Age of the Machine*. Westport, Conn.: Greenwood Press, 2003.

Johnson, Katie N. *Sisters in Sin: Brothel Drama in America, 1900-1920*. New York : Cambridge University Press, 2006.

King, Bruce, ed. *Contemporary American Theatre*. New York: St. Martin's Press, 1991.

King, Kimball. *Ten Modern American Playwrights: An Annotated Bibliography*. New York: Garland,1982.

—, ed. *Hollywood on Stage: Playwrights Evaluate the Culture Industry*. New York: Garland, 1997.

—, ed. *Modern Dramatists: A Casebook of the Major British and American Playwrights.* New York: Routledge, 2001.

Kinne, Wisner P. *George Pierce Baker and the American Theatre.* Cambridge: Harvard University Press, 1954.

Kirby, Michael. *Total Theatre.* New York: E. P. Dutton, 1969.

—, ed. *The New Theatre.* New York: New York University Press, 1974.

Klayer, Elizabeth. *Performing Television:Contemporary Drama and the Media Culture.* Bowling Green, Ohio: Bowling Green State University Popular Press, 2000.

Kolin, Philip C., ed. *American Playwrights since 1945: A Guide to Scholarship, Criticism, and Performance.* New York: Greenwood Press, 1986.

Krasner, David. *Beautiful Pageant: African American Theatre, Drama, and Performance in the Harlem Renaissance, 1910-1927.* New York: Palgrave Macmillan, 2002.

—, ed. *A Companion to Twentieth-Century American Drama.* Malden, Mass.: Blackwell, 2004.

—. *American Drama, 1945-2000: An Introduction.* Malden, Mass.: Blackwell, 2006.

Krutch, Joseph Wood. *American Drama since 1918: An Informal History.* New York: George Braziller, 1957.

Kubiak, Anthony. *Agitated States: Performance in the American Theater of Cruelty.* Ann Arbor: University of Michigan Press, 2002.

Lee, Josephine D. *Performing Asian America: Race and Ethnicity on the Contemporary Stage.* Philadelphia: Temple University Press, 1997.

Leiter, Samuel L, ed. *The Encyclopedia of the New York Stage.* Vol. 1:1920-1930; Vol. 2: 1930-1940. Westport, Conn.: Greenwood Press, 1985, 1989.

Levine, Ira A. *Left-Wing Dramatic Theory in the American Theatre.* Ann Arbor, Mich.: UMI Research Press, 1985.

Levine, Mindy. *New York's Other Theatre: A Guide to Off-Off Broadway.* New York: Avon, 1981.

Lewis, Allan. *American Plays and Playwrights of the Contemporary Theatre.* New York: Crown Publishers, 1965.

Lewis, Emory. *Stages: The Fifty-Year Childhood of the American Theatre.* Englewood Cliffs, New Jersey: Prentice-Hall, 1969.

Little, Stuart W. *Off-Broadway: The Prophetic Theater.* New York: Coward, McGann, & Geoghegan, 1972.

Locke, Alain L. *Plays of Negro Life: A Source-Book of Native American Drama.* New York: Harper & Brothers, 1927.

Long, E. Hudson. *American Drama from Its Beginnings to the Present.* New York: Appleton-Century-Crofts, 1970.

Lovell, John, Jr. *Digests of Great American Plays.* New York: Thomas Y. Crowell, 1961.

Macgowan, Kenneth. *Footlights Across America: Towards a National Theatre.* New York: Harcourt, Brace, 1929.

MacNicholas, John, ed. *Twentieth-Century American Dramatists.* Detroit: Gale Research, 1981.

Mantle, Burns. *American Playwrights of Today.* New York: Dodd, Mead, 1929.

—. *Contemporary American Playwrights.* New York: Dodd, Mead, 1938.

Marranca, Bonnie, and Gautam Dasgupta. *American Playwrights: A Critical Survey.* New York: Drama Book Specialists, 1981.

Marsh-Lockett, Carol P. *Black Women Playwrights: Visions on the American Stage.* New York: Garland, 1999.

Martin, Boyd. *Modern American Drama and Stage.* London: Pilot Press, 1943.

Mason, Jeffrey D. *Melodrama and the Myth of America.* Bloomington: Indiana University Press, 1993.

Maufort, Marc, ed. *Staging Difference: Cultural Pluralism in American Theatre and Drama.* New York: Peter Lang, 1995.

Mayorga, Margaret G. *A Short History of American Drama.* New York: Dodd, Mead, 1932.

McConachie, Bruce A. *Melodramatic Formations: American Theatre and Society, 1820-1870.* Iowa City: University of Iowa Press, 1992.

—. *American Theater in the Culture of the Cold War: Producing and Contesting Containment, 1947-1962.* Iowa City: University of Iowa Press, 2003.

McDonald, Robert L, and Linda Rohrer Paige, ed. *Southern Women Playwrights: New Essays in Literary History and Criticism.* Tuscaloosa: University of Alabama Press, 2002.

McDonough, Carla J. *Staging Masculinity: Male Identity in Contemporary American Drama.* Jefferson, North Carolina: McFarland, 1997.

McNamara, Brooks. *The American Playhouse in the Eighteenth Century.* Cambridge, Massachusetts: Harvard University Press, 1969.

Mersand, Joseph E. *American Drama Presents the Jew: An Evaluation of the Treatment of Jewish Characters in Contemporary Drama.* New York: Modern Chapbooks, 1939.

—. *American Drama, 1930-1940: Essays on Playwrights and Plays.* New York: Modern Chapbooks, 1941.

—. *American Drama since 1930: Essays on Playwrights and Plays.* New York: Modern Chapbooks, 1949.

Meserve, Walter J. *An Outline History of American Drama.* Totowa, New Jersey: Littlefield, Adams, 1965.

—, ed. *Discussions of American Drama*. Boston: D. C. Heath, 1966.

—. *American Drama to 1900: A Guide to Information Sources*. Detroit: Gale Research, 1980.

Miller, Jordan Y. *American Dramatic Literature: Ten Modern Plays in Historical Perspective*. New York: McGraw-Hill, 1961.

Miller, Jordan Y, and Winifred L. Frazer. *American Drama Between the Wars: A Critical History*. Boston: Twayne, 1991.

Moody, Richard. *America Takes the Stage: Romanticism in American Drama and Theatre, 1750-1900*. Bloomington: Indiana University Press, 1955.

Mordenn, Eric. *The American Theatre*. New York: Oxford University Press, 1981.

Moses, Montrose J. *The American Dramatist*. Boston: Little, Brown, 1917.

Moses, Montrose J, and John Mason Brown, ed. *The American Theatre As Seen by Its Critics*. New York: Norton, 1934.

Moy, James S. *Marginal Sights: Staging the Chinese in America*. Iowa City: University of Iowa Press, 1993.

Murphy, Brenda. *American Realism and American Drama, 1880-1940*. New York: Cambridge University Press, 1987.

—. *Congressional Theatre: Dramatizing McCarthyism on Stage, Film, and Television*. New York: Cambridge University Press, 1999.

—, ed. *The Cambridge Companion to American Women Playwrights*. New York: Cambridge University Press, 1999.

—, ed. *Twentieth-Century American Drama*: Critical Concepts in Literary and Cultural Studies. New York: Routledge, 2006.

Nannes, Caspar Harold. *Politics in the American Drama*. Washington, D.C.: Catholic University of America Press, 1960.

Novick, Julius. *Beyond Broadway*. New York: Hill and Wang, 1968.

O'Hara, Frank H. *Today in American Drama*. Chicago: University of Chicago Press, 1939.

Otero, Rosalie. *Guide to American Drama Explication*. New York: G. K. Hall, 1995.

Ozieblo Rajkowska, Barbara, and Miriam Lopez-Rodriguez, ed. *Staging a Cultural Paradigm: The Political and the Personal in American Drama*. New York: Peter Lang, 2002.

Ozieblo, Barbara, and María Dolores Narbona-Carrión, ed. *Codifying the National Self: Spectators, Actors, and the American Dramatic Text*. New York: Peter Lang, 2006.

Parker, Dorothy, ed. *Essays on Modern American Drama: Williams, Miller, Albee, and Shepard*. Toronto: University of Toronto Press, 1987.

Peterson, Bernard L. *Contemporary Black American Playwrights and Their Plays: A Biographical Directory and Dramatic Index.* New York: Greenwood Press, 1988.

Peterson, Michael. *Straight White Male: Performance Art Monologues.* Jackson: University Press of Mississippi, 1997.

Peterson, Jane T, and Suzanne Bennett. *Women Playwrights of Diversity: A Bio-Bibliographical Sourcebook.* Westport, Conn.: Greenwood Press, 1997.

Poggi, Jack. *Theater in America: The Impact of Economic Forces, 1870-1967.* Ithaca, New York: Cornell University Press, 1968.

Porter, Thomas E. *Myth and Modern American Drama.* Detroit: Wayne State University Press,1969.

Pradhan, Narindar S. *Modern American Drama: A Study in Myth and Tradition.* New Delhi, India: Arnold-Heinemann, 1978.

Price, Julia S. *Off-Broadway Theater.* New York, Scarecrow Press, 1962.

Proehl, Geoffrey. *Coming Home Again: American Family Drama and the Figure of the Prodigal.* Madison, New Jersey: Fairleigh Dickinson University Press, 1997.

Quinn, Arthur H. *A History of the American Drama, from the Civil War to the Present Day.* New York: Appleton-Century-Crofts, 1936.

Rabkin, Gerald. *Drama and Commitment: Politics in the American Theatre of the Thirties.* Bloomington: Indiana University Press, 1964.

Reynolds, R. C. *Stage Left: The Development of the American Social Drama in the Thirties.* Troy, New York: Whitston, 1986.

Richardson, Gary A. *American Drama from the Colonial Period Through World War I: A Critical History.* New York: Twayne, 1993.

Rigdon, Walter. *The Biographical Encyclopedia and Who's Who of the American Theatre.* New York: James H. Heinemann, 1966.

Robinson, Marc. *The Other American Drama.* New York: Cambridge University Press, 1994.

Rosefeldt, Paul. *The Absent Father in American Drama.* New York: Peter Lang, 1996.

Roth, Moira, ed. *The Amazing Decade: Woman and Performance Art in America, 1970-1980.* Los Angeles: Astro Artz, 1983.

Roudané, Matthew Charles. *American Drama Since 1960: A Critical History.* New York: Twayne, 1996.

Roudané, Matthew C, ed. *Public Issues, Private Tensions: Contemporary American Drama.* New York: AMS Press, 1992.

Ryan, Pat M. *American Dramatic Bibliography: A Checklist of Publications in English.* Fort Wayne, Ind.: Fort Wayne Public Library, 1969.

Sainer, Arthur. *The Radical Theatre Notebook.* New York: Discus Books, 1975.

—. *The New Radical Theatre Notebook.* New York: Applause, 1997.

Sanders, Leslie C. *The Development of Black Theatre in America: From Shadows to Selves.* Baton Rouge: Louisiana State University Press, 1988.

Sarlós, Robert K. *Jig Cook and the Provincetown Players: Theatre in Ferment.* Amherst: University of Massachusetts Press, 1982.

Sarotte, Georges Michel. *Like a Brother, Like a Lover: Male Homosexuality in the American Novel and Theater from Herman Melville to James Baldwin.* Translated from the French by Richard Miller. Garden City, New York: Anchor Press/Doubleday, 1978.

Savran, David. *In Their Own Words: Contemporary American Playwrights.* New York: Theatre Communications Group, 1988.

—. *A Queer Sort of Materialism: Recontextualizing American Theater.* Ann Arbor : University of Michigan Press, 2003.

Sayler, Oliver. *Our American Theatre.* New York: Brentano's, 1923.

Scanlan, Tom. *Family, Drama, and American Dreams.* Westport, Conn.: Greenwood Press, 1978.

Schanke, Robert A, and Kim Marra. *Staging Desire: Queer Readings of American Theater History.* Ann Arbor: University of Michigan Press, 2002.

Scharine, Richard G. *From Class to Caste in American Drama: Political and Social Themes Since the 1930s.* New York : Greenwood Press, 1991.

Schlueter, June, ed. *Feminist Rereadings of Modern American Drama.* Rutherford, New Jersey: Fairleigh Dickinson University Press, 1989.

—, ed. *Modern American Drama: The Female Canon.* Rutherford: Fairleigh Dickinson University Press, 1990.

Schmidt, Kerstin. *Theater of Transformation: Postmodernism in American Drama.* Amsterdam: Rodopi, 2005.

Schroeder, Patricia R. *The Presence of the Past in Modern American Drama.* Rutherford, New Jersey: Fairleigh Dickinson University Press, 1989.

Seller, Maxine Schwartz, ed. *Ethnic Theatre in the United States.* Westport, Conn.: Greenwood Press, 1981.

Shafer, Yvonne. *American Women Playwrights, 1900-1950.* New York: Peter Lang, 1995.

Shaland, Irene. *American Theater and Drama Research: An Annotated Guide to Information Sources, 1945-1990.* Jefferson, North Carolina: McFarland, 1991.

Shank, Theodore. *American Alternative Theatre.* New York: Grove, 1982.

Shuman, Robert Baird. *American Drama, 1918-1960: An Annotated Bibliography.* Pasadena, Calif.: Salem Press, 1992.

Sievers, W. David. *Freud on Broadway: A History of Psychoanalysis and the American Drama.* New York: Hermitage House, 1955.

Simard, Rodney. *Postmodern Drama: Contemporary Playwrights in America and Britain*. Lanham, Md.: University Press of America, 1984.

Smiley, Sam. *The Drama of Attack: Didactic Plays of the American Depression*. Columbia: University of Missouri Press, 1972.

Smith, Susan Harris. *American Drama: The Bastard Art*. New York: Cambridge University Press, 1996.

Smith, Wendy. *Real Life Drama: The Group Theatre and America, 1931-1940*. New York: Knopf, 1990.

Sternlicht, Sanford. *A Reader's Guide to Modern American Drama*. Syracuse: Syracuse University Press, 2002.

Stowell, Sheila. *A Stage of Their Own: Feminist Playwrights of the Suffrage Era*. Manchester, England: Manchester University Press, 1992.

Szilassy, Zoltán. *American Theater of the 1960s*. Carbondale: Southern Illinois University Press, 1986.

Taubman, Howard. *The Making of American Theatre*. New York: Coward-McCann, 1965.

Taumann, Beatrix. *"Strange Orphans": Contemporary African American Women Playwrights*. Würzburg, Germany: Königshausen & Neumann, 1999.

Taylor, Karen. *People's Theatre in America*. New York: Drama Book Specialists, 1972.

Taylor, William E, ed. *Modern American Drama: Essays in Criticism*. Deland, Fla.: Everett/Edwards, 1968.

Valgemäe, Mardi. *Accelerated Grimace: Expressionism in the American: Drama of the 1920s*. Carbondale: Southern Illinois University Press, 1972.

Vorlicky, Robert. *Act Like a Man: Challenging Masculinities in American Drama*. Ann Arbor: University of Michigan Press, 1995.

Wainscott, Ronald H. *The Emergence of the* Modern *American Theater, 1914-1929*. New Haven, Conn.: Yale University Press, 1997.

Wakefield, Thaddeus. *The Family in Twentieth-Century American Drama*. New York: Peter Lang, 2003.

Walker, Julia A. *Expressionism and Modernism in the American Theatre: Bodies, Voices, Words*. New York: Cambridge University Press, 2005.

Weales, Gerald C. *American Drama since World War II*. New York, Harcourt, Brace & World, 1962.

—. *Jumping-Off Place: American Drama in the 1960s*. New York: Macmillan, 1969.

Weber, Myles. *Middlebrow Annoyances: American Drama in the 21st Century*. Arlington, Va.: Gival Press, 2003.

Wertheim, Albert. *Staging the War: American Drama and World War II*. Bloomington: Indiana University Press, 2004.

Wertheim, Albert, and Hedwig Bock, ed. *Essays on Contemporary American Drama*. Munich: M. Hueber, 1981.

Wheatley, Christopher J, ed. *Twentieth-Century American Dramatists*. Detroit: Gale Group, 2000, 2002.

Williams, Dana A. *Contemporary African American Female Playwrights: An Annotated Bibliography*. Westport, Conn.: Greenwood Press, 1998.

Williams, Mance. *Black Theatre in the 1960s and 1970s: A Historical-Critical Analysis of the Movement*. Westport, Conn.: Greenwood Press, 1985.

Wilmeth, Don B, and Tice Miller, ed. *The Cambridge Guide to American Theatre*. New York: Cambridge University Press, 1993.

Wilmeth, Don B, and Christopher Bigsby, ed. *The Cambridge History of American Theatre*. Vol. 1: Beginnings to 1870. New York: Cambridge University Press, 1998.

Wilmeth, Don B, and Christopher Bigsby, ed. *The Cambridge History of American Theatre*. Vol. 2: 1870-1945. New York: Cambridge University Press, 2006.

Wilmeth, Don B, and Christopher Bigsby, ed. *The Cambridge History of American Theatre*. Vol. 3: Post-World War II to the 1990s. New York: Cambridge University Press, 2006.

Wilmer, S. E. *Theatre, Society, and the Nation: Staging American Identities*. New York: Cambridge University Press, 2002.

Wilson, Garff B. *A History of American Acting*. Bloomington: Indiana University Press, 1966.

—. *Three Hundred Years of American Drama and Theatre, from "Ye bare and ye cubb" to "A Chorus Line"*. Englewood Cliffs, New Jersey: Prentice-Hall, 1982.

Wittler, Clarence J. *Some Social Trends in WPA Drama*. Washington, D.C.: The Catholic University of America Press, 1939.

Woll, Allen. *Dictionary of Black Theatre*. Westport, Conn.: Greenwood Press, 1983.

Wolter, Jürgen C. *The Dawning of American Drama: American Dramatic Criticism, 1746-1915*. Westport, Conn.: Greenwood Press, 1993.

Young, William C. *Documents of American Theatre History*. 2 Vols. Chicago: American Library Association, 1973.

Zeigler, Joseph W. *Regional Theatre: The Revolutionary Stage*. Minneapolis: University of Minnesota Press, 1973.

CREDITS

First or Major Theatrical Productions and Film Adaptations of Plays Discussed (in alphabetical order)

Buried Child (1978), a play by Sam Shepard

Director: Gary Sinise
Scenic design by Robert Bril
Costume design by Allison Reeds
Lighting design by Kevin Rigdon
Sound design by Rob Milburn
Produced by the Steppenwolf Theatre Company on Broadway at the Brooks Atkinson Theatre
Opening date: April 30, 1996

Cast:
Bradley: Leo Burmester
Dodge: James Gammon
Tilden: Terry Kinney
Father Dewis: Jim Mohr
Shelly: Kellie Overbey
Halie: Lois Smith
Vince: Jim True
Shelly: Patricia Jones

La Cage Aux Folles (1983), a musical

Producer: Allan Carr, at Broadway's Palace Theatre
Music/Lyrics: Jerry Herman
Book: Harvey Fierstein
Director: Arthur Laurents
Choreographer: Scott Salmon
Scenic Design: David Mitchell
Costume Design: Theoni V. Aldredge
Lighting Design: Jules Fisher
Sound Design: Peter J. Fitzgerald

Opening date: August 21, 1983

Cast:
Georges: Gene Barry
Chantal: David Cahn
Monique: Dennis Callahan
Dermah: Frank DiPasquale
Nicole: John Dolf
Hanna: David Engel
Mercedes: David Evans
Bitelle: Linda Haberman
Lo Singh: Eric Lamp
Odette: Dan O'Grady

The Birdcage (1996), the film

Directed by Mike Nichols
Screenplay by Elaine May, based on the play by Jean Poiret and an earlier
screenplay by Francis Veber
Cinematography by Emmanuel Lubezki
Edited by Arthur Schmidt
Art direction by Tom Duffield
Production design by Bo Welch
Costume design by Ann Roth
Produced by United Artists

Cast:
Robin Williams: Armand Goldman
Gene Hackman: Sen. Kevin Keeley
Nathan Lane: Albert Goldman
Dianne Wiest: Louise Keeley
Dan Futterman: Val Goldman
Calista Flockhart: Barbara Keeley
Hank Azaria: Agador
Christine Baranski: Katherine Archer
Tom McGowan: Harry Radman
Grant Heslov: National Enquirer Photographer
Kirby Mitchell: Keeley's Chauffeur
James Lally: Cyril
Luca Tommassini: Celsius
Luis Camacho: Goldman Girl

Andre Fuentes: Goldman Girl

Running time: 117 minutes
Format: Color *(Technicolor)* with DTS sound

Death of a Salesman (1949), a play by Arthur Miller

Director: Robert Falls
Scenic designer: Mark Wendland
Costume designer: Birgit Rattenborg Wise
Lighting designer: Michael S. Philippi
Sound design: Richard Woodbury
Producer: Jujamcyn Theaters and Fox Theatricals, on Broadway at the Eugene O'Neill Theatre
Opening date: February 10, 1999

Cast:
Willy Loman: Brian Dennehy
Linda Loman: Elizabeth Franz
Biff: Kevin Anderson
Happy: Ted Koch
Charley: Howard Witt
Letta: Chelsea Altman
The Woman: Kate Buddeke
Uncle Ben: Allen Hamilton
Stanley: Kent Klineman
Miss Forsythe: Stephanie March
Howard: Steve Pickering
Bernard: Richard Thompson
Jenny: Tracy Thorne

Death of a Salesman (1985), the film

Directed by Volker Schlöndorff
Screenplay by Arthur Miller, taken directly from his play
Cinematography by Michael Ballhaus
Editing by David Ray
Production design by Tony Walton
Costume design by Ruth Morley
Music by Alex North
Produced by Bioskop Film, Punch Productions, and Roxbury Productions

Cast:
Dustin Hoffman: Willy Loman
Kate Reid: Linda Loman
John Malkovich: Biff Loman
Stephen Lang: Harold "Happy" Loman
Charles Durning: Charley
Louis Zorich: Ben Loman
David S. Chandler: Bernard, Charley's son
Jon Polito: Howard, Willy's Boss
Kathryn Rossetter: Woman from Boston
Tom Signorelli: Stanley the waiter at Frank's Chop House
Linda Kozlowski: Miss Forsythe
Karen Needle: Letta, Forsythe's friend
Anne McIntosh: Jenny
Michael Quinlan: Waiter

Running time: 130 minutes
Format: Color, with Mono sound

Dr. Faustus Lights the Lights (1938), a play by Gertrude Stein

Production conceived, designed and directed by Robert Wilson; Music by Hans
Peter Kuhn
Lighting by Heinrich Brunke and Andreas Fuchs
Dramaturge, Peter Krumme
Choreography, Suzushi Hanayagi
Costumes, Hans Thiemann, Andreas Auerbach, Anja Duklau, Marie Juliane
Friedrich, Peter Pelzmann and Petra Peters
Produced by Lincoln Center for the Performing Arts at Alice Tully Hall.
Opening date: July 9, 1992

Cast:
Dr. Faustus: Thilo Mandel, Christian Ebert, Thomas Lehmann
Mephisto in Red: Heiko Senst
Mephisto in Black: Florian Fitz
Marguerite Ida and Helen Annabel: Katrin Heller, Wiebke Kayser, Gabriele
Volsch
Little Boy: Matthias Bundschuh
Dog: Karla Trippel
Boy: Christian Ebert

Girl: Wiebke Kayser
Country woman: Martin Vogel
Mr. Viper: Moritz Sostmann
Man from over the seas: Thomas Lehmann

Edmond (1982), a play by David Mamet

Directed by Gregory Mosher
Scenery by Bill Bartelt
Costumes by Marsha Kowal
Lighting by Kevin Rigdon.
Produced by the Goodman Theater of the Art Institute of Chicago
Opening date: June 4, 1982

Cast:
Mission Preacher and Prisoner: Paul Butler
Manager, Leafleteer, Customer, Policeman, Guard: Rick Cluchey
B-Girl and Whore: Joyce Hazard
Peep-Show Girl and Glenna: Laura Innes
Man in a Bar, Hotel Clerk, Man in Back, Chaplain: Bruce Jarchow
Edmond's Wife: Linda Kimrough
Fortuneteller, Manager and Woman in the Subway: Marge Kotlisky
Shill and Pimp: Ernest Perry Jr.
Cardsharp and Guard: Jose Santana
Edmond: Colin Stinton
Barkeep, Bystander, Pawnshop Owner, Interrogator: Jack Wallace

Edmond (2005), the film

Directed by Stuart Gordon
Screenplay by David Mamet, based on his own play
Cinematography by Denis Maloney
Editing by Andy Horvitch
Music by Bobby Johnston
Produced by First Independent Pictures

Cast:
William H. Macy: Edmond Burke
Julia Stiles: Glenna
Joe Mantegna: Man in Bar
Ling Bai: Peep-Show Girl

Jeffrey Combs: Desk Clerk
Denise Richards: Allegro B-Girl
Mena Suvari: Whore
Dylan Walsh: Interrogator
Russell Hornsby: Shill
Debi Mazar: Atlantic Leisure Club Matron
Rebecca Pidgeon: Edmond's Wife
Lionel Mark Smith: Pimp
Marcus Thomas: Window Man
Jack Wallacc: Chaplain
George Wendt: Pawn Shop Guymore

Running time: 82 minutes
Format: Color, with Dolby Digital sound

Fool For Love (1983), a play by Sam Shepard

Director: Sam Shepard
Setting: Andy Stacklin
Costumes: Ardyss L. Golden
Lighting: Kurt Landisman
Sound: J. A. Deane
Producer: Circle Repertory Company Off-Broadway at the Beatrix Theatre
Opening date: May 18, 1983

Cast:
May: Kathy Whitton Baker
Eddie: Eddie Harris
Martin: Dennis Ludlow
Old Man: Will Marchetti

Fool for Love (1985), the film

Directed by Robert Altman
Screenplay by Sam Shepard, based on his play
Cinematography by Pierre Mignot
Editing by Luce Grunenwaldt and Stephen P. Dunn
Production design by Stephen Altman
Music by George Burt
Sound design by Catherine d'Hoir
Costume design by Kristine Flones-Czeski

Produced by Menahem Golan et alia

Cast:
Sam Shepard: Eddie
Kim Basinger: May
Harry Dean Stanton: Old Man
Randy Quaid: Martin
Martha Crawford: May's Mother
Louise Egolf: Eddie's Mother
Sura Cox: Teenaged May
Jonathan Skinner: Teenaged Eddie
April Russell: Young May
Deborah McNaughton: The Countess
Lon Hill: Mr. Valdes

Running time: 106 minutes
Format: Color, with Mono sound

The Front Page (1928), a play by Ben Hecht and Charles MacArthur

Director: Jerry Zaks
Set: Tony Walton
Costumes: Willa Kim
Lighting: Paul Gallo
Sound: Otts Munderloh
Producer: Lincoln Center, at the Vivian Beaumont Theatre
Opening date: November 23, 1986

Cast:
McCue, City Press: Trey Wilson
Endicott, Post: Bernie McInerney
Schwartz, Daily News: Lee Wilkof
Murphy, Journal: Ed Lauter
Wilson, American: Charles Stransky
Kruger, Journal of Commerce: Ronn Carroll
Hildy Johnson, Herald Examiner: Richard Thomas
A Woman: Amanda Carlin
Frank, a deputy: Philip LeStrange
Bensinger, Tribune: Jeff Weiss
Woodenshoes Eichorn: Jack Wallace
Diamond Louis: Raymond Serra

Jennie:Mary Catherine Wright
Mollie Malloy: Deirdre O'Connell
Sheriff Hartman: Richard B. Shul
Peggy Grant: Julie Hagerty
Mrs. Grant: Beverly May
The Mayor: Jerome Dempsey
Mr. Pincus: Bill McCutcheon
Earl Williams: Paul Stolarsky
Walter Burns: John Lithgow
Tony: Patrick Garner
Carl, a deputy: Michael Rothhaar
Policeman: Patrick Gamer
Policeman: Richard Peterson

The Front Page (1974), the film

Directed by Billy Wilder
Screenplay by Billy Wilder and I.A.L. Diamond, from the play by Ben Hecht
and Charles MacArthur
Cinematography by Jordan S. Cronenweth
Editing by Ralph E. Winters
Art direction by Henry Bumstead
Costume design by Burton Miller
Sound by Robert Martin
Music supervision by Billy May
Produced by Universal Pictures

Cast:
Jack Lemmon: Hildebrand "Hildy" Johnson
Walter Matthau: Walter Burns/Otto Fishbine
Susan Sarandon: Peggy Grant
Vincent Gardenia: "Honest Pete" Hartman Sheriff of Clark County
David Wayne: Roy Bensinger of the Tribune
Allen Garfield: Kruger
Austin Pendleton: Earl Williams
Charles Durning: Murphy
Herb Edelman: Schwartz (as Herbert Edelman)
Martin Gabel: Dr. Max J. Eggelhofer
Harold Gould: The Mayor/Herbie/Green Hornet
Cliff Osmond: Officer Jacobi
Dick O'Neill: McHugh

Jon Korkes: Rudy Keppler of the Chicago Examiner
Lou Frizzell: Endicott

Running time: 105 minutes
Format: Color *(Technicolor)*, with Mono sound *(Westrex Recording System)*

The Glass Menagerie (1944), a play by Tennessee Williams

Director: Frank Galati
Set: Loy Arcenas
Costumes: Noel Taylor
Lighting: Mimi Jordan Sherin
Sound: Richard R. Dunning
Projections: John Boesche
Music: Miriam Sturm
Producer: Roundabout Theatre Company, at the Criterion Theatre on Broadway
Opening date: November 15, 1994

Cast:
Tom: Zeljko Ivanek
Amanda: Julie Harris
Laura: Calista Flockhart
Jim: Kevin Kilner

The Glass Menagerie (1987), the film

Directed by Paul Newman
Screenplay from the play by Tennessee Williams
Cinematography by Michael Ballhaus
Editing by David Ray
Production design by Tony Walton
Costume design by Tony Walton
Music by Henry Mancini and Paul Bowles
Sound editing by Hal Levinsohn and Wendy Hedin
Produced by Burtt Harris and Joseph M. Caracciolo, Jr.

Cast:
Joanne Woodward: Amanda Wingfield
John Malkovich: Tom Wingfield
Karen Allen: Laura Wingfield
James Naughton: Jim O'Connor, the Gentleman Caller

Running time: 134 minutes
Format: Color, with Stereo sound

Glengarry Glen Ross (1983), a play by David Mamet

Director: Gregory Mosher
Scenic Design: Michael Merritt
Costume Design: Nan Cibula
Lighting Design: Kevin Rigdon
Producer: The Shubert Organization on Broadway at the John Golden Theatre
Opening date: March 25, 1984

Cast:
Richard Roma: Joe Montegna
Shelly Levine: Robert Prosky
John Williamson: J. T. Walsh
Dave Moss: James Tolkan
George Aaronow: Mike Nussbaum
James Lingk: Lane Smith
Baylen: Jack Wallace

Glengarry Glen Ross (1992), the film

Directed by James Foley
Screenplay by David Mamet, based on his play
Cinematography by Juan Ruiz Anchia
Editing by Howard Smith
Music by James Newton Howard
Production design by Jane Musky
Produced by Jerry Tokofsky and Stanley R. Zupnik

Cast:
Jack Lemmon: Shelley Levene
Al Pacino: Ricky Roma
Ed Harris: Dave Moss
Alan Arkin: George Aaronow
Kevin Spacey: John Williamson
Alec Baldwin: Blake
Jonathan Pryce: James Lingk
Bruce Altman: Mr. Spannel

Jude Ciccolella: Detective
Paul Butler: Policeman
Lori Tan Chinn: Coat check girl
Neal Jones: Man in donut shop
Barry Rossen: Assistant detective

Running time: 100 minutes
Format: Color, with Dolby sound

The Hairy Ape, a play by Eugene O'Neill

Directed by Elizabeth LeCompte
Sets by Jim Clayburgh
Lighting by Jennifer Tipton
Music by John Lurie
Sound by James Johnson and John Collins
Video by Christopher Kondek and Phillip Bussmann
Produced by the Wooster Group at the Selwyn Theatre
Opening date: April 4, 1997

Cast:
Yank: Willem Dafoe
Paddy: Scott Renderer
Long: Dave Shelley
Mildred Douglas: Kate Valk
Aunt: Peyton Smith
Prisoner on Video: Roy Faudree
I.W.W. Secretary: Paul Lazar

The Hairy Ape (1944), the film

Directed by Alfred Santell
Screenplay by Robert Hardy Andrews and Decla Dunning, from the play by
Eugene O'Neill
Cinematography by Lucien Andriot
Music by Michel Michelet & Eddie Paul
Art direction by James Sullivan
Editing by William H. Ziegler
Produced by Jules Levey

Cast:

William Bendix: Hank Smith
Susan Hayward: Mildred Douglas
John Loder: Tony Lazar
Dorothy Comingore: Helen Parker
Roman Bohnen: Paddy
Tom Fadden: Long
Alan Napier: MacDougald, Chief Engineer
Charles Cane: Gantry
Charles La Torre: Portuguese proprietor

Running time: 92 minutes
Format: Black and white, with Mono sound *(Western Electric Sound System)*

The Little Foxes (1939), a play by Lillian Hellman

Director: Jack O'Brien
Sets: John Lee Beatty
Costumes: Jane Greenwood
Lighting: Kenneth Posner
Sound: Aural Fixation
Score: Bob James
Producer: Lincoln Center, at the Vivian Beaumont Theater
Opening date: April 27, 1997

Cast:
Addie: Ethel Ayler
Cal: Charles Turner
Birdie Hubbard: Frances Conroy
Oscar Hubbard: Brian Kerwin
Leo Hubbard: Frederick Weller
Regina Giddens: Stockard Channing
William Marshall: Richard E. Council
Benjamin Hubbard: Brian Murray
Alexandra Giddens: Jennifer Dundas
Horace Giddens: Kenneth Welsh

The Little Foxes (1941), the film

Directed by William Wyler
Screenplay by Lillian Hellman, from her own play
Cinematography by Gregg Toland

Production design by Stephen Goosson
Editing by Daniel Mandell
Music by Meredith Willson
Produced by Sam Goldwyn

Cast:
Bette Davis: Regina Giddens
Herbert Marshall: Horace Giddens
Teresa Wright: Alexandra Giddens
Richard Carlson: David Hewitt
Dan Duryea: Leo Hubbard
Patricia Collinge: Birdie Hubbard
Charles Dingle: Ben Hubbard
Carl Benton Reid: Oscar Hubbard
Jessica Grayson: Addie
John Marriott: Cal
Russell Hicks: William Marshall
Lucien Littlefield: Sam Manders
Virginia Brissac: Mrs. Lucy Hewitt
Terry Nibert: Julia Jordan
Henry "Hot Shot" Thomas: Harold More

Running time: 115 minutes
Format: Black and white, with Mono sound

'night, Mother (1982), a play by **Marsha Norman**

Director: Tom Moore
Scenic Design and Costume Design: Heidi Landesman
Lighting Design: James F. Ingalls
Producer: The Shubert Organization on Broadway at the John Golden Theatre
Opening date: March 31, 1983

Cast:
Thelma Cates: Anne Pitoniak
Jessie Cates: Kathy Bates

'night, Mother (1986), the film

Directed by Tom Moore
Screenplay by Marsha Norman, based on her play
Cinematography by Stephen M. Katz
Editing by Suzanne Pettit
Production design by Jackson DeGovia
Costume design by Bob Blackman
Music by David Shire
Sound editing by Donald J. Malout
Produced by Aaron Spelling et alia

Cast:
Sissy Spacek: Jessie Cates
Anne Bancroft: Thelma Cates
Ed Berke: Dawson Cates
Carol Robbins: Loretta Cates
Jennifer Roosendahl: Melodie Cates
Michael Kenworthy: Kenny Cates
Sari Walker: Agnes Fletcher
Claire Malis: Operator (voice)

Running time: 96 minutes
Format: Color *(DeLuxe)* with Dolby sound

Of Mice and Men (1937), a play by John Steinbeck

Produced by Elliot Martin
Directed by Edwin Sherin
Scenic Design by William and Jean Eckart
Costume Design by William and Jean Eckart
Lighting Design by William and Jean Eckart
Incidental music by Mark Hardwick
Produced by Elliot Martin at the Brooks Atkinson Theatre, on Broadway
Opening date: December 18, 1974

Cast:
Curley's Wife: Pamela Blair
The Boss: David Clarke
Carlson: Pat Corley
Slim: David Gale

Candy: Stefan Gierasch
Curley: Mark Gordon
Lennie: James Earl Jones
Crooks: Joe Seneca
Whit: James Staley
George: Kevin Conway

Of Mice and Men (1992), the film

Directed by Gary Sinise
Screenplay by Horton Foote, based on the play by John Steinbeck
Cinematography by Kenneth MacMillan
Editing by Robert L. Sinise
Music by Mark Isham
Production design by David Gropman
Produced by Metro-Goldwyn-Mayer

Cast:
John Malkovich: Lennie Small
Gary Sinise: George Milton
Ray Walston: Candy
Casey Siemaszko: Curley
Sherilyn Fenn: Curley's Wife
John Terry: Slim
Richard Riehle: Carlson
Alexis Arquette: Whit
Joe Morton: Crooks
Noble Willingham: The Boss
Joe D'Angerio: Jack
Tuck Milligan: Mike
David Steen: Tom
Moira Harris: Girl in Red Dress
Mark Boone Junior: Bus Driver

Running time: 115 minutes
Format: Color *(DeLuxe)*, with Dolby sound

Our Town (1938), a play by Thornton Wilder

Director: Gregory Mosher
Musical Director: Michael Barrett

Sets: Douglas Stein
Costumes: Jane Greenwood
Lighting: Kevin Rigdon
Producer: Lincoln Center, at the Lyceum Theatre on Broadway
Opening date: December 4, 1988

Cast:
Stage Manager: Spalding Gray
Dr. Gibbs: James Rebhorn
Joe Crowell: Joey Shea
Howie Newsome: W. H. Macy
Mrs. Gibbs: Frances Conroy
Mrs, Webb: Roberta Maxwell
George Gibbs: Eric Stoltz
Rebecca Gibbs: Lydia Kelly
Wally Webb: Shane Culkin
Emily Webb: Penelope Ann Miller
Professor Willard: Bill Alton
Mr. Webb: Peter Maloney
Woman in the balcony: Marilyn Hamlin
Man in the auditorium: Steven Goldstein
Lady in the box: Katharine Houghton
Simon Stimson: Jeff Weiss
Mrs. Newsome: Mary McCann
Mrs. Soames: Marcell Rosenblatt
Constable Warren: Tom Brennan
Si Crowell: Christopher Cunningham, Jr.
Baseball Player: Steven Goldstein
Baseball Player: Jordan Lage
Baseball Player: Todd Weeks
Sam Craig: Roderick McLachlan
Joe Stoddard: William Preston
Farmer McCarty: Patrick Tovatt

Our Town (1940), the film

Directed by Sam Wood
Screenplay: Thornton Wilder, Frank Craven, and Harry Chandlee, based on
Wilder's play
Cinematography by Bert Glennon
Editing by Sherman Todd

Production design by William Cameron Menzies & Harry Horner
Music by Aaron Copeland
Produced by Sol Lesser

Cast:
William Holden: George Gibbs
Martha Scott: Emily Webb
Fay Bainter: Mrs. Julia Hersey Gibbs
Beulah Bondi: Mrs. Myrtle Webb
Thomas Mitchell: Dr. Frank F. Gibbs
Guy Kibbee: Charles Webb
Stuart Erwin: Howie Newsome
Frank Craven: Stage Manager
Doro Merande: Mrs. Louella Soames
Philip Wood: Simon Stimson
Ruth Tobey: Rebecca Gibbs
Douglas Gardner: Wally Webb
Arthur B. Allen: Prof. Willard
Charles Trowbridge: Rev. Dr. Ferguson
Spencer Charters: Const. Bill Warren

Running time: 90 minutes
Format: Black and white, with Mono sound *(Western Electric Mirrophonic Recording)*

A Soldier's Play (1981), a play by Charles Fuller

Director: Douglas Turner Ward
Scenic Design: Felix E. Cochren
Costume Design: Judy Dearing
Lighting Design: Allen Lee Hughes
Sound Design: Regge Life
Producer: Negro Ensemble Company Off-Broadway at Theatre Four
Opening date: November 10, 1981

Cast:
Tech/Sergeant Vernon C. Waters: Adolph Caesar
Private James Wilkie: Steven A. Jones
Captain Charles Taylor: Peter Friedman
Private Tony Smalls: Brent Jennings
Corporal Bernard Cobb: Eugene Lee

Captain Richard Davenport: Charles Brown
Private First Class Melvin Peterson: Denzel Washington
Private C. J. Memphis: Larry Riley
Corporal Ellis: James Pickens, Jr.
Lieutenant Byrd: Cotter Smith
Captain Wilcox: Stephen Zettler

A Soldier's Story (1984), the film

Directed by Norman Jewison
Screenplay by Charles Fuller, based on his own play
Cinematography by Russell Boyd & Peter Sova
Costume design by Robert Stewart & Chuck Velasco
Editing by Mark Warner & Caroline Biggerstaff
Production design by Walter Scott Herndon
Music by Herbie Hancock
Sound design by Charles Wilborn
Produced by Columbia Pictures

Cast:
Howard E. Rollins Jr.: Capt. Davenport
Adolph Caesar: Sgt. Waters
Art Evans: Pvt. Wilkie
David Alan Grier: Cpl. Cobb
David Harris: Pvt. Smalls
Dennis Lipscomb: Capt. Taylor
Larry Riley: C.J. Memphis
Robert Townsend: Cpl. Ellis
Denzel Washington: Pfc. Peterson
William Allen Young: Pvt. Henson
Patti LaBelle: Big Mary
Wings Hauser: Lt. Byrd
Scott Paulin: Capt. Wilcox
John Hancock: Sgt. Washington
Trey Wilson: Col. Nivens

Running time: 101 minutes
Format: Color *(Metrocolor)*, with Dolby sound

Way Down East (1920), the film

Directed by D.W. Griffith
Screenplay by Anthony Paul Kelly and D. W. Griffith, based on the play of the
same name by William A. Brady, Joseph R. Grismer, and Lottie Blair Parker
Cinematography by Billy Bitzer & Hendrik Sartov
Editing by James Smith and Rose Smith
Music by Louis Silvers and William Frederick Peters
Art direction by Charles Osborne Seessel
Produced by D. W. Griffith

Cast:
Lillian Gish: Anna Moore
Richard Barthelmess: David Bartlett
Lowell Sherman: Lennox Sanderson
Burr McIntosh: Squire Bartlett
Kate Bruce: Mother Bartlett
Mary Hay: Kate (the Squire's niece)
Creighton Hale: The Professor
Emily Fitzroy: Maria Poole (landlady)
Porter Strong: Seth Holcomb
George Neville: The Constable
Edgar Nelson: Hi Holler

Running time: 145 minutes
Format: Black and white; silent film

INDEX